NAMING GOD

Generations of Christians, Janet Soskice demonstrates, once knew God and Christ by hundreds of remarkable names. These included the appellations 'Messiah', 'Emmanuel', 'Alpha', 'Omega', 'Eternal', 'All-Powerful', 'Lamb', 'Lion', 'Goat', 'One', 'Word', 'Serpent' and 'Bridegroom'. In her much-anticipated new book, Soskice argues that contemporary understandings of divinity could be transformed by a return to a venerable analogical tradition of divine naming. These ancient titles – drawn from scripture – were chanted and sung, crafted and invoked (in polyphony and plainsong) as they were woven into the worship of the faithful. However, during the sixteenth century Descartes moved from 'naming' to 'defining' God via a series of metaphysical attributes. This made God a thing among things: a being amongst beings. For the author, reclaiming divine naming is not only overdue. It can also re-energise the relationship between philosophy and religious tradition. This path-breaking book shows just how rich and revolutionary such reclamation might be.

JANET SOSKICE is Professor Emeritus of Philosophical Theology in the University of Cambridge and a Fellow of Jesus College, Cambridge. She is presently the William K. Warren Distinguished Research Professor of Catholic Theology at Duke Divinity School. Her books include *Metaphor and Religious Language* (Oxford University Press, 1984), which is a classic work of metaphorical theology, and also the bestselling trade title *Sisters of Sinai: How Two Lady Adventurers Found the Hidden Gospels* (Chatto & Windus, 2009), which vividly recounts how the Ayrshire twins Agnes and Margaret Smith made in the Sinai desert one of the most important New Testament manuscript discoveries of the nineteenth century.

NAMING GOD

ADDRESSING THE DIVINE IN PHILOSOPHY, THEOLOGY AND SCRIPTURE

JANET SOSKICE

University of Cambridge

CAMBRIDGE
UNIVERSITY PRESS

CAMBRIDGE
UNIVERSITY PRESS

Shaftesbury Road, Cambridge CB2 8EA, United Kingdom

One Liberty Plaza, 20th Floor, New York, NY 10006, USA

477 Williamstown Road, Port Melbourne, VIC 3207, Australia

314–321, 3rd Floor, Plot 3, Splendor Forum, Jasola District Centre,
New Delhi – 110025, India

103 Penang Road, #05–06/07, Visioncrest Commercial, Singapore 238467

Cambridge University Press is part of Cambridge University Press &
Assessment, a department of the University of Cambridge.

We share the University's mission to contribute to society through the
pursuit of education, learning and research at the highest international levels
of excellence.

www.cambridge.org
Information on this title: www.cambridge.org/9781108834469

DOI: 10.1017/9781108993319

© Janet Soskice 2023

This publication is in copyright. Subject to statutory exception and to the
provisions of relevant collective licensing agreements, no reproduction of any
part may take place without the written permission of Cambridge University
Press & Assessment.

First published 2023

A catalogue record for this publication is available from the British Library.

Library of Congress Cataloging-in-Publication Data
NAMES: Soskice, Janet, author.
TITLE: Naming God : addressing the divine in philosophy, theology and
scripture / Janet Soskice, University of Cambridge.
DESCRIPTION: Cambridge, United Kingdom ; New York, NY, USA :
Cambridge University Press, 2023. | Includes bibliographical
references and index.
IDENTIFIERS: LCCN 2022062017 | ISBN 9781108834469 (hardback) |
ISBN 9781108993319 (ebook)
SUBJECTS: LCSH: God (Christianity) – Name. | God (Christianity) –
Attributes. | Theology.
CLASSIFICATION: LCC BT180.N2 S55 2023 | DDC 231–dc23/eng/20230515
LC record available at https://lccn.loc.gov/2022062017

ISBN 978-1-108-83446-9 Hardback

Cambridge University Press & Assessment has no responsibility for the
persistence or accuracy of URLs for external or third-party internet websites
referred to in this publication and does not guarantee that any content on
such websites is, or will remain, accurate or appropriate.

... have you not read in the book of Moses, in the story about the bush, how God said to him, 'I am the God of Abraham, the God of Isaac, and the God of Jacob'? He is the God not of the dead, but of the living ...

(Mark 12.26–7)

CONTENTS

vii

ACKNOWLEDGEMENTS

This book began with an invitation to do the Stanton Lectures at the University of Cambridge in 1997 and to give a public lecture during the same year as the Eugene McCarthy Visiting Professor at the Gregorian University in Rome. Further development came through delivering the Richards Lectures at the University of Virginia in 2006. To friends and colleagues from all these centres of wisdom, I am deeply indebted.

My dear friend Professor Gemma Corradi Fiumara read the whole, making helpful comments. David Burrell has been an abiding presence, especially championing *creatio ex nihilo*. Cambridge colleagues who gave me tips and steers include my Sinai guide, Andrew Macintosh, Diana Lipton, Andrew Davison, Vittorio Montemaggi, Elizabeth Powell, Barnabas Aspray and Nicholas Jackson. Others I have mentioned in notes. At the University of Virginia, Peter Ochs and Judith Kovacs were gracious and inspirational, as was the audience for the lectures. Others who read sections along the way included Morwenna Ludlow, Verna Harrison, Eugene Rogers and John Betz.

Appointment to the William K. Warren Professorship University at Duke Divinity School has brought new colleagues who were (and are) generous in conversation, especially Norman Wirzba and Peter Casarella, with special thanks to Marc Brettler and Richard Hays for reading parts of the manuscript. Brett Stonecipher, Anthony Gannaio, Sarah Neff and Jason Eslicker, my graduate research assistants at Duke, wrestled an untidy manuscript into a readable whole and have been insightful readers in its final stages.

Great thanks are due to my patient and encouraging editor at Cambridge University Press, Alex Wright, and to the anonymous readers at the Press.

I must of course thank my family – Catherine and Isabelle who named me 'Mum' and especially my husband, Oliver Soskice, for his willingness to read as many drafts as there seem to be names of God.

I

Introduction

~

Generations of Christians knew and named God and Christ with many names – hundreds of them: Messiah, Emmanuel, Alpha, Omega, Eternal, All-Powerful, Lamb, Serpent, One, Goat, Lion, Word, Worm, Bridegroom. These names, all drawn from Scripture, were said, sung and chanted in plainsong and polyphony, woven into the worship of the faithful. Today, a remnant of what we might call this 'piety of the names' remains in the popular Advent hymn, 'O Come, O Come, Emmanuel', where names come from the 'O Antiphons', each verse heralding the coming of Christ with one of the titles Christians took from the Old Testament: 'O come, Emmanuel! O come, Rod of Jesse! O Come, Dayspring from on High! O come, Key of David! Oh come, Adonai!'

It has long interested me that pre-modern theologians and spiritual writers seemed more concerned with how we name God than with how we might prove that God exists – not just in what names we use to speak of God, but in whether we can name God at all.[1] In this way titles first encountered in Scripture inspired theological and

---

[1] Although philosophers focus on Dionysius the Areopagite, Philo, Origen, Ambrose, Hilary of Poitiers, Albertus Magnus, Aquinas, Bonaventure and many others wrote on the names and the naming of God.

philosophical reflection about what it might be to 'name God' – what I will call the 'divine names tradition'.

At some time in the sixteenth century this changed. Jean-Luc Marion sees in Descartes a significant alteration. He writes:

> In the period when Descartes wrote, to offer a definition of God (whatever its status) still amounted to taking a position on the theological terrain of the divine names. In effect, he (Descartes) began from a rationality not theologically assured by Christian revelation, but metaphysically founded on the humanity of 'men purely men' (*Discourse on Method* AT VI, 3). The problematic of the divine names – originally a theological issue – is transposed *here*, perhaps for the first time, into the strictly metaphysical domain.[2]

Descartes believed that human reason alone can prove the existence of God and that this should be conjoined with a proof of divine attributes of which we find some trace in ourselves – 'infinite, eternal, immutable, omniscient, omnipotent'.[3] This project, by which Descartes thought he was saying nothing different from the theologians, has effect on its terms. Here 'eternal' and 'immutable', denominations familiar to earlier generations of theologians as names of God and as anchored in the realm of the

[2] Jean-Luc Marion, 'The Essential Incoherence of Descartes' Definition of Divinity', in *Essays on Descartes' Meditations*, ed. Amélie O. Rorty (Berkeley: University of California Press, 1986), 297–338 at 297.

[3] René Descartes, 'Discourse on Method', in *Descartes: Selected Philosophical Writings*, trans. John Cottingham, Robert Stoothoff and Dugald Murdoch (Cambridge: Cambridge University Press, 1988), 20–56 at 37. On this see Jean-Luc Marion, *On Descartes' Metaphysical Prism: The Constitution and the Limits of Onto-theo-logy in Cartesian Thought*, trans. Jeffrey L. Kosky (Chicago: University of Chicago Press, 1999), 206–9.

Bible, now come to stand as products of 'reason alone'. Seemingly we can define *what God is*, perhaps as one object amongst others, rather than say *who God is for us*.

Whatever credit or blame can be awarded to Descartes, at some time in the early modern period reflection on the divine names began to fade away, at least in philosophical theology, to be replaced by debates over the attributes or, as they became, the 'classical attributes of God' familiar to many from introductory courses in philosophy of religion.[4] These were defended or attacked as free-standing philosophical claims, removed from any anchorage in scripture or piety and, of course, from any reference to Christ – indeed, that was largely the objective in the Age of Reason. As such these attributes became hostages to debates as to whether the God of the philosophers could be the God of the Bible or the God of Jesus Christ, and much subsequent dispute over the doctrine of analogy and 'natural' theology, with patristic and medieval theologians and especially those who wrote of God as 'Being Itself', accused of paying scant heed to revelation and scripture and choosing instead the God of the philosophers. Nothing could be further from the truth.

My proposal is this: how might this picture look differently if we placed such titles as 'eternal', 'infinite' and even the much vilified 'Being Itself' in the wider family of divine names as did Patristic and medieval writers? To think about names, whether names of God or names more

---

[4] Marion believes Descartes should take the initial blame. 'For the very first time, Descartes transposes some of the divine names elaborated by medieval theology into the (primarily self-regulated) field of metaphysics of the modern era' ('Essential Incoherence', 328–9). Marion also thinks Descartes is at the origins of the 'perfect being' theology (320).

generally, means thinking about naming since naming is a universal human practice. Names work for us, and they do more than define and describe. We use names to call to and to call upon, to summon, to invoke and to beseech, to attest to kinship, as words of blessing and address. The names of God are used to do all these things and perhaps above all, to pray and to praise.

In Scripture the faithful found many names for God: 'Creator', 'Shepherd', 'Rock', 'Bread of Heaven', 'the One Who Is'. The names had, for earlier theologians, different statuses. Especially important were those regarded as 'divine self-denominations' – names which, in Scripture, God gives to Godself. But all the scriptural 'names' were regarded as gifts – given in Torah, Prophets and Psalms – acting as way marks in God's unfolding relation to his people, Israel and subsequently, with the New Testament, to the Christian church. They were signs of God's love and care in particular moments but with lasting importance. This is not then a 'biblicism' which is detached from context and community, but a reflection on the ongoing relation of God to the people, Israel. Names embedded and evolved in this history occur in new ways in their New Testament application to Christ: Lamb, Redeemer, Lord, Messiah.

'Names', then, as I am using the term, is a much broader category than 'attributes'. We can quickly see that many in the long list of 'divine names' (Wisdom, Day Spring, Root of Jesse, Key of David) could not be thought of as 'attributes' of God in our modern sense. 'Attributes' suggest to us qualities a bearer possesses, such as having red hair or being six feet tall. It has hardened, that is to say, into something like specification. But how could 'day spring' or 'key of David' or 'Lamb' be attributes of God or of anyone? But all were names – names held to have been given in Scripture and means by which to call upon the Lord in prayer, praise and supplication. It is here that we may find the greatest affinity between Christian, Muslim and some Jewish practices of meditation on the names of God.

The plenitude of names and naming was coupled with a certain modesty about what we could claim to know or say about God unaided. The apophatic in theology is thus not an occult strategy but the foundation of positive biblical reflection.

Paradoxical as it may seem, it was embracing the doctrine of creation, and specifically *creatio ex nihilo*, which compelled early theologians to insist that God is, strictly speaking, unnameable and, at the same time, the doctrine which underwrites the intimacy of God to all that God has created – which is, of course, everything.

We will never be far in this volume from the doctrine of creation, or from Moses at the burning bush.

Chapter 2, 'Naming God at Sinai', sets the stage and expands upon the text integral to the divine names tradition, Exodus 3, where God addresses Moses from the burning bush.

Chapter 3 considers the first century CE Jewish exegete, Philo of Alexandra, who wrote extensively on the names and the naming of God and whose work was influential on emergent Christian literature. Here the problematic of 'naming God' is disclosed as pendant on the Jewish (and then Christian and Muslim) teaching of *creatio ex nihilo*.

Chapter 4 Goes into the revolutionary importance of the doctrine of *creatio ex nihilo* for the Christian doctrine of God in general, and for naming God specifically.

Chapter 5, 'Is "God" the name of God?', considers more general philosophical concerns about what names are and what names do.

Chapter 6 returns to theology with a discussion of Gregory of Nyssa and his meditations on the story of Moses in Exodus.

Chapter 7 expands this set of concerns with naming and innominability in the work of Augustine, not only a great theologian but a substantial philosopher of language. In particular we consider his understanding of God as 'Being Itself'.

Chapter 8 takes us to Aquinas, suggesting a reading of the early stages of the *Summa theologiae* not simply as proofs for the existence of God but as a meditation on the divine names, and discusses Thomas's predilection for 'the One Who Is', or 'Being' as the most appropriate name for God.

Chapter 9, 'Calling and Being Called', brings us to Christ, the Name of God.

Naming God calls us back to the practice of *theologia* where *theologia* is not so much knowledge about God as knowledge of God, through contemplation, prayer and, above all, praise.[5] A reappraisal of the divine names tradition such as I am attempting is not, then, simply correcting errant readings of past texts but a re-understanding of theology as itself a practice.[6] Naming God is indeed about

[5] See Andrew Louth, *The Origins of the Christian Mystical Tradition: From Plato to Denys* (Oxford: Oxford University Press, 1981), 164.

[6] A number of important books have traversed elements of this story of naming and misnaming, often with pastoral intentions. Here especially

knowing God but knowing too in the sense of 'being in relation to God', for what is vital to the believer is not to know a great deal about God but to be in loving relation to God. Here epistemology and metaphysics come together. To call upon the Name of the Lord, to pray, is to be in relation with the One through whom all things have their being. To call upon the Name of the Lord is to call upon our Creator and Redeemer. Calling upon the name of the Lord does not disappear in the New Testament. Instead, Jesus is given many of the names ascribed to YHWH in the Hebrew Bible – Redeemer, Lord, Word. Paul in Philippians, famously, identifies Jesus with the Holy Name (Phil. 2.9–11).

Christians continue to 'call upon the Name of the Lord' who made heaven and earth and in doing so bring themselves into relation with God, with scripture, with one another and finally with the whole created order.

The present book is not a survey or a catalogue but a charting of the way. All the theologians discussed here deserve longer account. On Pseudo-Dionysius and the Divine Names there is excellent extant research to which readers may refer. I have not dealt with theologians of the eastern church where the divine names tradition did not suffer the deterioration of the west. I have not the competence to consider the Islamic tradition of the Ninety-nine Beautiful Names of God, although those aware of this tradition will find, I hope, helpful consonance. Each of the divine names touched upon deserves study in its own

I think of Elizabeth Johnson's ground-breaking feminist work, *She Who Is* and Kendall Soulen's, *The Divine Name(s) and the Holy Trinity*. My own book, *The Kindness of God*, was a contribution to the contemporary strains of inherited exclusive language.

right and welcome contemporary examples are appearing.[7] I hope, however, to provide a meeting place at the intersection of philosophy, theology, biblical studies and history on which others interested in naming God may continue to build.

---

[7] See, for instance, Brendan Thomas Sammon, *The God Who Is Beauty: Beauty as a Divine Name in Thomas Aquinas and Dionysius the Areopagite.* (Eugene, Ore.: Pickwick Publications, 2013). I will discuss later Cardinal Walter Kasper's *Mercy: The Essence of the Gospel and the Key to Christian Life* (New York: Paulist Press, 2014), a work endorsed and developed by Pope Francis in his own book, *The Name of God Is Mercy*. A valuable pastoral aid is Wilda C. Gafney, *A Women's Lectionary for the Whole Church* (New York: Church Publishing, 2021), which includes an appendix of God's names and divine titles.

2

Naming God at Sinai

The Gift of the Name

~

Is the Christian God a Metaphysical Monster?

'You are great, Lord, and highly to be praised (Ps 47.2): great is your power and your wisdom is immeasurable' (Ps 146.5). Man, a little piece of your creation, desires to praise you, a human being 'bearing his morality with him' (2 Cor 4.10), carrying with him the witness of his sin and the witness that you 'resist the proud' (I Pet 5.5). Nevertheless, to praise you is the desire of man, a little piece of your creation. You stir man to take pleasure in praising you, because you have made us for yourself, and our heart is restless until it rests in you.[1]

Saint Augustine begins the poem of love that is his *Confessions* by invoking and praising his God as a God of power and immeasurable wisdom. Augustine and his contemporaries had no difficulty calling upon a God who is powerful, eternal and immutable. Yet to many of us today, a God delineated by such perfections is entirely at odds with the God of loving kindness who, in the pages of Scripture, bends down to human need. Indeed, the God of these perfections appears no less a monster than the

---

[1] Saint Augustine, *Confessions*, Book I. Unless otherwise indicated, all excerpts from the *Confessions* are from the translation by Henry Chadwick (Oxford: Oxford University Press, 1998).

cruel and capricious God sketched by contemporary critics of Christianity – indeed God seems just a metaphysical monster.

Some modern theologians have argued that a mistake was made early on, that early Christianity never developed 'a consistent doctrine of God' but rather adopted 'the metaphysical tradition of Greek philosophy' and with it the attributes of a 'god' of natural theology. Jürgen Moltmann stated it thus:

If, in the manner of Greek philosophy, we ask what characteristics are 'appropriate' to the deity, then we have to exclude difference, diversity, movement and suffering from the divine nature. ... Impassible, immovable, united and self-sufficient, the deity confronts a moved, suffering and divided world that is never sufficient for itself. For the divine substance is the founder and sustainer of this world of transient phenomena; it abides eternally, and so cannot be subjected to this world's destiny.[2]

This God of what we have grown used to calling 'the classical attributes' is, on this argument, a philosophical cuckoo in the biblical nest – a remote deity that could not address our needs.[3] Talk of God's eternity

---

[2] Jürgen Moltmann, *The Trinity and the Kingdom: The Doctrine of God*, 1st US ed. (San Francisco: Harper & Row, 1981), 22.

[3] Katherine Sonderegger suggests that it was the Process Theologians who coined the category 'classical theism' by way of rejecting 'the God of classical theism'. 'Classical theism', she adds, is a category 'now so widely used as to seem self-evident'. *Systematic Theology*, Vol. I: *The Doctrine of God* (Minneapolis: Fortress Press, 2015), 165. See Sonderegger's book, and especially Part III, for an excellent analysis of the shortcomings of process theology and its ilk, and a robust defence of the divine perfections (attributes) firmly anchored in the Christian doctrine of God, deploying a nuanced understanding of religious language.

and immutability, his omniscience and omnipresence, conjures up a dictator, ruling in power and might, that most find impossible to love and, after several centuries of western imperialism and sexism, embarrassing if not impossible to own. What use in Christian life is one who is called *ipsum esse subsistens* or 'Being itself' whose attributes are unfolded as simplicity, infinity, eternity, omnipresence and so on?[4]

Some theologians have even argued that it is not just the God of the philosophers but God of the Bible itself – eternal, almighty and omniscient – who is a monstrous potentate. Gordon Kaufman, an extreme instance, insisted that Christianity must discard a God conceived as infinite and almighty, and was especially exasperated with Christian philosophers who defend a God whom he thinks no longer deserves defending.[5] The God who is 'an arbitrary, imperial potentate, a solitary eminence existing in glorious transcendence of all else' is, he tells us, a thing of the past. We can no longer think of God as 'an objectively existing powerful agent-self'.[6] We should no longer speak of God as creator/lord or father either, for these terms are infested with the anthropomorphism

---

[4] Cardinal Walter Kasper makes this point in his *Mercy: The Essence of the Gospel and the Key to Christian Life* (New York: Paulist Press, 2014), 10.

[5] See his exchange with Eleanor Stump and Norman Kretzmann in the issues of *Faith and Philosophy*, 1989 and 1990: Gordon D. Kaufman, 'Evidentialism: A Theologian's Response', *Faith and Philosophy: Journal of the Society of Christian Philosophers* 6, no. 1 (1989): 35-46, https://doi.org/10.5840/faithphil1989613.

[6] Gordon D. Kaufman, 'Reconstructing the Concept of God: De-reifying the Anthropomorphisms', in *The Making and Remaking of Christian Doctrine*, ed. Sarah Coakley and David A. Pailin (Oxford: Clarendon Press, 1993), 95–115 at 104.

responsible for much oppression (of the weak, of women, of the poor) in the past and even now.

If this is a warning against idolatry, then few will disagree, but Kaufman is not simply reminding us, as did almost every theologian before him, of the dangers of idolatry and anthropomorphic language. He goes further and suggests that we move beyond belief in a God altogether. His is a thoroughgoing abandonment – we once needed this 'God symbol', but so his argument goes, we do not need it now. In fact, its retention keeps us in a state of moral immaturity, forever waiting for a powerful deity to reassemble the pieces of our fractured world.

In the Bible God stands behind and governs all that exists. In this picture it was apparently the autonomous, free agent, the 'I' (ego) existing alone in its solitude that was the core model on the basis of which the image/concept of God was constructed. When Moses, in a very early story, asks the voice from the burning bush, 'Who are you? What is your name?' the answer that comes back to him is 'I Am; I Am Who I Am' (Exod. 3.13–14, paraphrased). God is identified here as the great 'I Am', the ego-agent *par excellence*, sheer unrestricted agential power. Given this model, it is not surprising that God has often been conceived of as an all-powerful tyrant, a terrifying arbitrary force before whom women and men can only bow in awe and fear.[7]

Kaufmann seems clear that his 'imperial potentate' is the one who addressed Moses at Sinai, but it is hard to believe that the God painted in such lurid colours could be the same God who awoke the love and devotion of Anselm or Aquinas, Augustine or Julian of Norwich – or, for that matter, that this could be the God of the Bible itself.

---

[7] Kaufman, 'Reconstructing the Concept of God', 104.

Exodus 3 Revisited

We have now reached a pivotal text – Exodus 3 with its famous account of Moses' encounter with God in the burning bush. The sequence in which Moses requests, and indeed, is given, the Holy Name, *YHWH*, was to be of immense influence in the history of Christian theology; however, to read it as presenting us with a divine tyrant, an 'ego-agent *par* excellence', is entirely misleading. For those thinkers we will examine in this book, Jewish and Christian, the story of Moses on Sinai is a foundational story of God's love and nearness – God's gift to God's people in their time of need.

Finding the God of the Bible to be a capricious tyrant, and even pointing the accusing finger at this passage from Exodus, is far from new – indeed, it is a favourite theme of modern atheism from the eighteenth century onwards. A tyrannical God was memorably sketched by David Hume in the *Natural History of Religion*. In one of the first attempts to provide a materialist and reductionist account of religious belief and bucking the eighteenth-century trend to see progress in matters of religion, Hume tells a story of decline. Hume's 'natural history' portrays religion created and fuelled from first to last by craven fear and blind hope. Since human society improves 'from rude beginnings to a state of greater perfection', Hume confidently concludes that 'polytheism or idolatry was, and necessarily must have been, the first and most ancient religion of mankind'.[8] Monotheism

---

[8] David Hume, *The Natural History of Religion* (1757, 1777), 1.1, Hume Texts Online (davidhume.org). Richard Dawkins is just one in a long line of critics of this unpalatable God.

is simply a refinement of polytheism. Simple and barbaric peoples will naturally choose a particular god as their patron and, having done so, endeavour to inflate his attributes to incomparable supremacy. Praise of their 'god' as the greatest god soon leads to praise of him as the 'only god' and, elevating their deities to the utmost bounds of perfection, at last beget the attributes of unity and infinity, simplicity and spirituality.[9]

Monotheism turns out to be the highest, and therefore best concealed, kind of idolatry, and the divine attributes – far from being the reasonable results of philosophical or spiritual reflection – are no more than distilled grovelling. Where God is so elevated, says Hume, (anticipating Marx, Nietzsche and Freud) the human mind is abased. It is a zero-sum game – if God is great, 'Man' is small. Monotheism is not morally preferable to polytheism – rather, the reverse. Polytheism, while untidy and primitive, is at least tolerant, but those religions which maintain 'the unity of God' are intolerant, implacable and narrow. Hume admits that a refined and reasonable religion would be quite acceptable to him, but as to religions as they are actually found – 'You will scarcely be persuaded that they are other than sick men's dreams.'[10]

With a capricious, inexorable God already made familiar by Enlightenment critics of religion, Freud was able to craft his own portrait of the overbearing heavenly father. Yet there's a certain irony in the fact that Freud's *Future of an Illusion*, while echoing Hume's contention that religion is little more than sick men's dreams, cannot dispense with

---

[9] Hume, *The Natural History of Religion*, 8.2.
[10] Hume, *The Natural History of Religion*, 15.6.

the myth of the Exodus. The God of Exodus becomes, in Freud's terms, the murdered primal father who is behind every divine figure, and the father who is giver of the law. Freud's talking cure revolved around 'our God, the word' and his late work, *Moses and Monotheism*, can be read as an extended, modern midrash on the Exodus story, in which Freud himself appears at times to be Moses, leading the people from pre-scientific slavery to the promised land of psychoanalysis. This borrowing of overtly religious terminology is even more apparent in Freud's famous French interpreter, Jacques Lacan (himself from a Catholic background). Lacan's essay 'The Function of Language in Psychoanalysis' is filled with reference to 'the Word' of the patient, with quotes from scripture (sometimes in Greek), and with theological terminology such as *anamnesis*, 'nature and grace' and so on.[11] Lacan provides his own psychoanalytic gloss on the famous Exodus 3 passage. Moses at the burning bush, according to Lacan, meets the symbolic father who is literally capable of laying down the law – of saying 'I Am Who I Am.' Here, analytically, is the fixed point of the law to which all who wish to enter psychic maturity must relate.

Since so many in the history of western philosophy and theology have glossed the story of this famous bush, it might seem to be only intellectual courtesy to allow Freud and Lacan their analytic allegories. The problem is that modern westerners, brought up on a diet of half-digested psychoanalytic theory, may take Freud's reading not as one reading of Exodus but as gospel truth.

[11] In *Speech and Language in Psychoanalysis* (Baltimore, MD.: Johns Hopkins University Press, 1981).

In this new gnosis the 'real meaning' of the God of Jewish and Christian origins is taken to be the Oedipal father, standing over and against us at the gates of psychic prehistory. Many who gag over fundamentalist interpretations of Scripture swallow without difficulty the exegeses of a Freud or a Lacan. Is perhaps Freud's God the real intellectual ancestor of Kaufman's 'ego-agent *par excellence*' before whom we must cower and grovel?

Meeting God at Sinai

Again, we must ask, is the God whom Moses meets on Sinai this domineering agent? I quote the relevant passage in full:

Moses was looking after the flock of Jethro, his father-in-law, priest of Midian. He led his flock to the far side of the wilderness and came to Horeb, the mountain of God. There the angel of Yahweh appeared to him in the shape of a flame of fire, coming from the middle of a bush. Moses looked; there was the bush blazing but it was not being burnt up. 'I must go and look at this strange sight,' Moses said 'and see why the bush is not burnt.' Now Yahweh saw him go forward to look, and God called to him from the middle of the bush. 'Moses, Moses!' he said, 'Here I am,' he answered 'Come no nearer,' he said. 'Take off your shoes, for the place on which you stand is holy ground. I am the God of your father,' he said, 'the God of Abraham, the God of Isaac and the God of Jacob.' At this Moses covered his face, afraid to look at God. (Ex. 3.1–6)

Then Moses said to God, 'I am to go, then, to the sons of Israel and say to them, "The God of your fathers has sent me to you." But if they ask me what his name is, what am I to tell them?' And God said to Moses, 'I Am who I Am. This' he added 'is what you must say to the sons of Israel: "I Am has sent me to you".' And God also said to Moses, 'You are to say to the sons of Israel: "Yahweh, the God of your fathers, the God of Abraham, the God of Isaac, and the God of Jacob, has sent me to you." This is my name for all time; by this name I shall be invoked for all generations to come.' (Ex. 3.13–15)

Moses as an infant is miraculously saved by Pharaoh's daughter, plucked from the Nile in his basket of reeds. The next we hear of him is as a grown man – educated as an Egyptian but showing some conscience about the conditions of his fellow Israelites. He is over-zealous and kills an Egyptian whom he sees striking a Hebrew, an action which does little for his reputation with the Egyptians or his fellow Hebrews. Moses, effectively outcast, removes himself to Midian, marries Zipporah whom he meets at the well and who is not a Hebrew, and takes employment as a shepherd for her father.

In the course of seeking new grazing land in 'the far side of the desert', Moses comes to Horeb (a place of double isolation, a mountain in a desert) – and his life is changed once and for all.

Moses looked, we are told, and there was the bush blazing but it was not being burnt up. 'I must go and look at this strange sight,' Moses said, 'and see why the bush is not burnt'. Then Yahweh called,

'Moses, Moses.'

'Here I am,' he answered.

'Come no nearer. Take off your shoes, for the place on which you stand is holy ground. I am the God of your fathers – the God of Abraham, the God of Isaac, the God of Jacob.'

He must have a closer look. But it is when God *speaks to him* from the bush that Moses is astonished. Lacan, for all the idiosyncrasies of his reading of Exodus, has at least noticed that this decisive revelation of God to Moses is in the medium of speech, *in words.*[12] More specifically is it a 'call' narrative. Moses is called by name and called to lead the Israelites out of their captivity, for 'to call' has this double sense.[13]

In the narrative of Exodus 3, names and naming are to the fore. God calls Moses *by name* and tells him to take off his shoes. God then gradually discloses to Moses a series of divine names. God does not begin with 'I AM WHO I AM.' Rather, in the first of a sequence of names, God says, '*I am the God of Abraham, Isaac and Jacob*', the God, that is, of Moses' ancestors. God tells Moses that he has seen the misery of his people, Israel, in Egypt and means to deliver them. Moses is to be the agent of this delivery. Moses is to go to Pharaoh and bring the sons of Israel out of bondage.[14]

---

[12] Walter Brueggemann notes that this is not so much a 'theophany' as a 'voice to voice encounter'. 'Exodus 3: Summons to Holy Transformation', in *The Theological Interpretation of Scripture: Classic and Contemporary Readings*, ed. Stephen E. Fowl (Cambridge, Mass.: Blackwell, 1997), 155–72 at 157.

[13] 'Call narratives' are an established form in the Hebrew Bible. Moses, Jeremiah, Isaiah and Ezekiel are all 'called' using similar narrative forms: introduction, commission, objection reassurance, sign. See Norman Habel, 'The Form and Significance of the Call Narrative', *Zeitschrift für die Alttestamentliche Wissenschaft* 77, no. 36 (1965): 297–323. For some widening of the 'call narrative' beyond Habel's model, see Fred Guyette, 'The Genre of the Call Narrative', *Jewish Studies Quarterly* 43, no. 1 (2015): 51–9.

[14] I am not happy with the use of male personal pronouns to refer to God in discussing this most cautious and numinous locus of biblical naming, but the English language lacks ways to express the personal nature of agency without using 'he' or 'she' at this juncture. It is the

Far from crumbling before the 'all-powerful tyrant' sketched by critics of the Bible from Hume through to Richard Dawkins, Moses becomes argumentative. He raises difficulties that perhaps God has not thought of – he is not a good speaker, he has a stammer, his brother Aaron might be better, Pharaoh won't listen to him, and to sum it up:[15]

'Who am I to go before Pharaoh?'

'I shall be with you' is God's reply.

This promise, 'I shall be with you', fails to satisfy Moses who is as uncertain of his reception among his fellow Israelites as before Pharaoh.

'What', he says, 'if the sons of Israel ask me what your name is – what am I to tell them?'

At this stage God gives a second name.

'And God said to Moses "*I Am Who I Am.*"'

And then a third – 'you must say to the sons of Israel "*I Am* has sent me to you".'

Then follows a fourth name, the four-lettered sacred name, or Tetragrammaton:

You are to say to the sons of Israel: 'YHWH, the God of your fathers, the God of Abraham, Isaac and Jacob, has sent me to you.' This is my name for all time; by this name I shall be invoked for all generations to come.

These names, three or four depending on how we count them, are given in sequence of text, names whose

---

personal nature of the God of Israel, not God's gender (which God does not have), which is the point.

[15] Brevard Childs speaks of the prophet's 'resistance to his inclusion in the divine plan' – *Exodus: A Commentary*, Old Testament Library (London: SCM Press, 1974), 71.

origins, Hebrew Bible scholars tell us, are lost in the overlapping and successive textual traditions, but whose significance in this final canonical form have been meditated upon for generations by Jews and Christians. Of these the Tetragrammaton (*YHWH*), is privileged. This is unpronounceable and, by pious Jews, the unpronounced name of God. This name appears over 6,000 times in the Hebrew Bible. When prophets and psalmists, 'call upon the name of the LORD', they invoke this name. Yet the Tetragrammaton's overwhelming presence in the Bible is masked for Christians by modern translations, which almost universally replace the *YHWH* in the original Hebrew with the capitalized 'LORD'. This is, of course, not without reason, for even at the time of Jesus the Tetragrammaton was not articulated. Instead, those reading aloud would substitute *Adonai*, the Hebrew word for Lord. Yet this translation practice obscures, for Christians, the importance of the Name (*YHWH*) in their own Bibles.

Exodus 3 marks the high point in a series of names and naming, of people and places, which began in Genesis with Abraham and ends with the first of the Ten Commandments in Exodus 20, 'I am YHWH your God who brought you out of the land of Egypt, out of the house of slavery.' It is not only God who is the subject of naming. Abram, who will be the father of nations, has been renamed 'Abraham'; Isaac is given his name from Sarah's 'laugh'. Naming in these texts is not simply a matter of tagging or simple denomination, it is, rather, a practice which locates a certain individual or place within the emergent, symbolic, remembered history of Israel.

It should be emphasised, however, that while naming and renaming are frequent features of the Hebrew Bible, divine self-naming is extremely rare. God is named, or called upon by name, hundreds of times by others – by Psalmists, Prophets and Moses himself – but rarely does God, as it were, name Godself. This is almost solely in the Book of Exodus and to Moses, hence the weight of the encounter of God and Moses at the burning bush. Here God not only gives Moses the Holy Name, *YHWH*, but glosses it, placing himself as the God of Israel's history. Moses is to know that whom he meets is the God of Israel's past (of Abraham, Isaac and Jacob), of its present who sees its suffering and of its future who will lead them from slavery to the promised land.[16]

While the Tetragrammaton should be privileged, the *'ehyeh asher ehyeh'* of Exodus 3.14–15 ('I AM WHO I AM') has fascinated Christian theologians, especially those whom we associate with 'negative' or mystical theology. The truncated form 'you must say to the sons of Israel "I AM has sent me to you"' (Ex. 3.14) with its suggestion of metaphysical ultimacy, of God as 'Being itself', was attractive to theologians of the early church. The Septuagint translation of the Hebrew (*ehyeh asher ehyeh*) as *Egô eime ho ôn* acted as an encouragement to just such a metaphysical reading, as did the Latin Vulgate's *Ego Sum Qui Sum*, and *Qui est*, for 'I AM'.

These renderings of the Hebrew in Greek and Latin, and the *'I Am Who I Am'* of the English Bibles, do not,

---

[16] See Jon D. Levenson, *Sinai and Zion: An Entry into the Jewish Bible*, New Voices in Biblical Studies (Minneapolis: Winston Press, 1985) in which Levenson points out that the encounter is not narrative as though 'it occurred on the level of mere fact …' but, rather, 'the writers enlisted history in the service of a transcendent and therefore metahistorical truth' (17).

however, do justice to the Hebrew text. *Ehyeh asher ehyeh* seems to be a gloss on the Name, *YHWH*, which is suggestive of the Hebrew verb, *hayah* 'to be', or better 'to become'. And while it would be incorrect to say, strictly speaking, that this is what *YHWH* means (for, technically, proper names do not have meanings), it is a commonplace of the Hebrew Bible that names may tell something of their bearers.[17] Walter Kasper suggests that the verb *hâyâh* here means not so much 'to be' as 'to effect' or 'to be effective'. The Name thus glossed is a promise that God will be with Israel in an effective way. For Brevard Childs, *ehyeh asher ehyeh* emphasises the actuality of God so that we might translate it as 'I am there, wherever it may be – I am really there.'[18]

Jewish writers emphasise the particularity of the disclosure on Sinai – God speaks at a specific time and for a specific purpose. I AM WHO I AM is not, in Exodus, a timeless abstraction derived from reason alone, as we saw with Descartes, but the God who Israel meets in her moment of need. It is the name of the God who delivers, the God who saves, who comes with everlasting love and that will continue throughout the Hebrew Bible as the faithful 'call upon the Name of the Lord'.

---

[17] See R. W. L. Moberly, *The Old Testament of the Old Testament: Patriarchal Narratives and Mosaic Yahwism*, Overtures to Biblical Theology (Minneapolis: Fortress Press, 1992), 95. Moberly mentions Gen 32.28, Ruth 1.20, I Sam 25.25.

[18] In personal correspondence, Andrew Macintosh suggests that 'to be' is an 'appropriate but not always accurate rendering. The verb implies transition, movement, intervention. I think the opening verses of Psalm 124 (Masoretic text ordering) give the best definition of the divine name: "If the LORD had not HAYAD-ed for us, we would have been clobbered by our enemies".'

This unfolding of Exodus 3 will prove the key to bringing together the biblical and the metaphysical, as can be seen when we look to the writings of the two Jewish philosophers most attentive to the Name and the naming of God in the twentieth century, Martin Buber and Franz Rosenzweig.

Buber and Rosenzweig on the Name and the Naming of God

No modern philosophers have worked harder to recover, indeed to rescue, the God of the Book of Exodus from the clutches of abstract philosophical speculation than Martin Buber and Franz Rosenzweig. Theirs was, at the same time, an attempt to recover for jaded readers, both Jewish and Christian, the vividness of the Hebrew original.

In 1925 Buber and Rosenzweig began work on a new translation of the Bible from Hebrew into their native German. Rosenzweig was already afflicted with the degenerative disease that would kill him in 1929 at only forty-three years of age, but he threw himself into the project with the intellectual vigour of a young man. This constituted a *volte-face*. Early in the same year he had declared himself entirely resistant to the project, being of the opinion that the reigning German translation (the Luther Bible) could not, or should not, be substantially changed and that to do so would be an affront to German language and culture. By the end of 1925 he had changed his mind. The plan was not simply to tweak the Luther Bible's translation of the Torah away from its Christian-inflected emphasis but to recover the power of the original Hebrew, and the beneficiaries would be Jews and

Christians alike.[19] Soon he and Buber were well into a free translation of the Torah which sought to catch the vigour of the Hebrew, and which departed radically from previous translations. In this project the Luther Bible was as much their inspiration and template as it was the subject of their criticism. In its day, Rosenzweig argued, the Luther Bible had been 'a trumpet-call in the ear of those who had fallen asleep', complacent with an accepted and familiar text.[20] Buber and Rosenzweig, already inducted into existential philosophy, sought the same 'trumpet-call' effect. Moments of divine address, of encounter and response were of particular importance to them, and thus the attention to Moses and the gift of the Name.

They had in Moses Mendelssohn a distinguished Jewish predecessor. This learned man translated the Pentateuch into German in the early nineteenth century and, with others, compiled the commentary known as the *Biur*. Mendelssohn's translation was indisputably elegant. Rosenzweig was to say, however, that, apart from its role in shaping German literary style, it had 'lasting effect on German and world Judaism only in one respect: translating the divine Name, YHWH, as "the Eternal"'.[21] The decision to use an abstract and philosophical term to translate the Tetragrammaton was, from Rosenzweig's point of view, a mistake and, moreover, one which was to influence

[19] Mara H. Benjamin, *Rozensweig's Bible: Reinventing Scripture for Jewish Modernity* (Cambridge: Cambridge University Press, 2009), 107–10.
[20] Franz Rosenzweig, 'Scripture and Luther', in *Scripture and Translation*, ed. Martin Buber and Franz Rosenzweig (Bloomington: Indiana University Press, 1994), 57–69 at 57.
[21] Franz Rosenzweig, '"The Eternal": Mendelssohn and the Name of God', in *Scripture and Translation*, ed. Martin Buber and Franz Rosenzweig (Bloomington: Indiana University Press, 1994), 99–113 at 100.

all 'Jewish piety of the Emancipation, even in orthodox circles'.[22] In his translational choice Mendelssohn shows himself under the sway of the 'rationalizing, classicizing spirit of his century'.[23] Rosenzweig takes the rendering of the Tetragrammaton as 'the Eternal' to be indicative of attenuated belief, and of Mendelssohn's apparently Enlightenment conviction that 'the notion of a being necessarily existent might inevitably imply the notion of a providential one'.[24] In a final ringing criticism, Rosenzweig suggests that in 'Mendelssohn's case the spirit of the age made alliance with the spirit of Maimonides, whom Mendelssohn had honoured all his life, against the sure instinct of Jewish tradition'.[25]

But how should a modern translator deal with the Divine Name? Buber and Rosenzweig wrote more on this topic than almost any other twentieth-century theologian, and certainly more than any philosophers. They were convinced that, alone amongst the biblical names for

[22] Rosenzweig, '"The Eternal"', 100.
[23] Rosenzweig, '"The Eternal"', 100.
[24] Rosenzweig, '"The Eternal"', 105.
[25] Rosenzweig, '"The Eternal"', 105. The disagreement over whether the God of the philosophers can have anything to do with the God of Scripture which we've marked in Christian writers is to be found amongst Jewish ones. Frequently, but not always, hostility to philosophy is aligned to criticism or dismissal of Maimonides such as we have here with Rosenzweig (for another contemporary example, see Michael Wyschogorod's *The Body of Faith: God and the People of Israel* (Northvale, NJ: Jason Aronson, 1996)). For a defence of Maimonides as both rabbi and philosopher, see José Faur, *Homo Mysticus: A Guide to Maimonides's Guide for the Perplexed* (Syracuse, NY: Syracuse University Press, 1998); Lenn Evan Goodman, *God of Abraham* (New York; Oxford: Oxford University Press, 1996); and Kenneth Seeskin, *Searching for a Distant God: the legacy of Maimonides* (New York; Oxford: Oxford University Press, 2000). Of these Faur is especially interesting since he writes as a scholar

God (*Elohim*, *El*, *El Shaddai*), *YHWH* had the status of a proper name and not a concept. Its truest form as a name is found in direct address – the 'I' which calls to 'You', that is, in the vocative. As a name it could be neither pluralised nor transformed into a noun. Yet it was also a meaning-bearing name, and this not just in the weak etymological sense in which the German name 'Friedrich' can be seen to be derived from *Friede* (peace). The Tetragrammaton was meaning-bearing in virtue of the revelation to Moses at the burning bush and the gloss given there for the Name.[26] The Name cannot be separated from the gloss, but how does the translator convey this to the non-Hebrew reader?

Mendelssohn, like other Jewish translators before him, had avoided the obvious translation 'my Lord' (Herr) because, although true to the Hebrew *adonai*, this had become too much associated in German language and through the Luther Bible with Christianity. Rosenzweig agreed, writing that through the Greek of the New Testament and its German translation, 'the Lord'

of Rabbinic literature, literary theory and Jewish law, and from an orthodox perspective. It is also worth stating that these defenders read Maimonides quite differently on different points. Seeskin, for instance, suggests that God cannot be spoken of as acting in the world, thus 'Revelation is not a case of God's choosing to speak with Moses but of Moses' coming to understand the will of God' (21), whereas Faur argues that Maimonides is above all anxious to defend God's providence and freedom to act. But both would agree with the suggestion, put by Seeskin that there is no tenable division between Maimonides the Rabbi and Maimonides the philosopher (20).

[26] Franz Rosenzweig and Martin Buber, 'A Letter to Martin Goldner', in *Scripture and Translation*, trans. Lawrence Rosenwald with Everett Fox (Bloomington: Indiana University Press, 1994), 189–92 at 190; Martin Buber, 'On Word Choice in Translating the Bible: In Memoriam Franz Rosenzweig', in *Scripture and Translation*, ed. Martin Buber and Franz Rosenzweig (Bloomington: Indiana University Press, 1994), 73–89 at 87.

has come to refer not to God but to the founder of Christianity – a reference that even today gives a Christian coloring to the Old Testament. When the devout Christian says, 'The Lord is my shepherd', he thinks not of God but of 'the Good Shepherd'.[27]

Rosenzweig has some sympathy for Mendelssohn's choice not to follow earlier Germano-Jewish translations, which used simply 'God'/*Gott* in place of the Tetragrammaton, for this loses the *particularity* of the Name. Yet 'the Eternal' was still an odd choice. Calvin had used it in his French translation, but it was 'biblical' only insofar as it appeared in the Apocrypha, texts written during the period of Hellenistic Judaism and not included in the Jewish canon. There in the Letter to Baruch *ho Aionios* appears several times as a name of God, and it was probably there that Calvin found this 'austere, sublime, genuinely "numinous" term' with which he rendered the name of God.[28]

Rosenzweig and Buber despaired of the ponderous metaphysical associations of the 'I AM WHO I AM' (in German, *ICH WERDE SEIN, DER ICH SEIN WERDE*) mediated to the west by the Septuagint and the Vulgate. Their resolution was to dispense with any single rendering of the Name but to translate the Name and its gloss in many variations, all of which favour the dynamic sense of *'becoming*, of *appearing*, and of *happening'*.[29]

Rosenzweig conceded that Moses Mendelssohn, despite a poor choice in translation, showed great insight on the Name. For instance, at the first use of the

---

[27] Buber, 'On Word Choice in Translating the Bible', 101.
[28] Buber, 'On Word Choice in Translating the Bible', 101.
[29] Rosenzweig, '"The Eternal"', 104.

Tetragrammaton in Genesis 2.4, Mendelssohn forbears to say *anything at all*, simply telling his readers to consult his later notes for Exodus 3.14, 'for there is the place to discuss it'.[30] This suggests that for Mendelssohn, as for Rashi, the significance of the Name is to be read 'backwards and forwards', so to speak, from the revelations to Moses at Horeb/Sinai.

When we reach Exodus 3.14 Mendelssohn paraphrases in this way:

God spoke to Moses: 'I am the being that is eternal.'
He said further: 'Say to the children of Israel,
"The eternal being, which calls itself, I-am-eternal, has sent me
    to you."'[31]

Mendelssohn's own comment on this is the following:

It says in a midrash,
'The Holy one, Blessed be He,' said to Moses: 'say to them, "I am the one who was, and now I am the same and will be the same in the future." And our teachers, may their memory be a blessing, say further: "I will be with them in this need, will be with them in their bondage in the kingdoms to come."' (Cf. Berakhot 9b)
Their meaning is the following: 'Because past and future time are all present in the creator, since in Him there is not change and dependence and of His days there is no passing – because of this all times are in Him called by a single name, which embraces past, present and future alike. Through this name he indicates the necessity of existence and at the same time the continuous and abiding character of providence. He says, then, by this name, "I am with the children of men, to be

---

[30] Rosenzweig, '"The Eternal"', 104.
[31] Buber, 'On Word Choice in Translating the Bible', 101.

well disposed and to have mercy on whom I will have mercy"
(Ex. 33.19). Say then to them, to Israel, that I am He who was,
is, and shall be, and who practices lordship and providence over
all. I shall be with them in this need and shall be with them
whenever they call to me.'[32]

Here we have 'omnitemporality, necessity of existence
and providence'. The word which best catches *all of these
meanings* is, Mendelssohn believes, 'the Eternal'.

This comment makes it altogether clear that
Mendelssohn *both knows and believes* the famous gloss on
the Name to be far more than 'a lecture on God's eternal
necessity'. He knows it to be *altogether* to do with the contingent, and with God's concern for the plight of the children of Israel at this narrative moment. Citing Onkelos,
Saadia Gaon and Maimonides, he says that the holy
Name in fact has three meanings: one concerning providence, another eternity and the third existential necessity.
All of these are caught up in the Name and its gloss, and
Mendelssohn sees no conflict between them.[33]

Mendelssohn's rationalism was by all accounts far
reaching, yet it is harsh to accuse him of ignoring the best

---

[32] Buber, 'On Word Choice in Translating the Bible', 101.

[33] Rosenzweig notes that the Talmud knows only the midrash of
'providence' and makes a distinction, alien to Mendelssohn, between
the 'classic religious philosophers' (Maimonides et al.) and 'the
genuine popular tradition' (Onkelos, Talmud, Rashi), (Rosenzweig,
'"The Eternal"', 103). Other modern Jewish writers are not so averse.
See the entry for 'God, Names of', in *The Oxford Dictionary of the
Jewish Religion*, ed. R. J. Zwi Werblowsky and Geoffrey Wigoder
(Oxford: Oxford University Press, 1997), 277–88, which notes that the
gloss is interpreted as denoting 'eternal existence'. See also Herbert
Chanan Brichto commenting on the 'I Am Who I Am' of Ex. 3.14 in
his *The Names of God: Poetic Readings in Biblical Beginnings* (New York;
Oxford: Oxford University Press, 1998), 24.

tradition of Jewish piety, or of being unduly swayed by the Vulgate or Septuagint. He would have been baffled by such a criticism. We could add that no one who was following Maimonides could possibly think the notion of a 'necessary existent' implied that of providence. Maimonides was committed to a theological notion without precedent in the philosophical theology of Plato and of Aristotle – *creatio ex nihilo* – which, as we shall see, defeats such an implication.

To bring these reflections on naming God at Sinai to a close, Exodus and Deuteronomy are not works of philosophical speculation. It would be anachronistic, to suppose that they were. But it is not unreasonable to read them as attesting to the disclosure of the One who is and was and will always be. This is what much subsequent Jewish and Christian reflection has done, and it was in order to secure this distinctive insight that Abrahamic understandings of divine eternity were developed. Providence here is not derived from some pre-existing philosophical commitment to a 'necessary existent.' The order is, if anything, the other way around: Scripture and its narratives come first, the text of Torah with the 'I Am Who I Am' and 'the One Who Is'. Philosophical reflection and Christian metaphysics can only follow what has been disclosed. The eternal God, ever free to act and be present to His people, is known as eternal God through his everlasting, providential concern.

It is this 'being present' of God that provides the point of departure for much late antique reflection on the giving of the Name to Moses. Those writing in this metaphysical register, whether Jews or Christians, were, as they saw it, defending the Bible's distinctive understanding. Moses Mendelssohn's explanation of why he translated the divine Name as 'the Eternal' stands in line with this tradition, even if it might not have been the best choice for a translation of the Holy Name.[34]

The genuine kinship between metaphysics and revelation was evident, it must be said, to Rosenzweig, as well. Writing of the giving of the Name to Moses he says:

Only because this one-becoming-present-to-you will always be present to you when you need him and call upon him – 'I *will* be there' – only for this reason does he become in our reflection, our after-thought, also the ever-being, the absolute, the eternal, separated thus from my need and my particular moment ... His eternity is made visible only in relation to a Now, to my Now; his 'absolute being' only in relation to my present being; his 'pure being' only in relation to the least pure being of all.[35]

Was Mendelssohn wrong then to translate the Name as 'the Eternal'? In the end Rosenzweig's best instincts allow him to be generous. The translator in him disapproves, but the religious writer concedes that such notions as 'being,' 'he-who–is' and 'the Eternal' are 'connected with the name, and latent in it, as philosophical consequences'.[36]

[34] My preference would be for the name to remain in Hebrew, or in transliterations such as *YHWH*. The New Jerusalem Bible uses 'Yahweh'; most other major English translations use LORD.

[35] Rosenzweig and Bubner, 'A Letter to Martin Goldner', 191.

[36] In the end his objections are those of a translator. He is as opposed to rendering the Name as 'he-who-is-present' as he is to translating it as 'the Lord' or 'the Eternal'. All of these reduce the Name to '*only* meaning' and lose the vocative sense. The Name should never seem just a noun. Rosenzweig and Buber, 'A Letter to Martin Goldner', 191.

Naming and Invocation

Pseudo-Dionysius begins his *Mystical Theology* with prayer. In direct allusion to Moses' ascent of Sinai, he prays that we will be led

> up beyond unknowing and light,
> up to the farthest, highest peak of mystic scripture
> where the mysteries of God's word
> lie simple, absolute and unchangeable
> in the brilliant darkness of a hidden silence.[37]

This is the kind of abstracting and allegorising that Jewish readers can find so annoying in Christian writings. What then are Christians to do with their inheritance of readings of the Exodus texts, readings dear to the mystical tradition? Certainly, Christians should take care not to interpret the disclosure at the burning bush as just a lesson in metaphysics. We must take to heart the Jewish insistence on the specificity of this particular moment in Israel's history. But, following Rosenzweig, we can say that the 'I *will* be there' who speaks to Moses is at the same time 'the ever-being, the absolute, the eternal'. In the hands of great theologians like Gregory of Nyssa, Augustine or Dionysius this 'ever-being' and eternal God of hidden silence is also *and always* the God of intimate presence, too.

Perhaps the most powerful and certainly the most effective of the western expositions of the divine perfections, or we might better say divine names, is to be found in Augustine's *Confessions*. Here God's omniscience and

---

[37] 'Celestial Hierarchy', in *Pseudo-Dionysius: The Complete Works*, trans. Colm Lubheid (Mahwah, NJ: Paulist Press, 1987), 134–91 at 135.

omnipresence, his unity and impassibility need scarcely be discussed, and indeed are not discussed in philosophical terms, for Augustine's text simply displays them. Augustine's God is 'omnipresent' because God is, simply, always present to Augustine – and was so even when Augustine was not aware of the fact. How do we know God is always there for Augustine? Because Augustine talks to his God, in any place, at any time – 'this, O Lord, you knew'. Augustine displays the presence of his God by his literary and doxological practice, retaining the vocative. He is calling upon his God and calls his God by many names. There is no time at which God is not, no place in which God is not, no secret centre to the soul where God is not. The God of these perfections is not remote but near, very near.

Who then are you, my God? What, I ask, but God who is Lord? For 'who is the Lord but the Lord', or 'who is God but our God?' (Ps 17:32). Most high, utterly good, utterly powerful, most omnipotent, most merciful and most just, deeply hidden yet most intimately present, perfection of both beauty and strength, stable and incomprehensible, immutable and yet changing all things, never new, never old ... you love without burning, you are jealous in a way that is free of anxiety ... You recover what you find, yet have never lost.[38]

One could of course suggest that Augustine simply *has not noticed* that he is mixing the language of philosophy (omnipotence, immutability) with the language of Psalms and Gospels. It is much more credible, however, to see him being deliberately provocative, rubbing our noses in

---

[38] Augustine, *Confessions*, 4–5.

the point he wants to make – he can only mix these words willy-nilly and without embarrassment because all are terms of God's intimacy with us.

The recognition that 'the One Who Is' or 'I AM' precisely **is** 'God with us' is the recognition Augustine makes when he moves from the schools of the Platonists to full Christian commitment. With the acceptance of the claim of the Jews that God has acted in their history, and of the even more startling Christian claim that the Word became flesh and dwelt among us, living a human life and dying a human death, Augustine comes to the recognition that history – lives as lived and deaths as died – far from being a distraction from things eternal is the only place where we can meet and know the God who is eternal, loving Lord.

When adumbrating these divine perfections, Augustine is not just speaking 'about' God but speaking to God. He is praying. The genre of the text performs the intimacy of his address. Augustine has begun *the* Confessions by invoking his God in prayer. Throughout the work Augustine will name God in hundreds of different ways, all scriptural, and in doing so he is participating in an already long-established practice which will endure for many centuries in theological reflection, worship and devotion. He is both naming and 'calling upon' God, as does Pseudo-Dionysius in beginning his 'Mystical Theology'.

The primary mode then for naming God is the vocative – calling, invoking, beseeching, praising. In earlier theological writings, ascriptions such as 'eternal', 'immortal' and 'all-knowing' stood not as lonely philosophical eminences but had their place amongst a host of divine names which were indeed discussed philosophically

34

but also invoked in prayer and praise.[39] They were, in short, attached to *practices* of naming, and these practices were in turn embedded in sustained meditation over many generations on the biblical texts and what it might be to name 'the Holy One of Israel'.

Naming and Calling Upon in Prayer

We are brought back to the words with which this chapter began, words of prayer with which Augustine opens his *Confessions*. It has often been remarked that Augustine begins this book with an epistemological quandary – how can he search for God if he does not yet know who or what it is he is searching for?[40] Yet Augustine has a prior question in his very first sentence – how, he wonders, can he praise God? 'How shall I call upon my God, my God and Lord?' How can he praise God if he does not know how to call upon him? Here the former professor of rhetoric agonises over how he *can speak at all* about the God who is beyond all naming. This is not just an epistemological and metaphysical question, it is a spiritual and a doxological one. For to name God is to risk making God into an object or an idol, and this is as true of the most seemingly non-idolatrous names that may be used for God, such as eternal, immutable and omniscient, as it is of the more obviously metaphorical names like king, shield and fortress.[41]

---

[39] Augustine uses the verb *invocare*, 'to invoke', six times in a few short sentences in *Confessions* Book I, i(1).

[40] See, for example, Denys Turner's discussion in *The Darkness of God: Negativity in Christian Mysticism* (Cambridge; New York: Cambridge University Press, 1995).

[41] Gordon Kaufman's 'God', or rather the one he credits to classical Christianity, would be just such a philosophical idol.

Augustine has already anticipated the dangers that Hume and Freud, and since them many theologians, have felt acutely – that our speaking of God may be a false speaking, simply exalted and disguised ways of speaking once more about ourselves. For someone setting out to write a spiritual autobiography this must be an ever-present danger.

He cannot speak if God does not call, and so Augustine begins with invocation. He beseeches his Lord, repeatedly, that he may find words, that God will give him words – 'Speak to me so that I may hear.' 'Allow me to speak.' The answer to his quandary is given in a practice, not a proposition – in the practice of prayer. God cannot be called down by human naming, however philosophically exalted this may be but surely, as Augustine says, 'you may be called upon in prayer that you may be known'. This prayer is itself already a gift.

My faith, Lord, calls upon you. It is your gift to me. You breathed it into me by the humanity of your Son, by the ministry of your preachers. (*Confessions*, Book I, i(1))

What those who diagnose servile terror in the account of Moses at the burning bush fail to notice is that when Moses asks God for a name, he is given one. Augustine's recognition is that we can speak of God only because, as with Moses and Israel, God has first spoken to us.

For 'those who have nothing to say or don't want to know anything', says Jacques Derrida, 'it is always easy to mimic the technique of negative theology'.[42]

[42] Jacques Derridak 'How to Avoid Speaking: Denials', in *Derrida and Negative Theology*, ed. Harold G. Coward and Toby A. Foshay (Albany: State University of New York Press, 1992), 73–142 at 75.

The language of the divine attributes is readily conceived either as painting a picture of a bullying God, or as vacuous. Yet despite its cautions and qualifications, this 'rhetorical of negative determination' is by no means vacuous and not, in the hands of theologians like Augustine or Dionysius, a technique for 'those who have nothing to say'.[43]

The agnostic Derrida proves an unexpected ally in that he does not find theological apophaticism to be trapped in a circle of negation. The reason for this is the place it gives to prayer. Why do the texts of Augustine, or Gertrude of Helfta, or any number of others, begin with invocation? The prayer which precedes these apophatic utterances is, as 'the address to the other', more than a pious preamble. One *must* begin with supplication, for the power of speaking and of speaking well comes from God.[44] Far from condemning the theological enterprise, there is in Derrida's essay the wistful implication that only the language of true theology, language whose destination is assured not by verbal domination but by grace, is truly language at all. To be a theologian, we might say, is always to stand under the primacy of the signified over the signifier (an exact reversal of what Derrida thinks to be the case for language in general) but at the same time to know the signified can only be

[43] Derrida, 'How to Avoid Speaking: Denials', 74.
[44] Derrida quotes Dionysius, 'to That One who is the Cause of all good, to Him who has first given us the gift to speak and then, to speak well' ('How to Avoid Speaking: Denials', 98). Derrida writes, 'This is why apophatic discourse must also open with a prayer that recognizes, assigns, or ensures its destination: the Other as Referent of a *legein* which is none other than its Cause' (98).

named through gift. The problem with which Derrida's reader is left is not one for theological language, but for any speaking or theory of speech which is atheistic. How, on Derrida's account, can anyone speak of God if he cannot first pray?

Above all this is true of course when speaking of God. The naming of God can never be, without risk of idolatry, a matter of simple denomination. Its foundation is gift – the gift of God's self-disclosure in history – and practice, the practice of prayer which is itself a gift. Our faith, Augustine says, is God's gift, through his Son. Augustine's search for self-knowledge and true speaking finds its conclusions not with 'cogito ergo sum' but rather in 'only say the word, Lord, and my soul shall be healed'.[45]

To conclude, instead of seeing a tension between detached philosophical reason on the one hand and scriptural warmth and intimacy on the other, we see bold theological commonality. Jews and Christians in the first centuries of the common era did not haplessly 'borrow' Greek metaphysics but, as we shall see, transformed it.

After Hume's *Natural History of Religion*, we are intellectually conditioned to think of philosophical monotheism as an intellectual notch above story-based, mythic religion. Attending to the textual and interpretative history of the Exodus narrative prompts a more demanding

---

[45] Liturgical response. See Matthew 8.8. For the continuing history of divine invocation in the writings of the mystics (or those we now call mystics), see Michel de Certeau, *The Mystic Fable*, Vol. I: *The Sixteenth and Seventeenth Centuries* (Chicago: University of Chicago Press, 1992), especially Ch. 5.

thought: from tribal henotheism and fledgling monothe-ism, Judaism moved to an account of divine transcend-ence more radical than any on offer in the philosophical monotheisms of Plato or Aristotle. The Bible provides the grounds for saying that God is 'Being Itself' – not a far-away God, but a God who is at the heart of everything and near to everyone. This philosophical transformation was built around the creator God as found in Scripture. This is not the 'god' of the philosophers but a God who is active, loving and free – a God who can call and be called upon and indeed 'be with the people'. To better see what transformation is involved it will be helpful to look back to the time of Christianity's origins and focus not on the Christians but on a Jew who interested himself greatly in naming God, Philo of Alexandria.

3

Philo on Knowing and Naming God

～

Philo, a Jewish Philosopher in the Age of Jesus and Paul

Much of what we find depends on our reason for seeking in the first place – for instance, a bottle of wine chosen to drink with cheese may present different merits than a bottle of wine (maybe even the same bottle) chosen as a makeshift cosh. The same is true, in more nuanced fashion, with philosophical texts and debates – what we find in them depends on what we were looking for in the first place. So it is with Philo of Alexandria. Approach him (as he was for many years approached) as a minor late Platonic philosopher, and you will find little of interest. However, if we consider him as a Middle Platonist, an expositor in the first century CE of his own Jewish scriptures and, in this case, as a Jewish philosopher who is very interested indeed in names, naming and in naming God, then startling new aspects of his thought appear.

Philo's work had considerable influence on early Christian thought, especially in what we now call 'negative' or apophatic theology, but this prodigious sage is nonetheless largely neglected by modern theologians and philosophers of religion.[1] Until relatively recent

---

[1] Even those who write on antecedents of negative theology pass him over, devoting attention to Plotinus and Porphyry in the third

times, even historians of philosophy treated Philo as something of a makeshift. Read just as a philosopher, Philo seems to say little that is original or novel.[2] He uses arguments standard to the Platonism of his time, much modified and a fluid mix of Stoic and Aristotelian ideas. Even John Dillon, who did much to recover interest in Philo, suggests that, apart from a heightened emphasis on divine transcendence and a 'greater personal reverence for God than one would expect to find

century CE and then leaping, in a single bound, back eight centuries from Plato himself while missing the Jewish and very biblical Philo. This is also true of those few philosophers who have been concerned with the divine names where the customary leap is from Pseudo-Dionysius to Proclus, and a rumoured lost text of Plotinus. See Olivier Boulnois, *Être et représentation* (Paris: Presses universitaires de France, 1999) and Olivier Boulnois, 'Les noms divins: Négation ou transcendence?', *Revue de Théologie et de la Philosophie* 150, no. 4 (2018): 315–33. This is, of course, to entirely miss the not lost writings of Philo. Historians are more receptive. Mark Edwards, in his *Origen against Plato*, Ashgate Studies in Philosophy and Theology in Late Antiquity (Aldershot: Ashgate, 2002), for example, devotes considerable attention to Philo.

[2] For instance, in *The Special Laws* (I.32) Philo uses an argument from Plato's *Timaeus*, without acknowledgement (as would be standard) and almost verbatim:

Doubtless hard to unriddle and hard to apprehend is the Father and Ruler of all, but that is no reason why we should shrink from searching for Him. But in such searching two principal questions arise which demand the consideration of the genuine philosopher. One is whether the Deity exists, a question necessitated by those who practise atheism, the worst form of wickedness, the other is what the Deity is in essence. Now to answer the first question does not need much labour, but the second is not only difficult but perhaps impossible to solve.

All the citations from Philo are from the Loeb edition, translated by F. H. Colson. I will give English names and Greek abbreviations for the texts. Those I use are the following:

in a Greek philosopher' there is little that marks Philo out from other Platonists of his day.[3] The other distinctive features of Philo's texts – his allegorising exegesis of scriptures and etymologies for proper names – seemed of merely antiquarian interest.[4]

Philo reads quite differently, however, if we approach him not as a mediocre philosopher but as an expositor of his own scriptures. This certainly is how Philo would have wanted to be read, for the vast bulk of his extensive writings is taken up with commenting on Jewish scripture. David Runia's work has been particularly important here. Runia even cautions us about styling Philo as a 'Middle Platonist' lest that obscure the fact that Philo

---

Abr. (De Abrahamo), On Abraham

Conf. (De confusione linguarum), On the Confusions of Tongues

Decal. (De Decalogo), On the Decalogue

de Cher (De Cherubim), On the Cherubim

Det. (Quod deterius potiori insidiari soleat), The Worse Attacks the Better

Deus (Quod Deus sit immutabilis), On the Unchangeableness of God

Fug. (De fuga et inventione), On Flight and Finding

Her. (Quis rerum divinarum heres sit), Who Is the Heir

L.A. (Legum allegoriae), Allegorical Interpretation

Mig. (De migratione Abrahami), On the Migration of Abraham

Mos. (De vita Moses), On the Life of Moses

de Mut. (De mutatione nominum), On the Change of Names

Op. (De opificio mundi), On the Creation

Somn. (De somnis), On Dreams

Spec. (De specialibus legibus), On the Special Laws

[3] John Dillon, The Middle Platonists: A Study of Platonism 80 BC to AD 220 (London: Duckworth, 1977), 155.

[4] The exception to this neglect by students of negative theology is Raoul Mortley's two-volume study From Word to Silence (Bonn: Hanstein, 1986), which does give Philo his due. But here we have an instance of the wine bottle as cosh phenomenon, as Mortley's interest in Philo is driven by his interest in the power of silence and the impotence of words as a strand in western philosophical thought rather than, as here, Philo's Jewishness and use of scripture.

saw himself not 'as a Greek philosopher, but rather as a devout and law-abiding Jew'.[5]

While reading Philo in the first instance as a biblical commentator might seem to lessen his importance to philosophy, I suggest that, on the contrary, it is when he grapples with his scriptures that he finds himself confronted with problems calling for innovative philosophical response.

For our purposes, however, Philo is important because of his interest in naming. More specifically, he is very interested in naming God, which is not surprising since in the Hebrew bible 'calling upon the name of the LORD' is idiomatic for prayer. Given what we have seen already of the centrality of the figure of Moses to this topic, we would expect to see Philo, if he is an attentive reader of Torah, turning frequently to Moses when he considers the question of naming God, and this is what we do find. Repeatedly, when his topic is the naming of God, Philo returns to Moses at Sinai. Furthermore, he does this when his topic is naming *and knowing* God, for Philo is one of the first to make this important link.

Philosophers before Philo had been fairly interested in naming. In the *Cratylus* Plato explores whether names (including common nouns like 'cow' and 'circle,' as well as proper names, like 'Catherine' and 'Isabelle') have a natural

---

5 See Runia's essay, 'Philo, Alexandrian and Jew', in *Exegesis and Philosophy: Studies on Philo of Alexandria* (Aldershot: Variorum, 1990), 1–18 at 16. Runia has transformed Philo studies by his insistence that Philo should be read as a Jewish expositor of his own scriptures. See also his *Philo of Alexandria and the Timaeus of Plato: Academisch Proefschrift ... Vrije Universiteit te Amsterdam* ([Amsterdam]: VU Boekhandel, 1983).

relationship to that which they designate or whether they apply by convention. Plato's suggestion is that 'correct' names reflect the nature of that which they name and he unfolds this by providing a list of etymologies of names for things, including the names for gods.[6] In a debate that would continue through the centuries, Aristotle plumped for convention.[7] Yet the notion that there might be 'correct' names for things lay behind a Greek fascination with etymologies as a guide to word meaning.[8]

Philo, too, is interested in etymologies of proper names – he provides etymologies for virtually everyone named in the biblical passages he discusses.[9] His warrant for doing so is less the Greek philosophical obsession with etymology than the biblical writings themselves, where meanings of names and of name changes are often given.[10] Where Philo stands out from the philosophers is in the difficulties he sees in naming God and, at the same time, the necessity that we should be able to do so. Should God be named as other things are named? How can any name for God be 'correct'? Most Greek philosophers took it for granted that naming the gods is similar

---

[6] See Robert van den Berg, 'Does It Matter to Call God Zeus?', in *The Revelation of the Name YHWH to Moses: Perspectives from Judaism, the Pagan Graeco-Roman World, and Early Christianity*, Themes in Biblical Narrative (Leiden: Brill, 2006), 169–83 at 174.

[7] On this see Mortley, *From Word to Silence*, Vol. I: *The Rise and Fall of Logos*, especially Ch. 5.

[8] Dillon, *The Middle Platonists*, 181.

[9] See David Winston, 'Philo of Alexandria', in *The Cambridge History of Philosophy in Late Antiquity*, ed. Lloyd P. Gerson (Cambridge: Cambridge University Press, 2010), 235–57 at 239.

[10] For instance, Philo discusses God's 'bestowing' upon those to whom he is dear new names. Abram ('uplifted father') becomes Abraham ('elect father of the sound') (*de Mut.* 60–9).

to naming the things about us. Plato, who touches upon it, thinks it is difficult to name God. For Philo it will be, strictly speaking, impossible.

Philo is our first source for certain distinctive divine epithets, for instance 'unnameable' (*akatonomastos*), 'unutterable' (*arrhêtos*), which subsequently find their way into Christian and pagan philosophical writings. We will find in Philo argumentative strategies that will subsequently characterise the 'divine names' tradition in Christian writings and which will reappear in the work of Moses Maimonides in the twelfth century and Thomas Aquinas in the thirteenth. It is vital to see already, in a Jewish writer of the first century CE, evidence of a shift that transformed western metaphysics, Christian and pagan. Philo, writing well before Christianity takes shape, strains every fibre to say that this 'One-who-is' is always already 'the-One-who-is-there', the One who is present to Israel. Furthermore, he argues this not because he is indebted to Plato or Aristotle (from whom he specifically distances himself), but because he is a Jew and because of what he believes as a Jew about God.

Jean Daniélou did not exaggerate when he said that Philo was 'unquestionably the first theologian to treat fully of divine transcendence'.[11] The alpha privative names are not mere pious detail but indicative of a radical shift in the understanding of God and God's relation to the world necessitated by Jewish believe in the creator God. Furthermore, it is because of – and not despite – the

---

[11] Jean Daniélou, *Gospel Message and Hellenistic Culture*, trans. John Austin Baker, A History of Early Christian Doctrine before the Council of Nicaea Vol. 2 (London: Darton, Longman and Todd, 1973), 236.

fact that his God is utterly transcendent that Philo's God is 'a personal being with which man has a reciprocal relation'.[12]

Ultimacy and Intimacy Are One

More should be said about Philo and his affinities with Christian writings of around the same period – that is, the books of the New Testament. Philo was a member of a flourishing Jewish community in Alexandria. Born around 20 BCE and dying perhaps in CE 50, he was a contemporary of Jesus and Paul although he seems to have no knowledge of this fledgling sect. Like the rest of Alexandrian Jewry and indeed like most Jews of the diaspora, his native language was Greek. He seems to have had little or no Hebrew.[13] As a member of an important and wealthy family, Philo received a Greek education, including strong grounding in grammar and rhetoric, about which he wrote appreciatively. As a respected figure, he headed a delegation to Rome in his later years, of which he left an account. Philo studied his own scriptures from the Greek Septuagint, the 'Bible' of Alexandria's Hellenised Jews. In his extensive writings, which for the most part take the form of allegorising and platonically informed readings of scripture, we discover that, for Philo, Moses anticipated all that was wise and good in the philosophers. For a number of reasons, not least the destruction of Alexandrian Jewry by the Romans, Philo's extensive writings are almost the sole

---

[12] Runia, 'Philo, Alexandrian and Jew', 11.
[13] See Runia, 'Philo, Alexandrian and Jew', 13.

witness to his Jewish milieu.[14] We have little basis to say what in them is original to Philo and what is common practice. We do know that his immersion in and embrace of Greek culture was by no means unusual for a Jew of the diaspora, and nor was Hellenism seen as an imposition, any more than a Jew in Manhattan today would regard the English language and the American way of life as alien.[15]

It seems likely that Philo had no wish to be an innovator. If so, his writings gain importance in that they may give us a clue as to how Greek-speaking Jews of the first century wrote, argued and – above all – read their scriptures.[16]

It is Philo's heightened and distinctly Jewish sense of the holiness and otherness of God that precipitates in him the crisis of language for the divine and leads him to say that God is unnameable and unknowable. As far as we know, Philo was the first to twin divine unknowability with divine unnameability, a standard pairing as late as Nicholas of Cusa in the fifteenth century. It is no

---

[14] Philo's writings were preserved by Christian sources. The Alexandrian theologians Clement and Origen both drew on Philo, as did (quite extensively) Saint Ambrose, Augustine's teacher. Gregory of Nyssa's Life of Moses is modelled on Philo's Life of Moses. Runia, 'Philo, Alexandrian and Jew', 13–14.

[15] See Tessa Rajak, *Translation and Survival: The Greek Bible and the Jewish Diaspora* (Oxford: Oxford University Press, 2009), 114–15. 'Hellenism' and 'Hellenistic Judaism' are today contested terms. Important here is to note that Philo is very 'Greek thinking' and very Jewish.

[16] See Henry Chadwick, 'Philo', in *The Cambridge History of Later Greek and Early Medieval Philosophy*, ed. A. H. Armstrong (Cambridge: University Press, 1967), 137–57, at 138. Since Philo is almost our only witness to the Alexandrian Jewry of his time, we have little basis to say what in his writings is original and what standard to his Jewish community.

accident, I shall argue, that it is a Jewish exegete and not a Greek philosopher who is our first source for many of our negative names for God.

By the time of Philo and the emergence of the New Testament, Greek rhetoric, philosophy and literature 'were the staple of elite education' in the eastern Roman empire, including the education of elite Jews.[17] St Paul, a native Greek speaker, writes with evident knowledge of Greek rhetorical structures. Although Greek metaphysics and cosmology presented difficulties for Jews, they had fewer problems with Greek grammar and rhetoric of which Philo, like Paul, is an adept.[18] Philo's writings show full acquaintance with the distinctions, tropes and categories of the antique grammarians. What most distinguishes his writings from his Greek philosophical sources is his reliance on scripture.

Philo is not a systematic exegete. He will frequently use a scriptural text as the stepping-off point for extended discussions of seemingly unrelated matters.[19] For instance, *On Flight and Finding*, one of twenty-one treatises dedicated to expounding Genesis, is ostensibly an exposition of the first few verses in Genesis 16 but is almost entirely given over to his discussion of thoughts triggered by just a few words – 'flight', 'found' and 'fountain'. Philo finds

---

[17] Rajak, *Translation and Survival*, 94–5.

[18] Of the period of Hellenised Judaism, Tessa Rajak writes, 'From the Jewish angle, this was a world in principle conducive to accommodation, even integration, without unwelcome compromise, let alone total submersion' (*Translation and Survival*, 94–5.).

[19] Thus manifesting what appears to us 'the strongest possible belief in the inspiration of the Scriptures with the freest possible criticism'. F. H. Colson, 'General Introduction', in *Philo*, Vol. I, trans. Colson, Loeb Classical Library (London: Heinemann, 1929), xii.

certain clusters of texts salient to particular problems and will return to them, throughout his writings, when that problem presents itself. Some of these clusters may be of his own devising, but others almost certainly mark inherited Jewish interpretative tradition – his ancestral philosophy.

Whenever it comes to the matter of naming God, Philo writes as one who is aware of the Greek philosophical literature and who also anticipates the difficulties of applying its accepted precepts to naming of the God of Israel. He is aware of the implications of the Jewish teaching on God as the Creator. Neither Plato nor Aristotle had a creator God, and certainly not one who creates 'all that is'. In the *Timaeus* Plato's demiurge moulds a pre-existent matter and Aristotle's impersonal deity is an everlasting correlate of an everlasting world. By contrast Philo, informed by the Psalms, Genesis and other scriptures, has a loving, willing, creator God, and this belief in a Creator God has a decisive influence on what Philo thinks about naming God.

Moving in a Greek intellectual milieu, he has need on occasion to distinguish his Jewish position from the common philosophy. He rejects Aristotle's view that the universe is ungenerated and eternal.[20] Philo believes that God has created all things. All things are dependent on God, but God is sufficient to himself and was so before the creation of the world.[21] Anticipating Augustine in the

---

[20] See the treatise *On the Creation of the Cosmos According to Moses* (*Op.*), especially §§170–1.

[21] 'How must it not be impossible to recompense or to praise as He deserves Him who brought the universe out of non-existence?' (*L.A.* III.10). 'He is full of Himself and sufficient for Himself. It was so before the creation of the world, and is equally so after the creation of

Confessions, Philo believes that God 'created space and place coincidentally with the material world' (*Conf.* 136). Anticipating Augustine, Philo holds that God created time itself, 'For there was no time before the cosmos, but rather it either came into existence together with the cosmos or after it' (*Op.* §26).[22] The cosmos is totally dependent on God and God is in no sense dependent on the cosmos. And finally, 'God, being One, is alone and unique, and like God there is nothing' (*L.A.. II.*1).[23]

This last is an altogether critical point for Philo when it comes to naming God. Since God cannot strictly *be like* any created being, we cannot *class* God or insert God into any category appropriate to our created kind. The philosophers known to Philo had said that God is 'eternal', 'imperishable' and 'unchanging', yet it is Philo who is our earliest surviving source for certain alpha-privatives which bear directly on naming and knowing: 'unname-able' (*akatonomastos*), 'unutterable' (*arrhêtos*) and 'incomprehensible under any form' (*kata pasas ideas akatalêptos*).

God is, for Philo, in the strict sense unknowable and unnameable by us. On the other hand, as a faithful Jew, Philo believes that God must not be left wholly in the

all that is. He cannot change nor alter and needs nothing else at all, so that all things are His but He Himself in the proper sense belongs to none' (*de Mut.* IV.27). 'Through His goodness He begat all that is, through His sovereignty He rules what he has begotten' (*de Cher.* 27–8). See also *Fug.* 46, *Mos.* II.267.

[22] Philo, *On the Creation of the Cosmos According to Moses*, ed. and trans. David T. Runia, Philo of Alexandria Commentary Series Vol. 1 (Leiden; Boston: Brill, 2001). See Runia's comment on this, p. 157.

[23] Debates concerning whether we find in Philo a consistent teaching of *creatio ex nihilo* rumble on and depend, often, on what elements of this 'raft' of teachings are taken as definitive. Frequently debate revolves around the question of whether Philo sees God as creating from some

realms of abstraction. In attempting to bridge this gap between the God who is totally *unlike* all created finitude and yet who is nonetheless present to us in the intimacy of disclosure, Philo anticipates a central problem which will occupy writers in centuries to come. For it is all very well to say that God is 'Wholly Other' – we have then to explain what justifies our language of prayer and praise and adoration. Jews (and Christians) do not characteristically want to say nothing at all about God – on the contrary theirs are amongst the most garrulous of religions. The God of the Pentateuch is personal and providential. How can our speaking be warranted? And if we cannot say how it is we *name* God, then can we claim to *know* God?

When questions about knowing and naming God arise, Philo turns to the example of Moses, 'sacred guide, most beloved by God'. He is not writing treatise in modern epistemology but as one who desires to see God's face. Philo's Moses is a seeker, the pre-eminent seeker, after God. Along with the story of the request for a name at the burning bush, Philo will revert again and again to Exodus 20 (where Moses ascends the mountain of Sinai and 'approaches the dark cloud where God was'), and to Exodus 33 where Moses asks to see God's glory.

---

primal matter, after the matter of the *Timaeus*, or by *divine fiat*. The two are not strictly incompatible, however, since it is possible to hold that God created the primal matter from which the world is fashioned. This seems to be Philo's position. Later thinkers would argue that this *could* be an eternal matter, without violating its total dependence on God. See Gregory E Sterling, '"The Most Perfect Work": The Role of Matter in Philo of Alexandria', in *Creation ex nihilo: Origins, Development, Contemporary Challenges*, ed. Gary A. Anderson and Markus N. A. Bockmuehl (Notre Dame, Ind.: University of Notre Dame Press, 2018), 99–118.

Exodus 33 is salient for there the cry of Moses leads to divine self-disclosure. Moses, Philo tells us, searched for God and cried out 'Reveal Thyself to me' (Ex. 33, *Spec.* I. 41). Moses' request to see God's glory was refused – he was allowed only to stand in a cleft in the rock and, mysteriously, to see God's back as God passes by. Philo's paraphrasing of the divine reply to Moses' request to 'see God's glory' makes clear that the obstacle is not modesty on God's part, but the impossibility for any creature to apprehend the Deity.

Thy zeal I approve as praiseworthy, but the request cannot fitly be granted to any that are brought into being by creation. I freely bestow what is in accordance with the recipient; for not all that I can give with ease is within man's power to take, and therefore to him that is worthy of My grace I extend all the boons which he is capable of receiving. But the apprehension of Me is something more than human nature, yea even the whole heaven and universe will be able to contain. (*Spec.* I.43–4)

When Moses asks that he might behold God's glory, he is told (according to Philo), that the 'powers' he seeks are altogether incomprehensible in their essence, but nonetheless, like a seal in soft wax, leave an imprint or copy that humans may see,

Do not, then, hope to be ever able to apprehend me or any of My powers in Our essence. But I readily and with right good-will will admit you to a share of what is attainable. That means I will bid you to come and contemplate the universe and its contents, a spectacle apprehended not by the eye of the body but by the unsleeping eyes of the mind. (*Spec.* I.49)

One of Philo's most extensive comments on knowing and naming occurs in the treatise *On the Change of Names* (*de Mut.*). His scriptural point of departure is Genesis 17.1 where Philo reads 'Abraham became ninety-nine years old and the Lord was seen by Abraham and said to him, "I am thy God"' (*de Mut.* I.1). But what can it mean to say 'the Lord was seen by Abraham'? Philo swiftly conducts his readers to Moses and Mount Sinai, and all three of the 'purple' passages mentioned are brought into play – Exodus 3.14, Exodus 20.21 and Exodus 33.13. We must not think, Philo says, that Abraham saw God with his eyes. No one, not even Abraham could see God with the eyes of the body. Nor yet can anyone fully apprehend God with the mind. When you hear 'that God was seen by man, you must think that this takes place without the light which the senses know'.

Do not however suppose the Existent (*to on*) which truly exists is apprehended by any man; for we have no organ by which we can envisage it, neither in sense, for it is not perceptible by sense, nor yet in mind. So Moses, the explorer of nature which lies beyond our vision, Moses who, as the divine oracles tell us, entered into the darkness (Ex. 20.21), by which figures they indicate existence invisible and incorporeal, searched everywhere and into everything in his desire to see clearly and plainly Him, the object of our much yearning, Who alone is good.' (*de Mut. II.*7)

When Moses despaired of this search he took refuge in prayer,

'Reveal Thyself to me that I may see Thee with knowledge' (Ex. 33.13)

This request is not granted for

To know what lies below the Existent, things material and immaterial alike, is a most ample gift even for the best sort among mortals ... for we read, 'Thou shalt see what is behind Me, but My face thou shalt not see' It means that all below the Existent (*to on*), things material and immaterial alike, are available to apprehension even if they are not all actually apprehended as yet, but He alone by His very nature cannot be seen. (*de Mut. II.*8–10)

Note that Philo includes amongst things that can be known in some way 'things immaterial' as well as things material. The unknowability of God is not simply the unknowability of things immaterial and unseen, like angels. All the Greek philosophers would agree the gods cannot be seen in this sense. But for Philo God is not a 'thing' at all. For Philo it is God alone who, by his very nature, cannot be seen. From this it follows for him that God cannot be named[24] The text continues,

It is a logical consequence that no personal name (*onoma kurion*) even can be properly assigned to the truly Existent. Note that when the prophet desires to know what he must answer to those who ask about His name He says 'I am He that IS' (*ego eimi ho on*), which is equivalent to 'My nature is to be, not to be spoken.' (*de Mut. II.*11)[25]

Some comment is needed on *onoma kurion*, here translated as 'personal name', in the course of which we will see something of Philo's indebtedness to antique grammar and its relation to metaphysics. Ancient Greek did

---

[24] Unnameability is a vice in Plato, a merit in Philo.
[25] See also *Somn.* I.230–1 where we read: 'Thus in another place, when he had inquired whether He that IS has any name, he came to know full well that He has no proper name, and that whatever name anyone may use of Him he will use by licence of language; for it is not the nature of Him that Is to be spoken of, but simply to be.'

not make a clear distinction between *name* and *word* but used *onoma* for both. Similarly, *onoma kurion* was used by Philo, as by Aristotle, without distinction to indicate both what we would regard as a 'common noun' (i.e. cat, tree, fish) and a 'proper name' (i.e. Fred, Fritz, Philo).[26] The nature of the argument is that God cannot be named with common names, or common nouns. We cannot, after the manner of Aristotle's account of naming, class God by genus or species for God is beyond both. Nor, after the manner of Plato's *Cratylus*, could any name be, in a strict sense, appropriate to God's nature. Names for humans and places may be of their nature 'fitting' to the essence of that which they name, but this cannot be so in the one special case of naming God. No name can represent God's nature, no name is correct.[27] This Philo takes to be the purport of God's reply to Moses, 'I Am He that Is.'

We need to remember that Philo's exegesis is driven by his understanding of who God is in Scripture. For while Philo's God is utterly transcendent, God is at the same time 'a personal being with whom man has a reciprocal relation.'[28] In his writings Moses is filled with longing and desire for God. We can see this in his very use of divine names, for while Philo will often designate God with the abstract Platonic title '*to on*' ('That Which Is' or

[26] See David T. Runia, 'Naming and Knowing: Themes in Philonic Theology', in *Exegesis and Philosophy: Studies on Philo of Alexandria*, Collected Studies (Aldershot: Variorum, 1990), 69–91 at 76. Runia suggests *onoma kurion* should be understood as a 'proper, legitimate name' (Runia, 'Naming and Knowing', 78.).

[27] See Dillon, *The Middle Platonists*, 181. Also Plato's *Cratylus* 430A–431E. Dillon says that it was the consensus, by Philo's time, that words were attached to things by nature and not convention.

[28] Runia, 'Philo, Alexandrian and Jew', 11.

'the Existent') he will also, following the Septuagint, use the personal masculine '*ho on*' – 'He Who Is' – a vacillation which, as Runia points out, would be problematic for a Greek philosopher.[29]

His next remark is one of Philo's most endearing – Jewish piety reinforced by the categories of classical grammar.

I am He that Is' (Ex. 3.14), which is equivalent to 'My nature is to be, not to be spoken.' Yet that the human race should not totally lack a title to give to the supreme goodness He allows them to use *by licence of language*, as though it were His proper name, the title of Lord God of the three natural orders, teaching, perfection, practice, which are symbolised in the records as Abraham, Isaac and Jacob. For this He says is 'My age-long name, ... (*de Mut. II*.12–13, my emphasis)

In the midst of metaphysics comes this non-sequitur of grace – God is unnameable but '*by licence of language*' gives Moses a name so that the human race should not be bereft. We should really pause to note the dynamic, vital for understanding the tradition of negative theology. Philo's commitment to the authority of scriptures compels him to say God is creator of all that is. His philosophy dictates that God cannot be 'named' as creatures are named (since not a being amongst beings). Yet, again his Jewish piety dictates that God must be named, for to pray is to name God. Thus, revelation is entirely necessary if we are to speak of God at all. This amounts to a philosophical argument, if not quite a proof, for the necessity of revelation for those who believe in the Creator God.

[29] Runia, 'Philo, Alexandrian and Jew', 11. The point, of course, is not the gendering of God but the invoking of a personal (and not abstract) deity.

It is interesting to note that the name which Philo thinks God has given to Moses to be used as a proper name is 'the Lord, the God of Abraham, and Isaac and Jacob'. This, Philo believes (textual critics would now say wrongly), is the name that is the name for all generations.[30] Philo explains what it means to be a name for the generations: those who are generated, those who live in time (generations) can have no grasp of the divine name in itself but

... those who are born into mortality must needs have some substitute for the divine name ...

Why?

so that they may approach if not the fact at least the name of supreme excellence *and be brought into relation with it.* (*de Mut.* II.13, my emphasis).

But in spite of and because of his exalted views of divine transcendence, Philo's deity is still a God of grace, for if God did not disclose a name, in Philo's terms, we could not name God at all. But Philo's God is a self-disclosing God and 'a personal being with which man has a reciprocal relation'.[31]

---

[30] Hebrew scholars take Exodus 3.15 to be saying that the Tetragrammaton is the name 'for all generations'. There is no reason, of course, why more than one 'licensed' name could not serve in this way. None of them, from Philo's point of view, is adequate.

[31] Runia, 'Philo, Alexandrian and Jew', 12. See also Roberto Radice, 'both the transcendence of God and His providential activity in the world are irrevocable dogmas for Philo', in 'Philo's Theology and Theory of Creation', in *The Cambridge Companion to Philo*, ed. Adam Kamesar (Cambridge: Cambridge University Press, 2009), 124–45 at 128.

Why then try to name God? Here we must recall Moses, the seeker. Despite the fact that the Existent is unknowable and unnameable, we should not cease to search after the essence of God, 'For nothing is better than to search for the true God, even if the discovery of Him eludes human capacity, since the very wish to learn, if earnestly entertained, produces untold joys and pleasures' (*Spec.* I.36). God has given, in Scripture, certain names by which we may call upon him. We can also know God through the trace that he has left, as Creator, on the cosmos.

Philo tells us often that we can only know *that God is* (*ei estin*) and not *what God is* (*ti estin*), and that even Moses is not granted a vision of the divine essence.[32] But Moses does see God's back! Philo's exegesis of Exodus 33.18–22 (that passage where Moses asks to see the divine glory and instead is placed in a cleft in the rock) is that, although we cannot see God's 'face' or essence, we can see his 'back' or rather what follows *after him*. David Runia clarifies the point:

God's existence is made known through what follows after him, that is through his *relationality*. God as τὸ ὄν is absolute (ὄν ᾗ ὄν), but through his powers and Logos stands in relation (πρός τι) to what has come into being. God is thus known through what he achieves in the cosmos via his powers ...[33]

If his scriptures push Philo towards the assertion that God is unnameable, then the same scriptures resolve the problem which then arises – 'How can God be named at

---

[32] David T. Runia, *Philo of Alexandria and the Timaeus of Plato* (Leiden: E. J. Brill, 1986), 436.

[33] Runia, *Philo of Alexandria and the Timaeus of Plato*, 436–7.

all?' This question is more pressing for Philo than it is for the philosophers. His Creator God is more truly 'other' than, for instance, the God of Aristotle who is in some sense a corollary of the universe.[34] Yet nonetheless, and guided by his scriptures, Philo wants to say that we cannot only 'speak about' ('name') God but also name God for the purposes of address. Our need to pray is to the fore. God must be 'named' if we are to be able to call upon Him. It is both because of our need and our incapacity that certain names have been 'vouchsafed to us' by God. He comments on the special honour that God paid to Abraham, Isaac and Jacob.

for He united them by joining His special name to theirs and calling Himself by one combined of the three. 'For this,' he said 'is my eternal name – the God of Abraham, the God of Isaac and the God of Jacob,' (Ex. 3.15) relative (*pros ti*) instead of absolute, and surely that is natural. God indeed needs no name; yet, though He needed it not, nevertheless vouchsafed to give to humankind a name of Himself *suited to them, that so men might be able to take refuge in prayers and supplications and not be deprived of comforting hopes.* (*Abr.* 51, my emphasis)

In philosophical terms, Philo sees God as supplying Moses with a rigid designation by which God may be named – that is, a referring expression ('the God of Abraham, Isaac and Jacob') which designates the deity not by any essential properties (for God need not have even created Abraham in the first place) but by what God has done for us (a *relative* name, not an *absolute* one).

---

[34] Aristotle's God is scarcely a 'who,' more a 'that' – in no sense a personal God.

God vouchsafed 'to give to humankind a name' so that they might pray, says Philo. We are here very far indeed from Aristotle's unmoved mover or Plato's demiurge. Philo's elaboration of this God of self-disclosure is again couched in the categories of antique grammar. The name given, he tells us, is 'relative instead of absolute' – here Philo shows his familiarity with distinctions of the grammarians between relative nouns (Greek *pros ti*, Latin *ad aliquid*) and absolute nouns or names.[35] For Philo, needless to say, *all* names for God were relative – they are names of the unnameable one for us. At the burning bush the name given is that for the generations 'Abraham, Isaac and Jacob'. In Genesis 17 (as in the text cited immediately above) it is *kyrios*, Lord, a title which, as Philo tells us, 'betokens sovereignty and kingship'.[36]

The difficulty in naming and knowing God is not new to Jews of the first century. In the Book of Isaiah we read

---

[35] Colson, translator of the Loeb edition of Philo, makes this point in an appendix to *De Abrahamo*, Vol. VI: '*Relative instead of absolute*. Philo, as often, shews his familiarity with grammatical terms. The distinction between relative nouns (πρός τι, Lat. *ad aliquid*) and absolute (usually ἀπολελυμένα, whence Lat. *absoluta*) is regularly given by Greek and Latin grammarians.' F. H. Colson, *Philo*, Loeb Classical Library (London: Heinemann; Harvard University Press, 1966), 597. It is interesting, in light of the Christian name for God '*Father, Son and Holy Spirit*' (one name not three), that Philo speaks of God calling Himself by one name combined of the three.

[36] See *De Abrahamo* where Philo discriminates between 'the Father of the Universe' (*ho ôn*) and the senior potencies powers nearest him (*presbytatai dynameis*), the 'creative and the regal'. 'The title of the former is God (*theos*), since it made and ordered the All; the title of the latter is Lord (*kyrios*), since it is the fundamental right of the maker to rule and control what he has brought into being' (*Abr.* 121).

To whom could you liken me
and who could be my equal? says the Holy One.
Lift your eyes and look.
Who made these stars
if not he who drills them like an army,
calling each one by name?

(Isa 40.18–26)

Nevertheless, it is a necessity of devout life that the followers of Moses be able to call upon God, and they are able to do so. They can name God according to what he has done as Creator, and also according to what he has done for Israel (the God of Abraham, of Isaac and of Jacob). In both cases we name the deity not according to the divine essence but relatively (*pros ti*), according to *who God is for us*. We can name God, so Philo believes, because God has chosen to give us the means of address.

Philo's exegesis is evidently informed by his Greek formation, but it is equally evident that this is not the God of the philosophers. This is the one Creator God and a God who speaks and is spoken to.[37] It is only by God's

---

37 Certainly not Aristotle or Plato. Later Platonists read or 'read into' Plato's texts (see *Republic* VI and VII) that 'God alone is true being, the source of being and knowledge for other existents.' Runia, *Philo of Alexandria and the Timaeus of Plato*, 435. However, it is possible these pagan philosophers were already influenced by Judaism's doctrine of God. Runia gives a good summary for philosophical parallels to some of Philo's beliefs, while cautioning against thinking he grounds them anywhere other than in the Pentateuch. Philo himself was by no means unhappy with overlap with the philosophers, since he reckons they got their best insights from Moses. It is in Philo, Runia suggests that 'for the first time, to our knowledge, the Platonic conception of the demiurge's goodness and the Judaeo- Christian conception of God the creator are brought together, an event of enormous implications for the history of ideas (Runia, *Philo of Alexandria and the Timaeus of Plato*, 441). The goodness of the God of the Bible and Platonic

gift of self-designation that we can truly 'name' God at all. Yet, even so, we name this God by grace and relatively – *pros ti*. We might put it thus: our ways of speaking do not legislate the *'qualities God has'* in some undesirably essentialist sense but, rather, designate *who God is for us*.[38]

For all their Hellenistic terminology, Philo and the Christian writers who followed were not so remote from the Rabbis. The Rabbis also understood the names, even the scriptural names of God as naming 'who God is for us'. Consider the Exodus Rabbah on Exodus 3.14:

And God said unto Moses (Ex. 3.14). R. Abba b. Mammel said: God said to Moses: 'Thou wished to know My name. Well, I am called according to My work; sometimes I am called "Almighty God", "Lord of Hosts", "God", "Lord". When I am judging created beings, I am called "God", and when I am waging war against the wicked, I am called "Lord of Hosts". When I suspend judgement for a man's sins, I am called "*El Shadday*" (Almighty God), and when I am merciful towards My world, I am called "*Adonai*" for "*Adonai*" refers to the Attribute of Mercy, as it is said: *The Lord, the Lord* (Adonai, Adonai), *God, merciful and gracious* (Ex. 34.6). Hence I Am That I Am in virtue

---

goodness, he adds, are quite different things: 'Platonic goodness is essentially *metaphysical*, signifying excellence of being, whereas the goodness of the God of the Bible is best described in terms of *grace*, the loving kindness and forebearance shown by a father to his children.'

[38] Richard Bauckham, writing more generally about the New Testament and not Philo, observes that 'for Jewish monotheistic belief in God what was more important was who the One is, rather than what divinity is'. Richard Bauckham, 'Monotheism and Christology in Hebrews 1', in *Early Jewish and Christian Monotheism*, ed. Loren T. Stuckenbruck and Wendy E. S. North, Journal for the Study of the New Testament Supplement series (London; New York: T&T Clark International, 2004), 167–85 at 167.

of My deeds.' R. Isaac said: God said to Moses: 'Tell them that I am now what I always was and always will be', for this reason is the word *eheyeh* written three times.[39]

There is no mention here of the divine *essence* but, drawing on the same Exodus texts to which Philo appealed, the Rabbis make the same conjunction between naming, knowing and 'being in relationship' which informs Philo's thought. God is named by his grace and not through comprehension of the divine essence. We know not 'what' God is, but Who God is for us.[40]

Conclusion

In a footnote, the philosopher John Dillon observes the oddity we have several times noted – that Philo will often

[39] Rabbi Dr S. M. Lehrman, ed., *Midrash Rabbah, Exodus* (London: The Soncino Press, 1939), 64. On this last remark of R. Isaac's, the editor comments in a note '*Eheyeh* denoting "I will be" or the eternal "I am".'

[40] N. A. Dahl notes that for the Rabbis 'no statement of scripture was haphazard or superfluous. They taught that even the two Hebrew words for God – *Elohim* and *YHWH* – were not synonyms but symbolised different aspects of God's providence. Wherever the Tetragrammaton appeared, God should be viewed as acting mercifully: where *Elohim* appeared, God's judgment should be understood. Between them, the two names expressed the totality of God's providence or, as they expressed it, His two *Middoth* or measures' ('Philo and the Rabbis on the Names of God', *Journal for the Study of Judaism in the Persian, Hellenistic, and Roman period* 9 (1978): 1–28). They note that 'Philo, too, privileges these names, but reverses them with *theos* (the LXX equivalent of *Elohim*) representing the beneficent and gracious, and *kyrios* (the equivalent of the Tetragrammaton in the LXX), standing for ruling power' (Dahl, 'Philo and the Rabbis on the Names of God', 1). They suggest similarities between Philo and the Rabbis on the names of God and demonstrate 'what few have denied, that Philonic and rabbinic interpretations are not independent variables but variants of one and the same tradition' (Dahl, 'Philo and the Rabbis on the Names of God', 5).

vary the Platonic title 'That Which Is' (*to on*) with a more personal form derived from the Septuagint, 'He Who Is' (*ho on*). 'This may be taken as influence from Judaism', Dillon adds, 'and so is of no concern to us'.[41] This is perhaps fair enough given Dillon's stated concern is with Middle Platonism broadly and his open admission that he will not go into what is Jewish or might be original philosophising in Philo's thought.[42] Yet we may see it quite differently if our concern is with Philo as a Jew and an expositor of his scripture.[43] We might then ask: how readily can we split what is philosophically innovative in Philo away from his Jewish convictions? Dillon himself notes that Philo's 'extreme transcendentalising' of God and his 'greater personal reverence for God' are both driven by his Judaism. These in turn, as I have argued here, bear directly on how Philo thinks we know and name God. Where Dillon sees, as a consequence of Philo's greater personal reverence for God, the occasional 'downgrading of the ability of the human intellect (unaided by God's grace) to comprehend truth', I suggest we might just

---

[41] Remarkably the context is God's relation to the world and the question whether, given Philo is our first extant source for certain negative names of God, Philo is responsible for introducing the notion of the 'unknowable' God into Greek thought (Dillon, *The Middle Platonists*, 155).

[42] He writes, 'Our concern in this work is not with Philo as a whole, ... but simply with the evidence he provides for contemporary Platonism. We cannot, therefore, go into the Jewish side of his thought, such as that was, or into any aspect of his philosophizing or which may possibly be original to himself' (Dillon, *The Middle Platonists*, 144). Philo, he believes, had little influence on the course of Middle Platonism, 'though he certainly influenced the Christian Platonists of Alexandria, Clement and Origen'.

[43] Dillon, *The Middle Platonists*, 163, 43.

as well speak of a *re-grading* of the ability of the human intellect – for if God is creator of all that is, and even of time itself, it is not a 'downgrading' of human capacity to say that we cannot grasp the divine essence. Indeed, as Philo insists, God alone cannot be classed among 'things', or creatures – no ontotheological story which folds God into such a sequence can obtain. With Philo's 'extreme transcendentalising' of God, we see a rupture in classical metaphysics which will allow Christians and Jews to confess a God who is both wholly other and nearer to us than our own heartbeat.

4

Creation *ex nihilo* as a Revolution
in Christian Metaphysics ...
and in Naming God

~

We've seen that Philo has a special interest in naming of
God. On his reckoning, God both cannot be named and
yet must be named for the purposes of prayer. Moses and
the divine self-disclosures in the Book of Exodus were
of central importance, as they would be for subsequent
Jewish and Christian tradition on naming God: not just
the divine self-naming at the burning bush. As important
is Exodus 33 where the LORD tells Moses to hide in the
cleft of the rock, and Exodus 34 where the LORD pro-
claims the Holy Name and provides a gloss:

The LORD (YHWH), the LORD,
a God merciful and gracious,
slow to anger,
and abounding in steadfast love and faithfulness ... (Ex. 34.6)

Later rabbinic tradition will say that it was God, not
Moses who at this juncture first 'called upon the name of
the LORD'. God taught Moses how to pray.[1]

Whenever Philo's concern is knowing and naming
God, he invokes Exodus 3 and the gift of the name to

---

[1] José Faur, *Golden Doves with Silver Dots: Semiotics and Textuality in
Rabbinic Tradition*, Jewish Literature and Culture (Bloomington:
Indiana University Press, 1986), 29.

Moses. Philo's God is one who both calls and wishes to be called upon. God has seen the sufferings of the Israelites in Egypt and declares (or names) himself as the God of their ancestors, 'the God of Abraham, and of Isaac, and of Jacob'). God is both 'the Existent' and the one 'who is and will be with them'. Philo understands the 'I Am Who I Am' of Exodus 3 to be the One who brought all things into being.[2] Above all we should stress that, unlike the god of Aristotle, his is a speaking God and one to whom Moses can speak. 'Scripture teaches that God has a name', writes the Rabbinics scholar José Faur, 'This means that God is semiologically accessible.'[3]

A linking of Exodus 3 with the creation narratives of Genesis was embraced early on by Christian theologians. 'The One Who Is' was understood as the one who confers being on all creation. Seeing the 'One Who Is' as the ground of all existence should not, however, be thought of as just an imposition on the Book of Exodus by Christian theologians marinated in Greek philosophy. The Palestinian Targums, Jewish texts written in Aramaic and within the Semitic milieu, provide us with the following glosses on the *ehyeh asher ehyeh* ('I Am Who I Am') of Exodus 3.15:

'He who spoke and the world came into being, spoke and everything came into being.' (Pseudo-Jonathan 14a)

---

[2] 'How must it not be impossible to recompense or to praise as He deserves Him who brought the universe out of non-existence?' (*L.A.* III.10). 'He is full of Himself and sufficient for Himself. It was so before the creation of the world, and is equally so after the creation of all that is. He cannot change nor alter and needs nothing else at all, so that all things are His but He Himself in the proper sense belongs to none' (*de Mut.* IV.27). 'Through His goodness He begat all that is, through His sovereignty He rules what he has begotten' (*de Cher.* 2.7–8). See also *Fug.* 46, *Mos.* II.267.

[3] Faur, *Golden Doves with Silver Dots*, 38.

'He who said to the world, "Be", and it came into being, and who will again say to it: "BE", and it will be. (Fragmentary Targum 14aV)

'I have existed before the world was created and have existed after the world has been created. I am he who has been at your aid in the Egyptian exile, and I am he who will be at your aid in every generation.' (Neofiti margin 2)[4]

These three texts link the 'I AM WHO I AM' of Exodus 3 to the Creator, an understanding which is elaborated in the doctrine of *creatio ex nihilo*.

This teaching is of such consequence for reflection on naming God, and more generally for the Christian theology, as to merit considerable attention here. I will take this as my working definition: *creatio ex nihilo* affirms that God, from no compulsion or necessity, created the world out of nothing – really nothing – no pre-existent matter, space or time. This central teaching (or 'doctrine', for that is just another word for 'teaching') is nonetheless still widely misrepresented and misunderstood. Heated disputes over 'creationism' have led the wider public to suppose that the central Christian doctrine of creation simply is that the world was made in seven days. Should you mention *creatio ex nihilo*, most churchgoers and most academic philosophers or scientists, if they have any view at all, will assume that '*creatio ex nihilo*' means the big bang theory; that is they will understand it to be a theory about cosmic

---

[4] For these citations see Graham Davies, 'The Exegesis of the Divine Name in Exodus,' in *The God of Israel: Studies of an Inimitable Deity*, ed. R. P. Gordon, University of Cambridge Oriental Publications (Cambridge: Cambridge University Press, 2007). This is not to say that the Targums themselves, while not written in Greek, are free of Greek influence.

origins at the beginning of time. But *creatio ex nihilo* is not just a cosmogonic theory happily coincident with the big bang theory. To put it bluntly, *creatio ex nihilo* is not just a teaching about the created order but about God.[5]

Central to the teaching is the power, goodness and freedom of God, and the dependence of 'all that is' (which, for the sake of convenience, I will call 'the world') on God or, more precisely, on God's free choice to create and to sustain, which comes to the same thing. It is thus, profoundly, a teaching about grace and gift, though it has other positive ramifications. The Christian teaching is that, were God to cease holding the world in being for a moment, it would not be.[6]

Creatio ex nihilo, like the doctrine of the Trinity, can be said to be an emergent Christian teaching – a reflection on what must be the case given scriptural texts and other beliefs. Once established as a mainstream Christian teaching (by the early fourth century at the latest), it was

---

[5] There are many excellent recent books on creation and *creatio ex nihilo* amongst which Kathryn Tanner's landmark *God and Creation in Christian Theology: Tyranny or Empowerment?* (Oxford: Basil Blackwell, 1988); Paul M. Blowers, *Drama of the Divine Economy: Creator and Creation in Early Christian Theology and Piety*, Oxford Early Christian Studies (Oxford: Oxford University Press, 2012); Ian A. McFarland, *From Nothing: A Theology of Creation* (Louisville, KY: Westminster John Knox Press, 2014); and see the essays in *Creation ex nihilo: Origins, Development, Contemporary Challenges*, ed. Gary A. Anderson and Markus N. A. Bockmuehl (Notre Dame, Ind.: University of Notre Dame Press, 2018), as well as those in the special edition of *Modern Theology* 29, no. 2 (April 2013), *Creation 'ex nihilo' and Modern Theology*.

[6] This teaching is fully compatible with there being an 'everlasting' universe, should one go down that route. Thomas Aquinas, for instance, thought that God *could* have created, *ex nihilo*, an everlasting world – that is, a world without beginning or end – although Aquinas believed, on the basis of scripture, that the world in fact had a punctual beginning.

rarely questioned. Unlike the doctrine of the Trinity, it is a teaching of Judaism and Islam as well as Christianity – Moses Maimonides believed it was the only teaching all three shared. From the time of the Cappadocians onwards, *creatio ex nihilo* has been, East and West, a foundational teaching of Christian thought. Major Reformation disputes involved grace, ecclesiology, sacraments, redemption and eschatology but not the doctrine of creation. The teaching is enshrined in the creeds: 'I believe in God the Father almighty, maker of heaven and earth.'

No doctrine is exempt from critical scrutiny, of course, and in recent years *creatio ex nihilo* has come under fire as antiquated and destructive, especially from thinkers influenced by process philosophy, by the work of Alfred North Whitehead and Charles Hartshorne. Common criticisms parallel those made of the 'God of the attributes' already discussed – that *creatio ex nihilo* presents us with a glacial god, lifted from the philosophers, with little to do with the Bible. The critics argue, variously, that *creatio ex nihilo* proposes a binarism which pits God against the world, drawing a picture of a deity indifferent and aloof. I suggest that the opposite is the case. The teaching in fact undergirds the intimacy and presence of God to us and to the whole created order. It is the doctrine of *creatio ex nihilo* which, in developed form, underwrites human freedom, providence and the spiritual conviction that God, far from being distant, is nearer to me than my own hands and feet. All of religious language, and not just naming, thus becomes radicalised by it.[7]

[7] I've engaged with some of this contemporary criticism directly in 'Why *creatio ex nihilo* for Theology Today?', in *Creation ex nihilo*, ed. Anderson and Bockmuehl.

As far as we can see from the scriptures, the ancient Israelites were not interested in metaphysics or in scientific cosmology. They were, however, interested in naming. In the creation narratives of the first chapters of Genesis, God calls light from the formless void, separating it from darkness. Significant for our interest, God *names* the light 'Day' and the darkness 'Night'. 'Calling' and 'naming' seem to come together, as they still do in modern European languages. Jean-Louis Chrétien observes that 'to call' in Greek has the same double meaning as in French – and we can add in English – 'to call, to call a name'.[8] God divides the waters from dry land, creates the sun and moon, living creatures and humankind, male and female, in God's own image. This sequence forms the prolegomena for the calling of Abram, renamed at that time Abraham, which marks the creation of the people Israel through whom God's blessings will be shed on the world. These narratives do not probe the metaphysics of space and time, or even present a consistent view on the origin of matter. They are more concerned to show the relationship of all things to God and to each other, and to establish that the creation is 'good' and the work of a beneficent God. They tell us something about the created order, but also something about the nature of God.

The Old Testament's reflections on creation are not, however, restricted to the Book of Genesis. Creation is a substantial theme in the theology of the Psalms: 'the sea is his, for he made it and the dry land, which his hands have formed' (Ps 95.5). The Psalms and the Book of Isaiah,

---

[8] Jean-Louis Chrétien, *The Call and the Response*, 1st English ed., Perspectives in Continental Philosophy (New York: Fordham University Press, 2004), 7.

biblical books which are amongst the Hebrew scriptures cited most frequently by the Qumran writings and the New Testament, both regularly link God's power as creator with God's faithfulness and power to save. Thus, in Psalm 121.1–2 we read:

> I will lift up my eyes to the mountains:
> From where shall come my help?
> My help shall come from the Lord
> Who made heaven and earth.

In Isaiah 45 an extended address from the LORD works the same theme of creation and salvation:

> Shower, O heavens, from above,
> and let the skies rain down righteousness;
> let the earth open that salvation may spring up,
> and let righteousness to sprout up also;
> I the LORD have created it. (Isa 45.8)

And in the midst of a stirring address on the need to turn to God and be saved:

> For thus says the LORD,
> who created the heavens
> (he is God),
> who formed the earth and made it
> (he established it;
> he did not create it a chaos,
> he formed it to be inhabited!):
> I am the LORD, and there is no other. (Isa 45.18)[9]

The earliest theology of creation seems to be, like the language of the Psalms, confessional and doxological,

---

[9] This passage of Isaiah is echoed in Paul's 'Christ hymn' of Philippians 2.

underscoring the freedom, power and goodness of *YHWH* (God) and this remains the tone of the New Testament and of the first Christian theologians.

But if you are to insist that God made 'everything', it will inevitably be the case, especially if moving in the philosophical culture of ancient Greece and Rome, that the question arises 'What do you mean by everything'?

Much of ancient philosophical theology, including that of Plato and Aristotle, was monotheistic. Greek philosophy had arrived, without any use of revelation, at a remarkable consensus concerning the unity of the divine essence and the nature of the divine attributes.[10] Such were findings of their science, for 'natural theology' was an aspect and requirement of science and a formal discipline akin to mathematics. There was no great division in antiquity between philosophy on the one side and religion or cult on the other. The philosophical schools offered 'ways' or wisdom and were willing to borrow and learn from other ways, including the way of the Jews when they saw fit.[11] Similarly, Jews and Christians, especially if Greek-educated, were happy to borrow from the findings of Greek science when it suited their purposes. If a philosopher could demonstrate the existence and unity of God, all to the good. This did not mean philosophy could

[10] See Lloyd P. Gerson, *God and Greek Philosophy: Studies in the Early History of Natural Theology* (London: Routledge, 1994). Greek intellectuals praised Judaism for being a 'philosophical' cult precisely because it was, like their own philosophical cosmology, monotheistic.

[11] Robert Wilken suggests that the philosopher and physician Galen, writing in the late second century, was the first to consider the Christian religion as a way of wisdom analogous to the various philosophical schools. *The Christians as the Romans Saw Them* (New Haven: Yale University Press, 1984).

dictate to what had been revealed. The Christian fathers, and Jews like Philo, regarded the austere and non-mythic discipline of Greek natural theology as a quarry to be mined, but with caution.

Within Greek philosophical monotheism was long-standing consensus that any divine craftsman would have worked with pre-existing materials. God did not create matter itself, or its corollaries of space and time. The cosmos had simply always existed. Aristotle regarded as absurd the notion that something could come from nothing (*Physics* 187a33–4), a view that remained the Greek philosophical consensus into early Christian times.[12] The logic is inexorable – there must always have been 'something' because if there ever was truly 'nothing', there would be nothing now. This is Aristotle's argument for the eternity of the universe.[13]

By strong contrast, however, Jews and Christians, driven by their scriptures, held to an 'intentional creation'.[14] God is understood to create freely and from no compulsion – in the Book of Genesis, by his word. God need not have created at all. This position is entirely at odds, for instance, with Aristotelian theology. Aristotle's deity is a corollary of the universe, something like its

---

[12] Wilken notes that the 'idea that the world came into existence out of non-being was abhorrent to the Greeks' (*The Christians as the Romans saw them*, 90).

[13] That there must always have been 'something' is the default view of many cosmologists today, and a driver is behind the theory of 'multiverses', which antedate any initial singularity. 'Multiverses' would, however, constitute no defeat of *creatio ex nihilo*, since God can still be seen as creator of the multiverses. C. S. Lewis played with this in fiction.

[14] David Burrell, 'Freedom and Creation in the Abrahamic Traditions', *International Philosophical Quarterly* 40, no. 158 (2000): 162–71 at 167.

DNA. We could not have the universe without god, but equally we could not have god without the universe. For Aristotle, the cosmos and the deity are both necessary and necessarily co-exist. Both are, in Aristotle's sense, 'eternal'. Although in this sense a 'necessary being', Aristotle's god is not providential – and indeed has no knowledge of actually existing things. Neither Aristotle nor Plato has a creator God in the Christian sense. Aristotle's god is the source of motion but not of being itself, and Plato's *Timaeus* has the demiurge moulding pre-existent matter.[15]

The Greek consensus that from nothing nothing comes – *ex nihilo nihil fit* – thus threatened not just Jewish and Christian cosmology but, more importantly, their teachings on divine freedom and love.

The consolidation of this teaching is more complex than a brief sketch allows. In some early Christian writings, the eternity of the world is rejected, but there remains ambiguity about matter itself. The Bible at times seems to speak of God moulding a pre-existent matter. The first verses of Genesis where the earth is described as 'formless void' (leaving it unstated as to whether formless void exists 'prior' to creation) is susceptible to such a reading, as is Wisdom 11.7 where we learn of 'the hand that from formless matter created the world'. Philo was inconsistent on this, and some early Christian writers seemed to be untroubled by such a reading and saw in it no threat to divine sovereignty. The Rabbis were in general

---

[15] David Sedley observes that 'even a divine creator would, like any craftsman, have to use pre-existing materials is an assumption that the ancient Greeks apparently never questioned.' *Creationism and Its Critics in Antiquity*, Sather Classical Lectures (Berkeley: University of California Press, 2007), xvii.

content to let variant understandings live at peace with one another. On the other hand, 2 Maccabees (composed around the beginning of the first century BCE) voices sentiments that seem to rule out any notion of the God of Abraham as a demiurge moulding pre-existing matter. There a mother, her son about to be martyred, encourages him in this way: 'my child, observe heaven and earth, consider all that is in them, and acknowledge that God made them out of what did not exist, and that mankind comes into being in the same way' (2 Maccabees 7.28).[16] It is hard not to see here a statement about the singularity of God's creative power.[17]

By the second century CE, both Christian and Jewish writers were differentiating their own, scripturally informed, view of creation from those of the philosophers.[18] In the dominant philosophy of this period (not Aristotelianism but Platonism or more properly a Middle Platonism which fused elements of Aristotelian and Stoic thought), the prevailing view remained that matter exists eternally and not as

[16] G. May, in his influential volume *Creatio ex nihilo: The Doctrine of 'Creation Out of Nothing' in Early Christian Thought* (Edinburgh: T&T Clark, 1994), which pushes hard at his case that *creatio ex nihilo* first arises in distinctly Christian confrontations with Greek philosophy, treats such verses as paraenetic and pre-ontological.

[17] An argument can also be made for an independent Jewish strand of development for the ideas which fed into the developed teaching. Menahem Kister sees interest amongst the Jewish sages in the question of whether the world was created 'out of primordial elements, out of matter (*ex hyles*) or out of nothing (*ex nihilo*)' as early as the second century BCE, in the Book of Jubilees. See Menahem Kister, 'Tohu wa-Bohu: Primordial Elements and Creatio ex Nihilo', *Jewish Studies Quarterly* 14 (2007): 229–56 at 229.

[18] The actual historical prompt for this may have been the need to rebut Gnostic heresies, as May demonstrates, but the net effect is a position quite distinct from philosophical cosmology.

the result of a creation. If this was unacceptable to Jews and Christians, even more so was the Neoplatonic conviction that 'being necessarily proceeded from the One', an assertion at odds with the idea that God creates freely.[19]

Over and against any formally necessitated 'creation', and in order to preserve divine freedom and creaturely contingency, theologians formulated *creatio ex* nihilo. This was not as a departure from the biblical account but in its clarification and defence. Thus, we find Rabbi Gamaliel II (c. 90/110) in dialogue with a philosopher who says to him 'Your God was indeed a great artist, but surely He found good pigments which assist him.' Rabbi Gamaliel replies – 'God made the colours, too!'[20] Although such statements are rarer in writings of the Rabbis than in those of early Christians, both aimed to protect God's sovereignty, freedom and action in the world.

It should be clear by now that it is not possible to maintain a strict opposition between philosophy and religion which puts all the metaphysics on the Greek side, and all the religion on the Jewish and biblical one. Some biblical claims entail metaphysical positions, above all those concerning God's relation to the creation. As soon as we ask whether space and time 'existed' prior God's creation of the world, Christians and Jews may feel compelled by their sacred texts to make a claim, at once theological and metaphysical, that God created 'all that is' including matter,

---

[19] May, *Creatio ex nihilo*, 5. Plotinus (204/5–70) is widely considered the father of 'Neoplatonism'. Philo and many early Christian writers antedated him, hence the term 'Middle Platonist'. This is contested nomenclature, but we should not assume that the influence on early Christian writings was 'Neoplatonist'.

[20] May, *Creatio ex nihilo*, 23.

space and time which, as the ancients knew and modern physics confirms, are functions of one another. It might be best to say that the Christian doctrine of *creatio ex nihilo* is both 'Greek', in the sense that it represents a defensive response to Greek philosophy, and 'biblical' in its desire to defend the God of Moses and the priority of scripture.[21] It is a scripturally driven piece of Christian metaphysics.

The prompt for *creatio ex nihilo* is theological. Its objective is not to explain the detailed order of the world. Nor is it, as I've said, principally an explanatory narrative about the beginning of the world. The theological questions to which it responds are not so much 'Where did the world come from?' as 'Who is the God to whom we pray?' or, more acutely, 'Who is the God we can call upon to come to our aid in times of need?' It is this One who 'is with us and will be with us' (Ex. 3), the One who made all that is, and the One who, the mother in the book of Maccabees believes, having created her son in the first place, can return him to life. The Psalms and Isaiah, books often referenced in early formulations of *creatio ex nihilo*, are full of reference to the Creator but also to the Redeemer and indeed the two are often wed. This tradition is scarcely interested in knowledge of God as an explanation, far more as a power to help accompany Israel both in practical matters and in matters of faith

---

[21] May, *Creatio ex nihilo*, viii. According to May (viii), 'The driving motive which underlines the Christian doctrine of *creatio ex nihilo* is the attempt to do justice to the absolute sovereignty and unlimited freedom of the biblical God acting in history... Christian theology has developed its doctrine of *creatio ex nihilo* from its own presumptions, albeit ... within the ambit of the philosophical teaching of world-formation.' May dates the full expression of the teaching well within the Christian period, probably in result of debates with Gnostics in the second century.

Returning to Philo, we can say, whatever his inconsistencies, that the building blocks for *creatio ex nihilo* are already evident in his writings: 'God, being One, is alone and unique, and like God there is nothing' (*L.A.* II.1).[22] God has created the world out of non-existence. All things are dependent on God, but God is sufficient to himself and was so before the creation of the world.[23] He creates from his goodness and governs what he creates. He does not change or alter. God, says Philo, 'created space and place coincidentally with the material world' (*Conf.* 136). God created time itself, 'For there was no time before the cosmos, but rather it either came into existence together with the cosmos or after it' (*Op.* §26).[24]

What is perhaps even more interesting, especially when our focus is naming God, is the importance Philo accords Exodus 3 and his linking, as also in the Targums, of the 'I AM' of Exodus to the Creator. His is a 'speaking' God – the God who speaks to Moses at Sinai is the One

---

[22] Philo seems inconsistent on the question of matter, as were some of the earliest Christian theologians. On this see Gregory E. Sterling, '"The Most Perfect Work": The Role of Matter in Philo of Alexandria', in *Creation ex nihilo*, ed. Anderson and Bockmuehl, 99–118.

[23] 'How must it not be impossible to recompense or to praise as He deserves Him who brought the universe out of non-existence?' (*L.A.* III.10). 'He is full of Himself and sufficient for Himself. It was so before the creation of the world, and is equally so after the creation of all that is. He cannot change nor alter and needs nothing else at all, so that all things are His but He Himself in the proper sense belongs to none' (*de Mut.* IV.27). 'Through His goodness He begat all that is, through His sovereignty He rules what he has begotten' (*de Cher.* 27–8). See also *Fug.* 46, *Mos.* II.267.

[24] See Runia's comment on this in Philo, *On the Creation of the Cosmos According to Moses*, ed. and trans. David T. Runia, Philo of Alexandria Commentary Series Vol. 1 (Leiden; Boston: Brill, 2001), 157.

who 'spoke' the world into being in the first place, who says 'Be' and it will be.

'I have existed before the world was created,' says Targum Neofiti, and 'I am he who will be at your aid in every generation.' Christians will naturally think of the prologue to the Gospel of John, 'In the beginning was the Word, and the Word was with God, and the Word was God. He was in the beginning with God. All things came into being through him, and without him not one thing came into being' (John 1.1–3).

Creatio ex nihilo, far from being lazy acquiescence with Greek philosophy, amounts to a revolution in western metaphysics. Returning specifically to naming God, *creatio ex nihilo* radicalises and transforms predicates which *were and are* used by the philosophers to describe the deity. Aristotle's god is eternal, but 'eternal' means, in Aristotle's scheme, without beginning or end – that is, everlasting. The Christian God – add Jewish and Muslim if you wish – is 'eternal' in being the Creator of time so wholly present to our temporal reality, but not in the way creatures are. The same logic transforms 'omnipresent'. God as Creator, who holds all in being at every moment, is more present to me, as Augustine and later John Henry Newman said, than my own hands and feet. The language of causation and existence is affected, too. The creator of time and space cannot be a 'cause' in the same way that I am a cause of my daughter's birthday cake. Indeed, God cannot 'exist' in the same way as does the apple before me. We can see that it is not just language but the very understanding of God that is revolutionised.[25]

---

[25] I will return to this when discussing Augustine and Aquinas.

Israel's God is a creator God. It is because God stands in radical and free relation to creation that God is intimate to creation in the way no element of the created order could be (omnipresence, eternity). Since God as the 'cause of being' is a cause of a different order from the causal agency of any creature, God's causation 'does not compete with a creature's causation' – human freedom is thus preserved.[26] God may 'act' in the miraculous without that being in violation of the created order.[27]

Although God does not need creation to be God, the creation stands in a real, if contingent, relation to God. God's creatures are gratuitously created from abundant love. In classical theology it is because God is always already abundance and fullness of life that creation is wholly gift and grace. It is not out of need but from pure love and delight that God creates.

In sum, *creatio ex nihilo* emerges as a core teaching when Jews and Christians felt a need to defend their understanding of God's relation to the cosmos, God's

---

[26] Burrell, 'Freedom and Creation in the Abrahamic Traditions', 169.

[27] We have the stuff of many great philosophical debates here. My purpose here is to show that thinkers like Augustine, Maimonides and Aquinas were trying precisely to defend the freedom of the God and of human kind as they saw it in scripture by developing their ideas about God's eternity, and not supplanting that God with a philosophical ghoul. On the coherence of *creatio ex nihilo* and human freedom, see Burrell, 'Freedom and Creation in the Abrahamic Traditions', also his *Aquinas: God and Action* (London: Routledge and Kegan Paul, 1979). An elegant recent treatment of Aquinas on the matter is found in Rudi te Velde, *Aquinas on God: The 'Divine Science' of the Summa Theologiae* (London: Ashgate, 2006). For a defence of the classical outline of divine eternity as fully compatible with and indeed necessary for the idea of a God who acts, see Eleonore Stump and Norman Kretzmann, 'Eternity', in *Concept of God*, ed. Thomas V. Morris (Oxford: Oxford University Press, 1987), 219–52.

power, freedom and love.[28] This teaching became integral to Christian theology. As we have seen from Philo, one of its effects was to transform the meaning of certain divine names which had enjoyed currency in Greek philosophical monotheism – those known to us as 'classical attributes' – and to impel the introduction of others.

---

[28] Although neither Plato nor Aristotle has a Creator god on whom 'all that is' wholly depends, we do find a 'One' that is the source of the 'many' in later Middle or Neoplatonist philosophy, but these are arguably influenced by Hellenistic Jewish writers like Philo, or by Christians. Numenius of Apamea, a second-century 'Middle' Platonist and known influence on Plotinus, has a 'first god' and a 'demiurge', and calls his first god 'ho on' He Who Is. But Numenius was openly interested in the Jewish writings and credits Moses with the 'revelation' that the First God is 'Being'. See Miles Burnyeat, 'Platonism in the Bible: Numenius of Apamea on Exodus and Eternity', in *The Revelation of the Name Yhwh to Moses: Perspectives from Judaism, the Pagan Graeco-Roman World, and Early Christianity*, Themes in Biblical Narrative, XIV (Leiden: Brill, 2006), 139–68, especially 158–60.

5

Is 'God' the Name of God?

~

We have seen that Philo, as a Jew and an exegete of his scriptures, had particular reasons for interesting himself in names and naming. Names and the renaming of people and of places are a distinctive feature of the Torah as well as elsewhere in Hebrew Scripture.[1] To pray, for a Jew, is to call upon the Name of the Lord. And then there is the mysterious and primal narrative of the gift of the Name to Moses at the burning bush.

Philo and early Christian theologians following him took a number of key teachings from that event, amongst which that God was, strictly speaking, unnameable and that he was so because he was not a 'creature' or a 'being' like other beings but the source of being itself – a view reflected in the Targums. Despite this transcendence, Philo sees that God chooses to bend down to the people in their need. His account of Moses and the naming of God is suffused with desire to see God. God reveals himself to Moses on Sinai and gives Moses a name by which the people may call upon him and be in relation.

---

[1] Marc Brettler has reminded me that naming and renaming is a feature of Isaiah and the early chapters of Hosea, amongst other places.

Naming and 'Proper Names'

But we may ask, for our own context and not just Philo's, what are names for? How do names work? Can we be in relation with someone just through naming? How much do we need to know about someone or something to name them or it?

For as long as the matter has been approached at all, it has been considered that the primary function of words is to name things – a thesis hard to sustain in simple form once we consider such words as *if, from, however,* or even *tomorrow* and *arcane.* Yet from Plato's *Cratylus* through to the present, philosophers have interested themselves in naming and have considered together, as aspects of the naming, both proper names (like *Aristotle* or *Olivia*) and common names like *dog* and *plumber.*[2] Naming is thus close to calling: we both 'call' someone by their proper name and 'call' something an anemone or a neutrino. Proper names are not always names of persons – they can name places (*Senegal, Madrid*), companies (*CocaCola*) or even boats. These are proper names because they are used to pick out only one individual, although as we shall see, proper names have more than this one, referential, function.

---

[2] The literature on this, both philosophical and linguistic, is extensive. Readers who wish to see more should look to John M. Anderson, *The Grammar of Names*, Oxford Linguistics (Oxford: Oxford University Press, 2007) for a comprehensive survey which maps out the differing but overlapping concerns of philosophers, linguists and philologists. See also Sam Cumming, 'Names,' in *The Stanford Encyclopedia of Philosophy*, ed. Edward N. Zalta (2019), https://plato.stanford.edu/archives/fall2019/entries/names/.

What Kind of a Name Is 'God'?

When it comes to naming God, we need to consider questions peculiar to the particular religious texts or traditions, as well as features common to naming more generally. For instance, *YHWH* needs to be seen as a name within the particularity of the Pentateuchal narratives, but what kind of name is 'God'? This doesn't seem to depend on the biblical text. Many people use it. We have seen that we can name using both common nouns and proper names, but which is 'God'? 'God/god' seems to resemble common nouns like 'dog' and 'plumber' more than proper names like 'Aristotle' or 'Abraham Lincoln'. 'God/gods' seems to name a kind of thing. But can we say that God is a 'kind of thing'? With dogs and carpenters, we can say what it is that makes something a dog or a carpenter. Can we do the same with God? How, then, does this fit with the ancient teaching that in the strict sense God is unknowable and unnameable? If we cannot say what kind of 'thing' God is, how can we be confident we are speaking about God at all? When doing theology these are usually seen as questions about God – and so they are – but they are also questions about the workings of language more generally.

The Name 'God'

I have already said that we are predisposed to think that words name things. This is the spirit in which John Locke, in the late seventeenth century, considers 'the name God'. 'The name God', writes Locke, being once mentioned in any part of the world, to express a superior, powerful, wise, invisible being, the suitableness of such a notion to the principles of common reason, and the interest men will always have to mention it often, must necessarily spread far and wide, and continue it down to all generations.[3]

Locke here uses 'name' to indicate any general term – his account here is of the name (general term) 'god', but it could be of the name (general term) 'cat', 'gold' or 'star'. In true Enlightenment spirit, and with a method much closer to the analytic method of Descartes than to the background in prayer and desire we have seen in Philo, Locke eschews any anchoring of this name in sacred text or traditions. Rather, and as with other general terms, his definition suggests that the name 'God' has an associated description and we have this description in mind when we use the term. To use 'god' to make an existential claim would be to say that a being with these attributes exists or to deny that such a being exists as the case may be. The divine *attributes* 'superior, powerful, wise', terms which earlier theologians might have considered to be more properly within the remit of *divine names*, are here laid out as predicates and qualities God 'has', all components of a description by which 'God' is identified.

This framework for discussing the divine attributes has continued to modern times in conjunction with proofs for the existence of God. Thus Anthony Kenny, introducing his classic, *The God of the Philosophers*, took care to place his study within the remit of a theory of meaning ('Sentences are composite, articulate, and their meaning

---

[3] John Locke, *An Essay Concerning Human Understanding* (Chicago: Gateway Editions, 1956), Book I, Ch. 3, §10.

and meaningfulness is a function of the expressions they contain'), and then indicates how this will apply to religious claims.

For this reason anyone who is interested in the question of the existence of God has to study first of all the divine attributes; *for to say that God exists is to say that there is something that has the divine attributes* and if 'God exists' is to be true, then the divine attributes must at least themselves be coherent and jointly compatible. The coherence of the notion of God, as possessor of the traditional divine attributes, is a necessary, though of course not sufficient, condition for God's existence.[4]

As with Locke the word *God* is treated as a common noun and correct use of the term involves being in possession of an idea of God, or a set of determining properties. Kenny speaks explicitly of the *attributes* which God *has*, presumably qualities of some sort not disanalogous to being six foot tall or having red hair, although in God's case these would be quite different.[5]

Now this initially seems to make sense. As a first step to determining whether God exists – or rather, to claiming that one can assert coherently that God exists – one must define the word and see whether its terms are consistent and compatible. The implication is that anyone who says or believes that 'God exists' makes a particular assertion based on what the word/name 'God' means. To speak about something we must know what it is. We must be able to provide defining properties of something if we are

---

[4] Anthony Kenny, *The God of the Philosophers* (Oxford: Clarendon Press, 1979), 5.

[5] Kenny goes on to discuss various attributes including omniscience, eternity and goodness.

to differentiate it from any other thing, and thus Kenny's conclusion that 'the coherence of the notion of God, as possessor of the traditional divine attributes, is a necessary, though of course not sufficient, condition for God's existence'.

This seemingly sensible way of proceeding has, however, some odd consequences. Many people believe or would say that 'God exists' without having a concept of God framed in terms of the 'traditional divine attributes' – probably most small children, elderly aunts, and ancient Israelites. It seems odd to suggest that these individuals do not understand what they are saying because they are bereft of a seventeenth-century definition like that of John Locke. Perhaps we might say that here there is a question of linguistic division of labour. Naive persons do not need to have a correct concept of God because somewhere in the community of language users are specialists, perhaps philosophers of religion, who know the correct definition which grounds the referential practice of the whole community. This has an oddly elitist ring to it. In general, one is more likely to trust the insights of pious aunts than philosophers in these matters. But in any case, what do we do if these religious specialists insist that neither they nor any of us can, without idolatry, provide a definition of God? Insistence on definition as the basis for existential claims seems to sound the death knell for those theological arguments, and they make up the bulk of pre-modern theology, which insists that the divine essence is, in a strict sense, unknowable and unnameable.

One apologetic strategy at this juncture is to provide a defence of the divine attributes. This is of course a worthwhile project and has been undertaken by a number of philosophers of religion.[6] But I suggest another way forward is to give consideration to the employment of the word *god* in religious speech as it hovers between use as common noun ('god') and as a proper name ('God').

Words and Reference

We are dealing with words. A 'word' might be a number of things – a particular vocalization, a sequence of letters bounded by a space (a *word-form*), and a grammatical notion as when we say that *found* and *find* are variants of the same dictionary word. To know the meaning of a word, one needs to know a great deal of its surrounding circumstances and its use. Single words (that is as sequences of letters bounded by spaces) *do not* on their own carry meaning. A colleague of mine was wont to demonstrate this point to students by asking them to write down all their associations with a word he would write on the board. The word was *pain* and as the students were all students of theology they wrote movingly of compassion, sorrow and so on, prior to being told by the professor that alas, all were mistaken as he had been writing in the French language and they might better think *baguette, crouton or croissant*.[7]

Reference, similarly, is not a feature of single words in themselves. Just as speech is a social possession, for we do not invent language, so reference is an utterance-bound

---

6 See, for instance, Richard Swinburne, *The Coherence of Theism*, 2nd ed. (Oxford: Oxford University Press, 2016), and Eleonore Stump, *The God of the Bible and the God of the Philosophers* (Milwaukee, Wisc.: Marquette University Press, 2016).

7 This colleague was Nicholas Lash.

notion. Words do not refer – it is speakers using words who make reference.[8] We can extend this to naming for it is not words which name but speakers using words who name. More of this later.

Is 'God' a Proper Name?

God is not technically a proper name – not in the sense that *George Washington* is the proper name of the first American president and *Barbados* the name of a country. *God* fails the standard tests for proper names – it can be pluralised (*gods*). We do not customarily translate proper names – English newspapers write of 'King Juan Carlos of Spain' and not 'King John Charles of Spain', yet *God* is translated when we speak in other languages Latin (*deus*), French (*dieu*), German (*Gott*) or Polish (*bog*).

The word *god* then seems more to resemble common nouns like *lemon* or *geranium*, even if monotheists believe there to be only one god. The word can be translated into any number of languages, although one should not assume it has the same connotations in all. Had the Aztecs been in possession of a dictionary, the entry for *god* might have read 'power that requires human sacrifice in order that the sun may rise'. Similarly had Parmenides possessed a Greek dictionary, the entry for *god/gods* would have been rather different from that which we find in the *Oxford English Dictionary* listed in the Christian sense – 'The One object of supreme adoration; the Creator and

---

[8] I went into this in some detail in *Metaphor and Religious Language* (Oxford: Oxford University Press, 1985).

Ruler of the Universe'. To be able to deploy the word *god* is to know, within the language community in which one is speaking, roughly the ways in which others are likely to use the term. This does not depend on exact agreement amongst speakers about meaning and nor does the shared meaning need to be factually accurate for the term to be used in successful referring expressions – speakers for years referred successfully to whales while believing them to be 'the largest fishes in the sea'. The common or stereotypical sense of a term plays a role in reference but is not solely determinative of it. Language is far more flexible than that.

The Greek and Latin common nouns for *god* and *gods* and those of other ancient near eastern religions were in place long before these languages were used to speak of the Holy One of Israel, and most had polytheistic overtones. Nonetheless, Jews and Christians did not hesitate to use these words for god to speak of their deity. Speakers are able to use terms referentially without using them existentially – they can speak of yeti and of unicorns. The ancient Israelites knew Chemosh as the god of the Ammonites. Elijah mocks the god Baal and has no time for him. Paul in Athens presumes that his listeners will understand him when he speaks of *god*, *gods* and the *unknown god*, even though he has a different message about God to give them. His intention is to tell them of the Christian God, but to do so he does not need to abolish the standard or dictionary sense of *god/gods* which he and his listeners share. Indeed, the comprehensibility of his speech depends upon this shared sense.

What we can say is that by custom the common noun *god* is employed by Jews and Christians as a proper name, a usage indicated textually in English and other European languages by its capitalisation as *God*.[9]

Why Name God?

Yet as we have seen, there is in the Hebrew Bible a candidate for the proper name of God, *YHWH*. If the Tetragrammaton is held to have been given in circumstances of such particularity and intimacy as Exodus describes, we may well wonder why it is not commonly used as the name for God. Jews, as is well known, do not for reasons of piety pronounce the Holy Name, although it is not well understood why this is so or when the practice began. Christian avoidance of the Name seems less readily explicable. But on the other hand, we may equally wonder why a monotheistic religion should have a proper name for the Deity at all. We use proper names to select particular people from a number of others – the phone book is a good example. We pick out individuals in other ways such as 'the short girl with fair hair who dances well', but descriptions are easily misunderstood and often wordy. A phone book with descriptive entries would be virtually impossible. Proper names are a succinct and effective means of picking out an individual. But how could this apply to God? 'Simply put,' says Herbert Brichto, 'monotheism has no need, possibly no room, for a name – a proper name – for Deity. If Deity is a class with but one member, then the common name or noun

---

[9] Marc Brettler reminds me that the Hebrew designation *elohim* is the plural of *eloah* (and related to a generic for 'gods'), whereas *YHWH* cannot be pluralised.

for the class is sufficient.'[10] One can go even farther, for God is not merely 'in a class of his own' but, in the formulations of classical theology, beyond genus and species altogether. God is not a 'thing' in the relevant sense to which our natural languages are suited. Yet if this *singularity* casts into doubt the need for a *proper name* for God, then naming of the Deity by means of the general term *god/gods* would seem to put us in even more of a quandary.

Naming and Context

It may be some consolation to those puzzled by the naming of God to find that the naming of even the most ordinary things and persons has generated a large and contentious philosophical literature. The capacity to use names is amongst the first and most readily acquired of human skills. The young child quickly knows how to name, using both proper names and common nouns, and yet explaining how *naming* works is fraught with difficulty.

The modern literature on naming, as mentioned, has been greatly concerned with meaning and reference and with questions such as 'how do proper names *pick out* particular individuals – even long-dead individuals like George Washington – or entities like the planet Venus. Why does *Aristotle* latch onto the ancient Greek philosopher who tutored Alexander the Great in one instance and a twentieth-century shipping magnate who married Jackie Onassis in another?'

---

[10] Herbert Chanan Brichto, *The Names of God: Poetic Readings in Biblical Beginnings* (New York; Oxford: Oxford University Press, 1998), 31.

The most important point to grasp is that *reference* is achieved at the level of utterance and that this is thus a social process. It is not, as I have stressed, words which refer but speakers using words who make successful reference. A speaker can successfully refer by means of a designation she knows to be false – 'Is the king in his throne room?' – when the speaker knows the 'king' to be a pretender. Successful reference has to do with context and presumed intention and does not depend on altogether accurate or unreviseable description, still less on a description of essence. That is why, in the appropriate context, we understand the referring expression 'the cabbage has been made premier' to refer to a human being and not some brassica.

Once we see that reference is an utterance-bound notion, the referential use of proper names becomes less puzzling. If words on their own do not 'have reference', then neither do proper names, but both can be used in referring expressions. Unlike normal nouns, however, proper names do not have *sense* (or dictionary meaning). Even where there is residual meaning in a proper name, as in *Jasmine* or *Joy* or *Victor*, it is not invoked when in normal speech someone is asked 'Victor, is there any more chocolate?' For this reason it is sometimes said that proper names are *directly referential* – that is, terms which are largely or entirely devoid of descriptive meaning and serve simply a referential function.[11]

---

[11] Biblical scholars will point out that certain proper names have deliberate sense, 'Isaac', for instance, from Sarah's laugh, and there is a whole branch of philology (onomastics) dedicated to the etymologies of names. However, when we look at the function of proper names it is not primarily attached to sense, and we can distinguish between

Other directly referential terms are indexicals – *I*, *you*, *now* and *tomorrow*. With these one can see that it is not quite the case that there is no meaning to the term (*he* is not *you*), but the descriptive sense is minimal. When it comes to reference, indexicals depend on their context of utterance. You and I may both say words, 'I am going to the cinema' and in doing so will pick out different individuals. True demonstratives (*that*, *this*), a subset of indexicals, may depend on a gesture 'that man over there' (pointing).

Proper names, unlike demonstratives, preserve their referential force across changed circumstances. In this sense they more closely resemble the referential use of descriptive phrases.[12] Yet unlike descriptive phrases, speakers who have little shared knowledge of an individual may successfully refer to the same person by means of a proper name – a great part of their usefulness is indeed that they enable us to refer across a broad range of acquaintance and circumstance. I may know little more of Jane Jamieson than that she is a person who has phoned and asked me to phone her back, and you may know her only as your dentist, but we can both, by using her name, successfully refer to her. Proper names, as John Searle puts it, seem to be pegs on which to hang descriptions.[13]

'baptism' or 'giving of a name' and its subsequent use. For instance, a child may be named as 'Hope' or 'Victor' of 'Joy' for a particular reason and with a definite meaning, but that meaning will not be to mind when, some years later, he is asked 'Victor, is there any chocolate?' The concerns of historical linguists are, of course, somewhat different from those of contemporary analysts. On this, and on onomastics, see Anderson, *The Grammar of Names*.

[12] Palle Yourgrau, *Demonstratives*, Oxford Readings in Philosophy (Oxford: Oxford University Press, 1990), 1.

[13] John R. Searle, *Speech Acts: An Essay in the Philosophy of Language* (London: Cambridge University Press, 1969), 172.

Proper names are attended by conventions and learning how to use them involves learning these conventions. In written English and other European languages, one of these is capitalisation – by convention we assume 'Daisy' in a written text refers to an individual of some sort (maybe a person, maybe a dog or a boat), and we assume that 'daisy' does not.

In speech a good deal of information is assumed in using a proper name. What the child learns is not the meanings of proper names but their *use*. Effective use of proper names involves shared practice, expectations, context and knowledge. For instance, one must at least know that the term in question is (or is being used as) a proper name. Children make mistakes here. One of mine on a trip to an art gallery had several paintings of Venus and Adonis pointed out to her and asked, with some puzzlement, 'but what is a donis?'

In addition to knowing certain linguistic conventions, to use a proper name referentially we need to have at least some 'discriminating conception' of the individual to whom we wish to refer. This may be very minimal – *the person who has asked me to return their call* – and it certainly does not need to be the same discriminating conception for every successful user of the name.

When you fully understand my reference, you know and understand what or whom I intend to pick out. The referential use of proper names thus has an indexical aspect. At work we might assume that 'Peter was just looking for you' referred to our colleague of that name. At home we might assume the same phrase referred to our neighbour, Peter. Referential ambiguity in proper names is usually resolved by context without much need of explanation. David

Kaplan notes that when his wife says to him, 'It's up to you to punish Jordan for what happened today',

It is by means of various subtle contextual clues that I understand her to be charging me to administer discipline to our son and not to be calling on me to act where the United Nations has failed.[14]

Successful referential use of a proper name thus involves picking out the individual or bearer in question. In this respect the proper names of fictional characters, or of those whose existence is contested is not much different. If what is called for is a clear indication of the person or bearer under discussion, then there is no attendant difficulty in the use of proper names to 'pick out' fictional characters like David Copperfield, or even individuals about whose historical reality we may wish to suspend judgement, like Robin Hood or Jonah. There is no reason why this should be viewed as misuse of language. Human speech is almost infinitely complex and varied because we wish to say complex and varied things. References to fictional characters are vetted and contested in much the same way as those to non-fictional – *Jane Eyre finally married Mr Knightley ... No, that was Emma!* Sometimes we wish to refer to an individual without clarifying troublesome questions as to whether they existed. I can successfully refer to Job's comforters without clarifying whether I think they, or indeed Job himself, were historical figures.

---

[14] David Kaplan, 'Dthat', in *Syntax and Semantics*, Vol. 9, ed. Peter Cole (New York: Academic Press, 1978), 221–43 at 220. See also François Recanati, *Direct Reference: From Language to Thought* (Oxford: Blackwell, 1993).

What Is Involved in Naming
and Referring to God?

Let us first be clear what is at issue. When we are asked the question of how God can be named or referred to, given that God cannot be described, we are not being asked to *prove that God exists*. The questions is rather *how can one speak coherently of God if any discriminating concept we should seize upon is either inadequate or incoherent?* What the religious believer needs to block is the insistence that their claims are incoherent insofar as they cannot say what God *is*. This is a serious criticism insofar as it dovetails with theology's own long-standing insistence that God's essence cannot be comprehended or defined.[15] Accounts of 'naming' in the Lockean mode seem to rule out this diffuse way of proceeding. To have a 'name' (here a general term like *cow* or *geranium*) is to have an idea, and in the case of the idea of God this includes certain qualities (attributes) God 'has'.

The reply to this is twofold. First, we need to be aware of the slippage here between the use of *god* as a common noun and as a proper name. Capitalisation is an indication that the term in question is being used as a proper name. But if *God* is used as a proper name we do not here, any more than with the proper names of human individuals, need to be in possession of a list of essential properties or even one discriminating conception *shared* by

---

[15] See, for instance, Aquinas in the *De Potentia Quae*. 7, article 3 where we read, 'God cannot be defined, because whatsoever is defined is comprehended by the intellect of him that defines it; and God is incomprehensible to the intellect. Hence it is not a definition of God when we say that he is pure act' (pp. 17–18).

all other users of the name in order to use *God* successfully in referring expressions. We do, as with all proper
names, need some discriminating conceptions, although
this can be minimal and far from providing a definition
in terms of essential properties. The Book of Exodus, for
instance, refers to God by means of a number of definite
descriptions such as *the God of Abraham and of Isaac and of
Jacob*. Indeed, *characteristically it is by means of such descriptions that the God of Israel is referred to in the Biblical literature* – not in terms of what God '*is*' (at least not if that
means a metaphysical essence) but in terms of what God
does or has done (the One who rescued us from Egypt,
the One who made heaven and earth). These are held by
the faithful to be 'facts' about God, but they are 'facts' of
a particular sort – they are contingent and not necessary
truths about God. Just as I may refer to Jane Jamieson
as 'the one who phoned me earlier', even though it is
a contingent fact that she did so, so I may refer to God
as creator and redeemer, even though God might have
not rescued the Israelites, or loved them or even created heaven and earth. As with other proper names, different individuals may use the name successfully while
associating it with different discriminating conceptions.
Moses could speak of God as 'the One who led us out of
Egyptian captivity'. Abraham, since he lived before this
stated event, could not – nonetheless both can refer to
the same God.

If I'm told to 'return the phone call to Jane Jamieson',
I may know nothing of *Jane Jamieson* other than that she
called earlier but, we might say, a great deal is smuggled
in here under the *nothing*. I recognise from the phrase that
this is a proper name, I assume her to be an individual,

and a human being, or perhaps a shop. Although I cannot give an account of who this person is exactly, but I can say what, in general, human beings are like.

But must we not have some idea of what or who *God* is, or at least, (since this seems to be a noun used as a proper name), some idea how the noun, *god*, works in ordinary speech?[16] The answer is that we do. The word *god* has a dictionary entry like any other noun, and the faithful today, like Paul at the Areopagus, are fully able to invoke that common meaning. That is why it is not redundant to say 'The Lord is my God, YHWH is his Name.' It is not the case, however, that the sense of the word (*god*) gives a full description of what 'god' must be like. Nor does the sense of the word fix the reference in by supplying a list of attributes every member of the denotata must have. This sense is important, for obviously one who says 'God made heaven and earth' is not saying a giant squid or even a magician made heaven and earth, but the nature of the 'god' referred to has yet to be filled in, and this is what is done in the countless qualifying stories of divine acts that make up the Old and New Testaments. These specify that it is not just a god, but this particular god who has called Abraham from Ur, spoken to Moses from the bush and freed Israel from Babylonian captivity.

That the faithful are altogether capable of using the word *god* (in whatever language) in its shared sense, while retaining distinct views as to the truth about *god* and *gods* is shown in the comic story of Elijah and the prophets of

---

[16] Here meaning just a noun that serves to 'sort' the referents into countable items.

Baal in 1 Kings 18 in which *god* is used both as a general term and as a proper name. With the wavering children of Israel before him, Elijah throws down the gauntlet:

'How long', he said 'do you mean to hobble first on one leg then on the other? If Yahweh is God, follow him; if Baal, follow him.' (v.21)

This is mocking generosity, however, and what follows makes it clear that Elijah thinks the worshippers of Baal are deluded. Elijah and the prophets of Baal are to prepare altars with slaughtered bulls:

You must call on the name of your god, and I shall call on the name of mine; the god who answers with fire, is God (*Elohim*) indeed. (1 Kgs 18: 24)

When midday comes with no result for the prophets, Elijah taunts them:

Call louder for he is a god: he is preoccupied or busy ... perhaps he is asleep and will wake up. (1 Kgs 18: 27)

Nothing happens until Elijah's supplication to 'YHWH, God of Abraham, Isaac and Israel' is met with immediate fiery success.

The faithful have no difficulty using the word *god*, although they would then wish to clarify who exactly their god might be. Paul does the same thing on the Areopagus, speaking of *gods* while himself having no truck with polytheism. To provide a dictionary definition for a term does not determine the exact nature of everything that might reasonably fall in its denotation. A parallel to the word *god* in this respect might be the word *government*. This has a dictionary definition, and it is on this basis that we call a set of relations and operations *a government*; however, in the individual case clarification will need to be made as to what kind of government it is – a tyranny, a monarchy, a parliamentary democracy, a federal government and so on. Similarly, with *god* the common or dictionary sense provides a basis for shared understanding, but groups and individuals will qualify more exactly what it is they intend in their particular religious use of the term. Complementing such an account with narratives, citations and eulogy is neither digressive nor irrelevant but altogether necessary for clarifying *who or what* this particular god is. Those who insist on a consistent and coherent definition of *god* in order to speak meaningfully of God, or refer to God, confuse providing a definition for *god*, which can after all be easily done, with providing an account of who or what a particular faith community might mean by *God*, a matter which requires a greater exposition than a dictionary entry.

Consider how this might work in a particular instance: suppose that one of the prophets of Baal were to have said, 'Elijah, your god is a great god', Elijah would have understood this, and both would have seen that the Prophet of Baal is referring successfully to the God of Israel, even though the Baal-worshipper might have little or no understanding of who or what this god might be. Agreement that they were referring to the same god might then be the beginning of the refinement of the Prophet of Baal's understanding. And how would this be done? Then as now through the telling of stories, the relating of sacred histories, by being taught how to pray and make to religious observance, and so on. The Prophet of Baal at the end of it might decide after all that this God, *YHWH*, did not exist but he would have then a good understanding of what Elijah means when he invokes *YHWH*, God of Abraham, Isaac and Israel.

Naming and Relationship

To sum up: naming is a practice. We use names to refer to individuals and to kinds of things, and this need not involve existential commitment: we can refer to Moby Dick and to unicorns. We do not need to use proper names to refer to individuals – this can successfully be done by definite descriptions (*the first president of the United States, the heroine of Pride and Prejudice*) and indexically (*that man over there*). To use the word *god* effectively, one does not need to be in possession of a metaphysically or scientifically 'correct' concept, but only to know the commonplace meaning the word has in the community using it.

Speakers can both use *god/gods* in standard dictionary senses and use *God* as a proper name. This is characteristic of western monotheism. Speakers may refer to their god by means of a definite noun phrase, for instance *the One who made all that is* and indeed believe this to be a 'fact' about God. Although using this description as a means of reference, even as a definite description, they are not thereby committed to the belief that it is in any way a description of God's essence or of 'what God is' per se. God need not have created anything at all. The same can be said of the definite noun phrase much favoured by the Pentateuch, 'the God of Abraham, and of Isaac and Jacob'. This, if it picks out any god, it picks out only the God of Israel – yet it does so without recourse to essential properties. It is entirely contingent that God should have made Israel and, in formal terms, that God should have loved her.

Analogy and Metaphor

When the ancient writers say that no words are capable of expressing God, they do not mean that nothing can be said of God at all. 'All things', as Augustine was quick to say, 'can be said of God', that God is bread, water, light, a house 'but nothing can be said about God worthily. You seek a suitable name; you do not find it. Whatever way you seek to speak, you find he is all things.'[17] We can say certain things *concerning* God without qualification and in that sense, literally – for instance, we might say 'many people believe in God' or even 'churches are dedicated to the worship of God', but these are statements *about* God only in a trivial sense. As to what we can say about the divine nature, the line from the Greek and Latin fathers through to medievals, is clear and insistent – we can predicate nothing unequivocally of the Creator and of creatures. Minimally our language is 'stretched' when it comes to God. Augustine, perhaps in a moment of rhetorical excess, goes so far as to insist that we cannot even say God is *unspeakable,* for even to say that is to have said something. This stretched speech is not difficult to understand. If we understand the standard senses of *cause/causes/caused*, we can grasp the semantic intent of a sentence like, 'God caused all that is to come into being' and readily paraphrase it – 'Without God, nothing would be that is.' What we cannot say is, in God's case, what the nature of the *causing* might be. We can comprehend the utterance but not *apprehend* what the nature of this

---

[17] Augustine, *Tractates on the Gospel of John*, The Fathers of the Church, 5 vols. (Washington, DC: Catholic University of America Press, 1988), Tractate 13, 5.

causing would be in the divine life. Aquinas marks this as a distinction between the *res significata* and the *modus significandi* – that which is signified and our way of signifying. We can catch much of the same flexibility by noting that speakers can know the *meaning* of (dictionary definition) *cause/caused* and recognise, when predicated of God, that these are being used in a special way. The same may be said of other descriptive terms we use of God; for indeed we do need descriptive terms if we are to say not only what God does but, in some way, what God is. 'The cause of all' is one such, and another is that God is a 'person' and this, too, used analogically, for speakers know various senses of the word *person* – 'an individual, a mode of being of the Godhead' – and so on. A speaker can readily see that when one speaks of a *personal* God, the intention is to say that God is an individual who can be addressed and who may respond, and so on. To say that a person *must* be a material being is to beg the question. To say that 'God is personal' is literal, if analogical speech, for a moment's reflection will show that qualification is needed even if we are to say that 'God is an individual'. God cannot be an individual as individual creatures are, for God is not a creature. Nonetheless, the speaker intends to say that God relates to us as a person to persons.

Now drawing attention to the 'stretched' (or analogical) and metaphorical nature of our speaking of the divine is in modern discussions often treated as the last redoubt of the philosophically embarrassed – once metaphysics gives way, it is suggested, believers beat a retreat to mystery and obfuscation. This is clearly not what Augustine and Aquinas had in mind. These writers did not doubt God's existence nor invoke the inadequacy of our language in order to retreat from sceptical fire. That all our speaking falls short of the divine reality was not for them an admission of defeat but the primordial religious insight on which all our *true speaking* of God must depend. The background for this, in Judaism as in Christianity, is an overwhelming awareness, mediated by Scripture, of the *holiness* and Otherness of God before whom even the prophets speak as those with unclean lips. To this is added in the Christian period the teaching of *creatio ex nihilo*, which makes the distinction between God and the world more radical (and at the same time the relation more intimate) than any to be found in the texts of the ancient philosophers – a distinction not just between God and world but between Creator and creatures. Strictly speaking, God cannot even be said to *exist*, since this for us has the connotations of materiality and temporality. God is beyond existential categories, yet we do say 'God exists' and in doing so speak analogically.

As Sr Verna Harrison points out, apophaticism is not an excuse for agnosticism.[18] Whether there is a God is not what is at issue, but how could we speak of One so wholly other as to be not 'a being' at all. Even our saying that 'God is One' needs qualification if not to place God within a cardinal series – this is why 'One' is regularly capitalised in these contexts (Arabic even has a different word for the Oneness of God from the *one* which is in the cardinal series of numbers).

These strategies of negation or qualification are a means of un-naming, a reminder always of the limitations

---

[18] Verna E. F. Harrison, 'The Fatherhood of God in Orthodox Theology', *St Vladimir's Theological Quarterly* 37, no. 1 (1993): 185–212 at 187.

of human knowing and speaking when it comes to God. What we grasp when we grasp the classical attributes (One, eternal, omniscient) is not a set of recondite truths about how things are *chez God*, but a practice of unknowing, not baseless conjecture but a reasoned response to what we know of the Godness of God whom we know to be creator of all that is. We can see all this at work in this excerpt from Gregory Nazianzen. He is speaking about the birth of Christ and mentions in this context the giving of the Name to Moses:

God was manifested to man by birth. On the one hand Being, and eternally Being, of the Eternal Being, above cause and word, for there was no word before The Word; and on the other hand for our sakes also Becoming, that He Who gives us our being might also give us our Well-being.

And a little later:

God always was, and always is, and always will be. Or rather, God always Is. For Was and Will be are fragments of our time, and of changeable nature, but He is Eternal being. And this is the Name that He gives to Himself when giving the Oracle to Moses in the Mount. For in Himself He sums up and contains all Being, having neither beginning in the past nor end in the future; like some great Sea of Being, limitless and unbounded, transcending all conception of time and nature, only adumbrated by the mind, and that very dimly and scantily ... not by his Essentials.[19]

---

[19] Gregory of Nazianzus, 'On the Theophany, or Birthday of Christ', Oration 38 in *A Select Library of Nicene and Post-Nicene Fathers of the Christian Church: Second Series*, Vol. VII, ed. Philip Schaff and Henry Wace (Edinburgh; Grand Rapids, Mich.: T&T Clark; William B. Eerdmans, 1988), 345–51 at 346.

Augustine, in the *De Trinitate*, says we should not be surprised, given the difficulty of understanding even the workings of our own intellect, that we are unable to grasp the nature of God. But why then speak at all?

We should understand God, if we can and as far as we can, to be good without quality, great without quantity, creative without need or necessity, presiding without position, holding all things together without possession, wholly everywhere without place, everlasting without time, without any change in himself making changeable things, and undergoing nothing. Whoever thinks of God like that may not yet be able to discover altogether what he is, but is at least piously on his guard against thinking about him anything that he is not. (*de Trin.* Book V, Prologue)

Naming, Calling Upon and Being in Relation

Names are used to pick out individuals in a phone directory, but that is only one use of names, and not the one that interested Philo or the other religious writers I am considering. Their concern is with names used to praise, to invoke and to call in moments of love, intimacy, anger and even distress: consider 'Captain, the ship in sinking!' and Elijah's 'Answer me, LORD, answer me, so that this people may know that you, O LORD, are God, and that you have turned their hearts back' (1 Kgs 18.37; NRSV translation).

The Elijah text emphasises the fact that, along with *referring to*, naming is important to *calling to* and *calling upon*. What goes on when we call upon someone, and why do we do so? This returns us, as does the Elijah text, to the question of why it is we call God *God* – why use a generic when there is a unique proper name at hand, *YHWH*?

As mentioned before, and much to the diminishment of Christian theology, English translations of the Hebrew Bible, as in the New Revised Standard Version quoted for I Kings 18 above, largely efface the presence of the Tetragrammaton in the text, leaving instead only the orthographic convention of writing 'LORD' in capitals. But the God to whom Elijah has cried out is *YHWH*: 'Answer me, YHWH, answer me, so that this people may know that you, O YHWH, are God.' Yet the translators are in a bind, since in the New Testament, God and Christ are called Lord, with evident anchorage in the Hebrew tradition of replacing the Tetragrammaton with the Hebrew word for Lord (*Adonai*).

However, just as proper names are not the only means by which we refer to individuals, they are also not the only or even the most intimate means by which we call upon someone. Characteristically we call upon some of those closest to us by common names. Consider *Mom*. *Mom*, like *God*, is not a proper name after the fashion of *Thomas Jefferson*. The title *Mom* carries some descriptive content (*female parent*) – but it would be curious to say that *Mom* just means 'female parent' – to know this term's significance is to grasp its use as an appellative.

As with the indexicals (*this, you, here*), appellatives are context sensitive. In the playground a dozen children call out to a dozen women -'Mom!' – and no confusion arises. Understanding who it is that is 'picked out' by the name depends not just upon the sense of the term but pre-eminently upon who it is that is speaking or calling. In a family gathering of a number of cousins and aunts, no one is confused by my saying 'Mom, would you like a drink?' once they are clear who it is that has spoken.

With this, and the playground example, we have locutions as much concerned with address as with reference. The children calling 'Mom!' do not have as their main intention the identification of a particular individual for third parties although that may be an unintended effect. Their intention is to draw their own mothers' interest. No one could reasonably insist that this playground communication would be improved if each child addressed the relevant mother by her proper name. The mother hearing her child cry 'Mom!' is unlikely to think anyone else is intended. Use of a proper name might even represent a loss of information for those overhearing the exchange for they would not know if the child were calling to an aunt, a sister or a baby-sitter. *Mom* tells us of a relationship, not necessarily a biological relationship between a speaker and one spoken to – it also, for the speaker and the one spoken to, reinscribes this relationship.

Mom like *God*, is a name for an office-holder (consider also *Boss*, *Captain* and *President*). That *Mom* names an office-holder is borne out by the effective, if inelegant practice, of young children who say 'but my mom told me'. And this vernacular use gives the clue to another important feature – that the primary use of *Mom*, the most common and directive use of *Mom* is as a vocative, as a means **to call out to or to call upon someone**. In this *Mom* and other appellatives are much like *God*. As with other vocative naming, one who calls out to *God* inscribes a relationship in doing so. Here we may find a reason why *God* may be preferred in prayer to *YHWH*. *God, my God* inscribes a relationship as does *my Mom* and *my Lord* – a relationship between the one who calls and the one who is called. The language of love and desire will be replete with such names – my beloved, my dearest, my Saviour.

Conclusion

It is a profound truth, but one easily neglected, that no one of us 'invents' language. Infants learn language by being spoken to, usually by those who love and care for them. Even those who cannot speak are spoken to and named and become members of the community of speakers.

If language is social, then naming is a profoundly social practice. Naming, as we have seen, needs a context and a purpose. Naming other persons involves being in relationship with them, whether trivial (as with the phone book), belligerent (as with derisory names) or lovingly in the language of desire by which we call upon our beloved, or a child calls to her mother. All this can tell us something about God.[20]

---

[20] Rowan Williams explores this in *The Edge of Words: God and the Habits of Language* (New York: Bloomsbury Continuum, 2021) and develops the themes in *Looking East in Winter: Contemporary Thought and the Eastern Christian Tradition* (New York: Bloomsbury Continuum, 2021), 86, where he also speaks of 'the need to challenge reductive models of knowing that assume the normative status of non-relational, descriptive and external modes of understanding the environment and fail to deal with the mutual "implication" of knower and known'.

Naming is almost never simply a matter of labelling, for to be 'in language' at all means that we have been addressed by other people in the first place.

We speak because we have been spoken to, and we speak of God and to God because we believe God has spoken to us, usually through the words of Scripture. Moses at the burning bush speaks because God first spoke to him. To speak at all, as Rowan Williams observes, is to 'gesture towards a prior reality of *address*'.[21]

---

[21] Williams, *The Edge of Words*, 33.

6

Gregory of Nyssa – Naming and Following God

From Mystic Vision to Ethics

~

> Trinity! Higher than any being,
> any divinity, any goodness!
> Guide of Christians
> in the wisdom of heaven!
>
> Lead us up beyond unknowing and light,
> up to the farthest, highest peak
> of mystic scripture,
> where the mysteries of God's Word
> lie simple, absolute and unchangeable
> in the brilliant darkness of hidden silence.

This prayer opens Denys the Areopagite's famous treatise, *The Mystical Theology*. His advice to one seeking spiritual growth

> is to leave behind you everything perceived and understood, everything perceptible and understandable, all that is not and all that is, and, with your understanding laid aside, to strive upward as much as you can toward union with him who is beyond all being and knowledge. (Pseudo-Dionysius, *The Mystical Theology*, 997A–1000A)

This directive to move beyond the perceptible into a union beyond knowledge is redolently Neoplatonic, but the opening prayer is framed by Moses' ascent of Mount Sinai. That same mountainous ascent informs the

Prologue to John's Gospel with its talk of darkness and light, a 'tabernacling' deity, and of seeing and not seeing, God. Denys, writing sometime in the sixth century, already stands in a long tradition which links the way of unknowing to the theophanies of Moses at Sinai.

While Denys the Areopagite is credited with first speaking of 'apophatic theology', the way of negation is well trodden before him by the Cappadocians, by Athanasius, and by Plato himself, and this indeed is the genealogy traced in many contemporary accounts of the origins of mystical theology. What such accounts often leave out is any reference to the Hellenistic Judaism for which Philo is an eminent source.[1] Why does this matter?

It is true that some of the philosophical strategies characteristic of negative theology were already present in Plato and can be found in later pagan Neoplatonist writings. But what most evidently we do not find anywhere in Plato is Moses, a figure everywhere present in Christian mystical writings.

We might ask if the Moses narrative does no more for the early Christian writers than provide a convenient biblical story to frame what is essentially a platonic ascent. Might another story have done just as well – perhaps that of Jonah who is ejected from the darkness of the whale's belly into the light? But the patristic authors did not choose Moses

---

[1] See, for instance, the otherwise wonderful Vladimir Lossky, *The Mystical Theology of the Eastern Church* (Cambridge: Clarke, 1991). See also Denys Turner, *The Darkness of God: Negativity in Christian Mysticism* (Cambridge; New York: Cambridge University Press, 1995). Historians of the early church are better. See, for example, the concise insistence on the importance, and the Jewishness, of Philo in M. J. Edwards, *Origen against Plato*, Ashgate Studies in Philosophy and Theology in Late Antiquity (Aldershot: Ashgate, 2002), 15–17.

arbitrarily. They had a precursor in Philo for whom the story of Moses at Sinai is the quintessential narrative for the knowing, naming and desirous seeking of God.

As mentioned earlier, when Philo addresses knowing and naming God, he invariably returns to Moses and the Exodus. Amongst the early Christian writers Origen, Clement and Gregory of Nyssa all write on the life of Moses. All stand indebted to Philo or his milieu, and all connect knowing with naming God.

Gregory of Nyssa's *Life of Moses* is one of his late works, written sometime in the early 390s. It is a landmark in the literature of negative theology. While a contrast has sometimes been drawn between Gregory's earlier (philosophical) writings and the later (spiritual) ones, concern for divine transcendence, unnameability and unknowability runs clearly throughout his works. The philosophical writings are shot through with glimpses of the God beyond human knowing, and his later spiritual texts are underpinned by philosophy. While we may be looking at different genres of theological writing in earlier and later works, we are looking at the same theological mind.[2]

Gregory writes as one constantly mindful of the radical distinction between the uncreated and all that is created. Some background will allow us to see what Gregory inherited, as well as to appraise how he develops the tradition. *Creatio ex nihilo*, by his day largely taken for granted, was an achievement of the early centuries after Christ. Where

---

[2] In their foreword to *Gregory of Nyssa: The Life of Moses*, ed. and trans. Abraham J. Malherbe and Everett Ferguson, Classics of Western Spirituality (New York: Paulist Press, 1978), Malherbe and Ferguson describe the work accurately as a 'philosophical theology of the spiritual life' (xvi).

earlier Christian writers wobbled, as did Philo, on the question of whether matter pre-existed the creation, the second century, with its debates over Gnosticism, proved a forcing house. A God who created by moulding pre-existing matter, or from whom the universe emanated ineluctably, did not have the freedom of the God who brings about the activity of existing as such. By the time of the Council of Nicaea in 325, the teaching was fully articulated. Both Athanasius, champion of the orthodox, and his opponent Arius affirmed the distinction between uncreated and created, while differing as to which side to put the Son.[3]

As we have seen, *creatio ex nihilo* puts pressure on religious language. Philo in his eagerness to differentiate the God of Moses from that of the polytheists on the one hand and the philosophers on the other is pressed to neologism. Many of the predicates that are distinctive of later negative theology make their first appearance in Philo's writings – others, which suggest Philo is not alone amongst Hellenistic Jewish exegetes, appear in the Greek texts of the New Testament.

Where terms are Greek and 'philosophical', it is easy to assume that they were, in the first instance, terms of philosophy subsequently borrowed by Jewish or Christian

[3] On this see Peter Bouteneff, *Beginnings: Ancient Christian Readings of the Biblical Creation Narratives* (Grand Rapids, Mich.: Baker Academic, 2008), 86–7, who writes, of the second-century Apologists: 'These writers came to see the importance of declaring that creation was not an emanation from God or a shaping by God of pre-existing matter. This, too, was clearest in Irenaeus, who faced the most obvious (gnostic) opposition to the *ex nihilo* view … The clarity with which they affirmed that creation was a total event, in the sense of denying any existing material substrate, effected the clearest delineation yet between created and uncreated – two categories that would prove of decisive importance throughout the formative period of Christian theology.'

thinkers. As we have seen, however, borrowings went both ways – terms and ideas (maybe even that of God as 'beyond being') which originated in Jewish apologetics were later picked up by pagan Neoplatonism.[4] And as we have seen with 'the eternal', the same terms used across Platonic, Jewish, Christian and gnostic texts do not necessarily carry the same significance.[5] *Creatio ex nihilo* means a whole new context for talk about God.

The second century CE saw a flowering of negative predication when speaking of God, not only in the Christian writings but in gnostic texts and writings of the philosophical movements. While often assumed to be the result of 'oriental' and Platonist influence, the drive to negation seems to be as much indebted to Hellenistic Judaism. It is to Jewish sources that we can trace the first use of *agenetos*/uncreated, self-sufficient, uncontainable and invisible (*aoratos*). Philo himself is our first source for unnamable (*akatonomastos*), ineffable (*aratos*) and incomprehensible (*akataleptos*).[6] Christian

---

[4] Daniélou notes that *invisible* (*aoratos*) is not applied to God by Plato nor by any of the later philosophers dependent only on Middle Platonism, but that it *does* occur in St Paul. See Jean Daniélou, *Gospel Message and Hellenistic Culture*, trans. John Austin Baker, A History of Early Christian Doctrine before the Council of Nicaea, Vol. 2 (London: Darton, Longman and Todd, 1973), 326.

> He is the image of the unseen God
> and the first-born of all creation. (Col 1:15)

Morwenna Ludlow has pointed out to me that although Plato does not use the term directly of God, he does use it of the invisible world or 'heavenly realm' (*Sophist* 246a, *Theatetus* 155e). Gregory could reasonably be influenced by both.

[5] Daniélou, *Gospel Message and Hellenistic Culture*, 324.

[6] A term which was to become of great importance to Christian writers in the fourth century.

apologists like Justin Martyr pick these terms up from Philo or his milieu, and by the time we read them in the works of the non-Christian Celsus, it is likely that he has taken them from Christian texts with which he is in dispute. The very emphasis on naming God, a topic of middling to low importance to Plato himself, seems to come into later Platonic traditions through the influence of Jewish sources for whom, as we have seen, the Holy Name, calling upon the Name and the various names for the Holy One in scriptures are established points of concern.

According to Andrew Louth, creation *ex nihilo*, with its 'fundamental ontological divide' between God and creatures, forced a crisis in Christian Platonism. Not only did it precipitate the Arian controversy, it had deep implications for mystical theology, and 'it was there that it found its most fundamental resolution'.[7] For a Neoplatonist like Plotinus, the soul has a natural kinship with the divine which facilitated the philosopher's quest and, in some rare cases, the philosopher's success in merging with the divine. Earlier Christian Platonists such as Origen had allowed for continuity of soul and deity, but *creatio ex nihilo* rules this out absolutely. In its terms the soul, like the body, is a creature. The soul is 'not in any way connatural' with the divine and cannot by any philosophical exercise lift itself up into the One. We can be lifted up only by grace, and for the Christian apologists this means through the Incarnation, death and resurrection of Christ.[8]

---

[7] Andrew Louth, *The Origins of the Christian Mystical Tradition: From Plato to Denys* (Oxford: Oxford University Press, 1981), 77.

[8] Louth, *The Origins of the Christian Mystical Tradition*, 78.

In the realm of religious language, this absolute onto-logical difference between created and uncreated puts God beyond knowing in a way which subtly contrasts with that of the Neoplatonists. Vladimir Lossky puts it thus, thinking perhaps of Plotinus:

> To a philosopher of the Platonist tradition, even though he speaks of the ecstatic union as the only way by which to attain to God, the divine nature is nevertheless an object, something which may be explicitly defined – the ἐν – a nature whose unknowability lies above all in the fact of the weakness of our understanding, inseparable as it is from multiplicity.[9]

The One of Plotinus is beyond knowing and naming because with true philosophical simplicity comes the collapse of the multiplicity of subject and predicate, and even of knower and known. Nonetheless, for the Platonist the kinship of mind (*nous*) and the divine makes a certain grasp of the divine possible. Jean Daniélou points out that for the Neeoplatonist to say God is ineffable means that God 'surpasses any conception of him that the mind can form in terms of the sensible world; but it is also to affirm that, if only the mind can shake itself free from all conceptions of that kind, it will be able to grasp his essence'.[10] For the Christians, however, the biblical God transcends not only what could be known by the senses but what could possibly be grasped by the mind. For Gregory of Nyssa, God must be profoundly unknowable and unnameable and our speaking of God at all made possible only by God's gift, as Philo had expressed it, 'by licence of language'.

---

[9] Lossky, *The Mystical Theology of the Eastern Church*, 32.
[10] Daniélou, *Gospel Message and Hellenistic Culture*, 2, 336.

We see a merging of residual Platonism with the truly Christian apophaticism in Clement of Alexandria:

For on account of his greatness he is ranked as the perfect, and is the father of the universe. Nor are any parts to be predicated of him. For the One is indivisible ... therefore it is without form and name. And if we name it, we do not do so properly ... we understand the unknown, by divine grace and by the word alone that proceeds from him; as Luke in the Acts of the Apostles relates that Paul said ... Whom you ignorantly worship, Him declare I unto you.[11]

If God cannot be known by our efforts, then, as Eric Osborn put it, the divine condescension which is grace comes 'not as a compromise but as an assertion of transcendence'.[12] This God of Abraham is a speaking and teaching God.

Gregory's most sustained philosophical treatment of the names and the naming of God comes in an early work, *Contra Eunomium*, aimed at a latter-day Arian called Eunomius. His transgression appears to be to make the Son less than the Father, and to do so on the basis of linguistic arguments. Gregory answers in kind, his rebuttal displaying his own fine philosophical formation. He chides Eunomius for fancy rhetorical footwork while at the same time showing himself skilled in deploying the rhetorician's tactics and the grammarian's distinctions.

---

[11] Clement, *Stromateis* 5.12.81. Cited in Eric Osborn, 'Negative Theology and Apologetic', in *The Via Negativa*, ed. Raoul Mortley and David Dockrill, Supplement to Prudentia (Auckland: Prudentia, 1981), 49–63 at 49.

[12] Eric Osborn, *The Beginning of Christian Philosophy* (Cambridge: Cambridge University Press, 1981), 59, here speaking of Tertullian.

According to Gregory, Eunomius is led into the error of subordinating the Son to the Father by his poor theology *and* bad philosophy of language. Eunomius ignores, or twists the meaning, of gospel names when 'he passes over in silence the name of the Father and of the Son and of the Holy Spirit' (Matt 28, 19). Instead of 'the *Father*', Eunomius speaks of some 'highest and most authentic being' and, instead of 'the *Son*', of 'one which exists because of that being and after that being has supremacy over the rest'.[13] This is not just a matter of names, says Gregory, and we should be suspicious of one who prefers terms of his own coinage to those of scripture (I, XIV, §160). Eunomius, 'frequent contemplator of incomprehensible things' (I, XXXVIII, §575), seems not to see the distinction evident even to 'quite a small child just learning verbal skills under a teacher of grammar ... that some nouns are absolute and unrelated, and others are used to express a relation' (I, XXXVIII, §568). All his linguistic and theological failings come together in his presumptuous opinion that the divine essence can be known and is expressed by the term 'ungenerate' (*agenetos*). The Son's essence can equally be designated, so Eunomius argues, as 'begotten' and is therefore less than the Father.

Gregory's objection to this, as throughout, rests on his conviction of the absolute distinction between the created and the uncreated, which poses 'what is ultimately an

---

[13] Gregory of Nyssa, *Contra Eunomium I: An English Translation with Supporting Studies*. Vigiliae Christianae, Supplements, Vol. 148, ed. Miguel Brugarolas, trans. Stuart George Hall (Leiden: Brill, 2018), XIV, §156 (e-book).

insuperable barrier to knowledge of the Divine essence'.[14] Because we cannot have that knowledge, we cannot adequately *name* the Divine essence. Eunomius' presumption is to think 'ungenerate' stands as a true definition of God, a rationalistic theology based on an account of language in which 'names designate essences'.[15] Against this Gregory argues that:

We … following the suggestions of Holy Scripture, have learned that His nature cannot be named and is ineffable. We say that every name, whether invented by human custom or handed down by Scriptures, is indicative of our conceptions of the divine nature, but does not signify what that nature is in itself.[16]

The names given in Scripture, and especially the Trinitarian names of Father, Son and Holy Spirit, have special status for Gregory, but even they do not name the divine essence. Our names are 'names for us', and for the most part name God's activities, or *energeiai*. With God

what is named by those who speak of him is not what he actually is, for the nature of him who Is is ineffable; but he gets his titles from the actions he is believed to perform for our lives.[17]

---

[14] James Le Grys, 'Names for the Ineffable God: St Gregory of Nyssa's Explanation', *The Thomist* 62, no. 3 (1998): 333–54 at 336.

[15] Le Grys, 'Names for the Ineffable God', 337. See Chapter 5.

[16] *Ad Ablabium* (*That We Should Not Think of Saying that There Are Three Gods*), III. 1:42–3. Cited in Le Grys, 'Names for the Ineffable God', 337.

[17] *Contra Eunomium II: An English Version with Supporting Studies*, ed. Lenka Karfíková, Scot Douglass and Johannes Zachuber; trans. Stuart George Hall (Leiden: Brill, 2007), 149 (e-book). 'Father,' 'Son' and 'Spirit' are in a special class of names, not naming operations (which are always of the Triune God) but relations among the persons. On this see Le Grys and also Verna E. F. Harrison, 'The Care-Banishing Breast of the Father: Feminine Images of the Divine in Clement of Alexandria's *Paedagogus I*', *Studia patristica* 31 (1997): 401–5.

The similarities to Philo will be apparent. God is not nameable by essence but is named by those who call upon him. The same dynamic will be apparent in Gregory's later 'mystical' writings.

The Life of Moses

The Life of Moses, read most often as a work of mystical theology, is addressed to its readers as a treatise on 'perfection in virtue'. Any apparent tension here is eased by the recollection that 'the mystical' for Gregory, as still for the Eastern Church, does not have the subjectivist connotations it later acquired in the West, but remains a Christological term. All Christians are called to the way of mystery, which is Christ.[18] To follow this way involves a knowing and an unknowing, for its end is not acquisition of a body of knowledge but a deepening and, from Gregory's point of view, never-ending journey into God. As such mystic knowledge is pre-eminently practical.

Any easy assumption that *The Life of Moses* is 'spiritual' in a subjectivist or privatising way is confounded by Gregory's concern throughout for moral teaching. 'Perfection in virtue', it transpires, concerns perfection in its broadest sense. The spiritual way is not directed to the amassing of arcane spiritual knowledge or experiences, nor is it the life of the solitary. Love of neighbour is inseparable, in this journey, from love of God.[19]

---

[18] See Lossky, *The Mystical Theology of the Eastern Church*, Ch. 1., and J. Meyendorff, 'Preface', in *Life of Moses*, ed. and trans. Malherbe and Ferguson (hereafter Nyssa, *Life of Moses*.)

[19] The work shows clear indebtedness to Philo. Just as Philo's *Life of Moses* is divided into an exposition of the Moses narrative followed by

But why should Gregory write a life of Moses as a guide to Christian perfection?[20] To say that he does so because Clement, Origen and Philo did so before him is just to push the question back. True, Gregory, like Philo, makes Moses into something of a peripatetic philosopher whose ascent of Sinai recalls the stages of illumination in Platonic mysticism. But if we are looking for an ideal seeker, why not choose Abraham, father of the Jewish people, a smasher of idols and seeker of God? Indeed, both Philo and Gregory do speak of Abraham in this way and can find in his life the stages of ascent.[21] But it is the story of the Exodus which, pre-eminently, addresses a time when Israel comes to 'know' the Lord and his Name, and with this knowing and naming comes following – or discipleship.

The three stages of mystic ascent are mapped by Gregory onto just those points in the Book of Exodus

an edifying commentary, so Gregory, between brief introduction and conclusion, divides his text into two main sections – an *historia* in which he expounds the text, and a *theoria*, or contemplation, which addresses its meaning. Parallels with Rabbinic exegesis can be found throughout in what is, nonetheless, a thoroughly Christian reading of the Moses story.

[20] Gregory himself notes the oddity of fashioning our life after the pattern of one who was raised by a daughter of Egypt but concludes that all these stories of 'sublime individuals' are recorded by scripture in detail to direct us in conducting our lives to the good (Nyssa, *Life of Moses*, 32).

[21] Consider, for instance, Philo: 'Now he who is in the intermediate stage is always pressing forward to the summit, employing the gifts with which nature has blessed him' (*de Mut.* 2). The reader might be forgiven for thinking that the one 'pressing towards the summit' is Moses; in fact, here it is Abraham. In Book II of the *Contra Eunomium*, Gregory breaks off to give an account of the life of Abraham which has as its intention to show, as Verna Harrison puts it 'how the patriarch, unlike Eunomius who claimed to have knowledge of the divine essence, acknowledged God's incomprehensibility and lived by faith' (*Grace and Human Freedom According to St Gregory of Nyssa* (Lewiston, NY: Edwin Mellen Press, 1992), 64).

which Philo, and very likely a broader Jewish tradition, took as central to knowing and naming God: Exodus 3, the burning bush (*Moses began with light*); Exodus 20, where Moses 'drew near to the thick darkness where God was' (Ex. 20.21) and Exodus 33, *where Moses asks to see God's glory*. It is around these three episodes that Gregory develops his doctrine of God in *The Life of Moses*.[22] In Gregory, as in Philo, knowing and naming are connected to following. For Gregory this means that *theologia*, in the sense of contemplation of the things of God, and right action cannot be separated.

For Gregory, as for Philo, the true lover of God is one who is always seeking. The guiding text of his *Life* is Paul from Philippians, who 'never ceased *straining towards those* things *that are still to come*'.[23] In expanding upon this in his prologue, Gregory shows sensitivity to questions of language:

The Divine One is himself the Good (in the primary and proper sense of the word), whose very nature is goodness. This he is and he is so named and is known by this nature.[24]

Since there is no limit to good but evil, and the Divine does not admit of an opposite, Gregory concludes God is unlimited and unlimited virtue, and our journey into God has no stopping place. It is thus impossible to attain perfection, not simply because we backslide but because perfection is not marked off by limits – it is endless. Gregory's anthropological vision is not one of crimpling limitation of stricken souls but of endless growth made

[22] Malherbe and Ferguson, 'Foreword', in Nyssa, *Life of Moses*, 14.
[23] Nyssa, *Life of Moses*, 30. Citing Phil 3.13.
[24] Nyssa, *Life of Moses*, 31.

possible by the infinite horizon of the goodness of God. Although what one seeks is in some sense unattainable, we should nonetheless strive, he tells us, after the perfection which is attainable: 'To that extent let us make progress within the realm of what we seek. For the perfection of human nature consists perhaps in its very growth in goodness.'[25] We are very near the heart of Gregory's theology here: God's perfection is limitless. To seek God is to be always growing. This philosophy of growth, as Daniélou points out, is in strong contrast with the Greek conception according to which change involves imperfection. The follower of God is always moving forward.[26]

Gregory's God, like Philo's but unlike that of the Platonists, is a speaking and teaching God. Gregory has the Platonist's preference for visual metaphors and the three moments he privileges in the life of Moses are indeed visions, but all three are at the same time moments at which God teaches Moses something. Commenting, for instance, on the theophany of the burning bush, he tells us that the 'light's grace was distributed to both senses, illuminating the sight with flashing rays and lighting the way for hearing with undefiled teaching'.[27]

At the burning bush Moses learns that God cannot be compared to any other. Gregory takes the divine self-designation, 'I Am Who I Am', as the opportunity to discuss 'real Being'. Gregory says:

[25] Nyssa, *Life of Moses*, 31. This is, by the way, close to Philo's suggestion in *The Special Laws* that perfection is found in progress itself.

[26] On this *epektasis*, the soul's continual stretching to God, see Morwenna Ludlow, *Gregory of Nyssa, Ancient and (Post)modern* (Oxford: Oxford University Press, 2007), especially Ch. 7 'Spirituality: Perpetual Progress in the Good'.

[27] Nyssa, *Life of Moses*, Book 1.

the definition of truth is this: not to have a mistaken apprehension of Being. Falsehood is a kind of impression which arises in the understanding about non-being, as though what does not exist does, in fact, exist. But truth is the sure apprehension of real Being.[28]

True being is 'what possesses existence in its own nature, that is only God, 'I Am'.'[29]

It seems to me that at the time the great Moses was instructed in the theophany he came to know that none of those things which are apprehended by sense perception and contemplated by the understanding really subsists, but that the transcendent essence and cause of the universe, on which everything depends, alone subsists.

That which is always the same, neither increasing nor diminishing, immutable to all change whether to better or to worse, standing in need of nothing else, alone desirable, participated in by all but not lessened by their participation – this is truly real Being. And the apprehension of it is the knowledge of truth ...[30]

For Gregory, the theophany at the burning bush, and indeed all theophanies are Christological. He makes the connection between the burning bush story and the opening verses of John's Gospel. The burning bush was a manifestation of truth and light, 'sublime names', by which the Gospel testifies to 'the God who makes himself visible to us in the flesh'.[31] This light reaches down to us in material substance, here from an 'earthly bush' and in the Incarnation through Mary.

---

[28] Nyssa, *Life of Moses*, 60. It is interesting to note that Gregory makes no mention of the Tetragrammaton; very likely, as with Philo, he is unaware of its presence behind his Greek text.

[29] Nyssa, *Life of Moses*, 60.   [30] Nyssa, *Life of Moses*, 60.

[31] Nyssa, *Life of Moses*, 59.

Note that for Gregory the ascent of Moses does not begin when he enters the 'dark cloud where God was', as those who wish to emphasise the Platonic elements in Gregory's mysticism have sometimes suggested. Unlike Origen for whom the mystic way is one from darkness to greater and greater light, for Gregory the journey begins with the blazing light of the bush. It begins not from human initiative but with gift: we are addressed by God. This is an address in truth and light – a light which reveals at the same time how shadowy is human understanding compared to the 'I Am' which is its object. From there the seeker progresses into darkness, the one who seeks to associate with God must go beyond all that is visible and ascend, as to a mountaintop, to the invisible and incomprehensible and 'believe that the divine is *there* where the understanding does not reach'.[32]

'What does it mean', Gregory asks, 'that Moses entered the darkness and saw God in it?'[33] Does this second theophany (Ex. 20) conflict with the earlier where God is seen in light? Not at all, says Gregory, for Scripture teaches us that 'religious knowledge comes at first to those who receive it as light'.[34] As the mind progresses, 'it sees more clearly what of the divine nature is uncontemplated'.[35] As we learn more, we realise that we know less, and this is because the object of our knowledge is the God whose wonders are unfathomable. This is not only a twist to the Platonic story but a daring Christological insight. The Light which comes into the world does not make things less mysterious. Mystery would evaporate if Jesus were

---

[32] Nyssa, *Life of Moses*, 43.   [33] Nyssa, *Life of Moses*, 94.
[34] Nyssa, *Life of Moses*, 95.   [35] Nyssa, *Life of Moses*, 95.

only man and not truly God. According to the Nicene orthodoxy to which Gregory adheres, God in Christ must remain eternal mystery even while he is for us the Gate, the Way, and the very cleft in the rock in which we shelter.

Thus, the journey which begins with light moves on into darkness, but we are not left without guidance. In the second theophany Moses 'gains access to the invisible and incomprehensible ... the seeing which is not seeing' in a 'luminous darkness', but at the same he is taught.[36] Moses after all *ascended* into the darkness of Sinai, but he *descended* with the Ten Commandments. The positive teaching does not contradict the apophatic moment. On the contrary, the commandments, or 'religious virtues', as Gregory sees it, are divided into two parts. The first are 'the things which must be known about God (namely, that none of those things known by human comprehension is to be ascribed to him)'. Note that Gregory extends the prohibition on graven images to all conceptions of God, 'since every concept which comes from some comprehensible image by an approximate understanding and by guessing at the divine nature constitutes an idol of God and does not proclaim God'.[37]

The second set of commandments tell us of our duty to our neighbours – not to kill, not to commit adultery and so on. Proper love of God and love of neighbour are laid down here.[38]

Barely mentioned in Book I, the 'historical' book of the *Life of Moses*, the third theophany (Ex. 33–4) is the

---

[36] Nyssa, *Life of Moses*, 95.   [37] Nyssa, *Life of Moses*, 96.

[38] See also his elaboration on the second theophany in Book I: 'He was commanded to heed none of those things comprehended by notions with regard to the divine nor to liken the transcendent nature to any

theological climax of Book II and indeed of the whole work. Quite a lot has happened to Moses by this time. He has met God in the burning bush, led the Israelites out of Egypt, gone up into the darkness into the divine presence, and received the Law. Outraged that the people have built the golden calf in his absence, Moses shatters the tablets of the Law, only to be instructed by God to cut two more tablets of stone and ascend Mount Sinai again. It is then that Moses asks to see God's face, 'Show me your glory, I pray' (Ex. 33.18). This seems an even more astonishing request than the earlier request for a name, and Gregory is struck by the same difficulty which troubled Philo before him – why should one with whom, we are told, God has spoken face to face 'as one speaks to a friend' (Ex. 33.11) make this bold request to see face to face? Gregory concludes that the ardent soul always desires more: 'He still thirsts for that with which he is constantly filled himself to capacity, and he asks to attain as if he had never partaken, beseeching God to appear to him, not according to his capacity to partake, but according to God's true being.'[39]

'Such an experience,' says Gregory, 'seems to me to belong to the soul which loves what is beautiful'. The ardent lover of beauty is drawn forward, he says, echoing the Song of Songs, and longs 'to enjoy the Beauty

of the things known by comprehension. Rather, he should believe that the Divine exists, and he should not examine it with respect to quality, quantity, origin, and mode of being, since it is unattainable. The word also adds what are right moral actions, presenting its teaching in both general and specific laws. General is the law which is destructive of all injustice, namely that one must love his neighbour ... Among the specific laws was established honour for parents, and there was a list of prohibited deeds' (Nyssa, *Life of Moses*, 43–4).

[39] Nyssa, *Life of Moses*, 114.

not in mirrors and reflections but face to face'.[40] God does not quench this desire 'since the true sight of God' is 'that the one who looks up to God never ceases in that desire'.

God gives only life. The cryptic *'You cannot see my face, for man cannot see me and live'* does not mean that God, Medusa-like, would cause the death of those who saw Him. In an epistemological turn Gregory says:

> He who thinks God *is something to be known* does not have life, because he has turned from true Being to what he considers by sense perception to have being. ... True Being is true life. This Being is inaccessible to knowledge. ... He learns from what was said that the Divine is by its very nature infinite, enclosed by no boundary.[41]

Yet Moses' petition is answered, an extra grace is given. God tells him that there is a rock with a cleft in it which Moses must enter. God places his hand across the cleft and calls out to Moses as he passes by. Moses sees the back of the One who called him. In this way he thought he saw what he was seeking, and the promise of the divine voice did not prove false.[42]

Philo, we may recall, understood 'seeing God's back' to mean that we see the traces of God in creation. Gregory finds something more personal. In seeing God's back (which Gregory understands figuratively since God lacks body parts in this way), Moses gets even more than he asks for:

[40] Nyssa, *Life of Moses*, 114–15.
[41] Nyssa, *Life of Moses*, 115. My emphasis.
[42] Nyssa, *Life of Moses*, 112. Might Emmanuel Levinas have adapted the notion of 'trace' from Philo?

So Moses, who eagerly seeks to behold God, is now taught how he can behold Him: to follow God wherever he might lead is to behold God.[43]

When the Lord who spoke to Moses 'came to fulfil his own law,' says Gregory, he explained the meaning of this figure. Jesus did not say 'if anyone wants to go before me' but, rather, 'if anyone wants to follow me':

And to the one asking about eternal life he proposes the same thing, for he says *Come, follow me.* Now he who follows sees the back.[44]

God, it seems, does not want epistemologists, but followers.

In another late work, his *Commentary on the Song of Songs* (*c.* 389), Gregory gives us a lengthy disquisition on Moses:

The much desired face of the Lord once passed Moses by, and thus the soul of the lawgiver kept on going outside its present condition as it followed the Word who led the way. Who does not know those ascents which Moses attained? He was always becoming greater and never stopped in his growth. [*here Gregory gives or provides some account of Moses' early life in Egypt*]. Next, he was enlightened by the fire upon the bush, and his hearing was illumined with the beams of life by means of the Word. ... He heard the trumpets, braved the burning mountain, touched the peak, and became an unapproachable sun to those who came near because light radiated from his face. Indeed, how could anyone relate all his ascents and various theophanies? Nevertheless, this man who had experienced such things ... still was not satisfied. He besought God to see

---

[43] Nyssa, *Life of Moses*, 119.   [44] Nyssa, *Life of Moses*, 119.

him face to face, although Scripture had already testified that he was counted worthy of speaking with God face to face. But neither his speaking as friend with friend nor the intimate conversation with God stopped his desire for more. Rather, he says, *If I have found favour in your sight, make yourself known to me.* God granted this requested favour. He who said, *I have known you above all men*, passed by him while he was shadowed by God's hand at that divine place in the rock so that after God passed by he could only see his back. Scripture teaches by this, I think, that he who desires to behold God sees the object of his longing in always following him. The contemplation of his face in the unending journey accomplished by following directly behind the Word.[45]

This recapitulation of the life of Moses in the midst of a commentary on quite another biblical text (and one in which Moses does not make an appearance), shows his importance for Gregory, whose reading of the Song of Songs is continually refracted through the story of Moses. The 'cleft in the rock' (*Come, my dove, in the cleft of the rock next to the wall*) is at the same time the cleft in which Moses stood, the rock on which he stands the Gospel which is Christ.[46] The bride is the soul, like Moses 'constantly making progress and never stopping at any stage of perfection', and the Spouse is God, 'Whom she loves with all her heart and soul and strength.'[47]

---

[45] Gregory of Nyssa, *Commentary on the Song of Songs*, Vol. 12 (Brookline, Mass.: Hellenic College Press, 1987), 354, 56.

[46] *Commentary on the Song of Songs* 2.14. See Gregory of Nyssa, *From Glory to Glory: Texts from Gregory of Nyssa's Mystical Writings*, ed. Jean Daniélou and Herbert A. Musurillo (Crestwood, NY: St Vladimir's Seminary Press, 1979), 191.

[47] Nyssa, *From Glory to Glory*, 197, 201.

The stream of the divine names seems to have gone underground here but it is never far from the surface when the Moses is our guide. The verse, 'Upon my bed at night / I sought him whom my soul loves; I sought him but found him not: I called him, but he gave no answer' (Song of Songs 3.1 NRSV) draws from Gregory these reflections. Here the bride finds herself

surrounded by the divine darkness, searching for Him Whom I desired – though the Beloved Himself resists the grasp of our thoughts. And so *I sought him in my bed by night (Cant.* 3.1), to learn of His substance, His beginning and His end, and in what His essence consists. But *I found Him not.* I called Him by name – as though it were possible to find Him in a name when he cannot be named.

No name would have a meaning that would reach Him Whom we seek. For how can He be discovered by a name when He is *beyond all names?*[48]

While at first glance oddly metaphysical in a commentary on the Song of Songs, these insights are of a piece with the arguments of the early *Contra Eunomium* and, of course, *the Life of Moses.*

What, then, can our relation be to a God who is beyond naming and knowing? For Gregory it is one of unimaginable intimacy and delight, but it is not we who forge the way between created and uncreated. God comes first to us in the address of love:

Since that which is by nature finite cannot rise above its prescribed limits, or lay hold of the superior nature of the Most High, on this account He, bringing His power, so full of love for humanity, down to the level of human weakness, so far as it was possible for us to receive it, bestowed on us this helpful gift of grace.[49]

For Gregory, like Philo, the Divine bends down to speak to us but for the Christian writer God's supreme Word is Christ. This is the Word who creates, who teaches and who leads. To see God's face is to be set upon the 'unending journey accomplished by following directly behind the Word'.

Gregory finds Christ to be present everywhere in the Exodus narrative. It is Christ who speaks from the burning bush which Gregory himself is the first to take as a figure of the Virgin Mary, God-bearer, as fully physical in her womanhood as is the bush in its spiky materiality.[50] The bitter waters at Marah (Ex. 15.22–5) are made sweet by the Cross ('You of course understand the "cross" when you hear "wood",' says Gregory). The rock Moses strikes at Horeb and from which fresh water flows is Christ (Ex. 17.5–7), 'For the *rock*, as the Apostle says, is *Christ*.'[51]

The Word is both our teacher and our Way to participate in the infinite divine Goodness. Le Grys notes that there are two sides of divine infinity, 'It means both that

---

[49] *Contra Eunomium* II, 418–19. Cited in Le Grys, 'Names for the Ineffable God', 343.

[50] Nyssa, *Life of Moses*. This association of Mary with the burning bush became a feature of Orthodox liturgy and iconography. The icons attached to this theme show Mary variously, as flanked by Moses and Elijah (the two prophets who experienced theophanies on Sinai), or with the burning bush inside her body, or sometimes as seated with the Christ Child on the bush.

[51] Nyssa, *Life of Moses*, 87. Gregory is citing I Cor 10.1–4 'I do not want you to be unaware, brothers and sisters, that our ancestors were all under the cloud, and all passed through the sea, and all were baptized into Moses in the cloud and in the sea, and all ate the same spiritual

God is ultimately incomprehensible, and that there is no end to our progressive initiation into the mystery of God. Thus, it is not that we know simply nothing of God, but rather that there is always more to be known.'[52]

God is beyond our grasp not just because our knowing is flawed but because knowledge of God cannot be of the 'commercial' kind. As he says in *Contra Eunomium*, 'Knowledge acts, as it were, in a commercial spirit, dealing only with what is known. But the faith of Christians acts otherwise. For it is the substance, not of things known, but of things hoped for....'[53]

Verna Harrison cautions us against contrasting faith with knowledge here, in a way that suggests the true seeker is finally wise enough to give up on knowledge as she 'humbly settles for faith'. It is not all knowledge but this possessive, Eunomian knowledge that Gregory discounts. We genuinely know God through his creative activity, but this falls short of the divine essence.[54] Faith brings us beyond knowledge into relation with the divine essence. This participation is Gregory's mysticism, in the Christological sense, and it is in this participation through Christ that we are endlessly to progress – 'deified' not through our own lives but through sharing in his. As Gregory understands the theophany at the burning bush,

---

food, and all drank the same spiritual drink. For they drank from the spiritual rock that followed them, and the rock was Christ.' Philo's interpretation of the same Exodus passage (*Det.* 31) is that the water from the rock is Wisdom (logos). It is not surprising that the Fathers found the exegesis of Hellenistic Judaism so sympathetic.

[52] Le Grys, 'Names for the Ineffable God', 349.

[53] *Nicene and Post-Nicene Fathers, Series* 2, Vol. V, 259; GNO 1.254, cited in Harrison, *Grace and Human Freedom According to St Gregory of Nyssa*, 67.

[54] Harrison, *Grace and Human Freedom According to St Gregory of Nyssa*, 67.

'real Being' alone 'possesses existence in its own nature'. It stands in need of nothing else, 'participated in by all but not lessened by their participation'.[55]

But central though the theme of individual seeking and questing may be, the story of Moses is not, for Gregory, a template for solitary spiritual perfection. Gregory is after all a bishop. Moses ascends in the darkness of God, but he descends to his people with the Law. Following God, as in the book of Exodus, is not a private fancy but a communal spiritual journey.

[55] Nyssa, *Life of Moses*, 60.

7

Augustine, Moses and God as Being Itself

~

Desiring and Speaking

we should understand God, if we can and as far as we can, to be
good without quality, great without quantity, creative without need
or necessity, presiding without position, holding all things together
without possession, wholly everywhere without place, everlasting
without time, without any change in himself making changeable
things, and undergoing nothing. Whoever thinks of God like that
may not yet be able to discover altogether what he is, but is at least
piously on his guard against thinking about him anything that he
is not. (Augustine, *de Trin.* Book V, Prologue)

Have I spoken something, have I uttered something worthy of God?
No, I feel that all I have done is to wish to speak; if I did say something, it is not what I wanted to say. How do I know this? Simply
because God is unspeakable. But what I have spoken would not have
been spoken if it were unspeakable. For this reason God should not
even be called unspeakable, because even when this word is spoken,
something is spoken.[1]

Augustine, throughout his writings, is concerned with how
it is we can name and know God, preoccupations which
are especially evident in the *Confessions*. There, as we have
seen, he weaves together titles of metaphysical ultimacy
(eternal, immortal, immutable) with tokens of fragility
and intimacy. By now, in this study, it should be evident

[1] Augustine, *The Trinity*, trans. Edmund Hill, O.P. (Brooklyn, N.Y.: New
City Press, 1991), 190. *De doctrina christiana*, trans. R. P. H. Green,
Oxford Early Christian Texts (Oxford: Clarendon Press, 1995), 17.

that in this regard Augustine is not an innovator but stands in a well-established tradition of Christian reflection. In this chapter we will see that, while Augustine's God is 'Being Itself', this is not the 'supreme being' of the philosophers and it is the distinctly Christian teaching of *creatio ex nihilo*, and not any Neoplatonic vision of 'divine supremacy', which is key to his Christian metaphysics.

Augustine is a younger contemporary of Gregory of Nyssa but wrote in the Latin West rather than the Greek-speaking East. He did not read Greek, or not very well, and there's no reason to believe Gregory's writings were known to him. All the more interesting, then, is it to see how much they share when it comes to naming God. This is particularly the case if we do not read him, as does some contemporary philosophy, as one whose conception of God is fundamentally that of the philosophers, only thinly and inconsistently draped with biblicisms.[2]

Augustine never concealed his gratitude to the books of the Platonists. He read the *Enneads* of Plotinus, or at least some parts of it, while in Milan and during a time of

---

[2] See Scott MacDonald, 'The Divine Nature: Being and Goodness', in *The Cambridge Companion to Augustine*, ed. Eleonore Stump and Norman Kretzmann (Cambridge: Cambridge University Press, 2001), 71–94 at 80. MacDonald speaks of Augustine's new beliefs, following his encounter with Platonism as based on 'the argument from divine supremacy': 'In Augustine's hands the argument from divine supremacy yields an impressive list of divine attributes: incorporeality, eternality, immutability, incorruptibility, inviolability, life, and wisdom, among others' (81) MacDonald speaks of God as being 'the topmost being on the hierarchy of natures' and that Augustine received, in his intellectual vision, 'a glimpse of God's inmost nature', which is 'deeply explanatory of both the manifold divine attributes and the universe in which God ranks supreme' (81). MacDonald's language is at best incautious, suggesting God is, for Augustine, a being amongst beings, if the supremely ranked one.

anguished searching. It was through reading these that he learned that God was 'another reality, that which truly is' (*Conf.* III.7). Yet many have puzzled over his precise debt to 'the Platonists'. He may have found in Plotinus a 'One' that is the self-caused cause of all, but Plotinus' 'One' is very different from Augustine's Creator. The 'One' of Plotinus is neither personal nor intimate. Plotinus' One, beyond all differentiation, cannot be named or even spoken about. Augustine, on the other hand, spends his whole time speaking about God and extolling God's mercies to us even if, as he admits, we can never speak adequately of God. Above all, the One of Plotinus cannot call out to our hearts or be addressed, whereas the *Confessions* is all about divine address – God's address to us and our address to God in prayer. Augustine's God, like the God of Gregory and Philo but unlike that of the Platonists, is a speaking and a teaching God.

Although he never wrote a life of Moses, Augustine returns again and again to the disclosure at the burning bush. Writing in the fourth century, Augustine is heir to a Christian consensus, configured around Moses and Exodus 3, that the Creator is unnameable and in the divine essence unknowable.[3] What Augustine, the great theologian of the Latin West, brings to the table is an intense interest in language itself – not just our speech about God but how it is that we can speak at all, and what that implies for our speaking not only 'of' God but 'to' God.

---

[3] See, for example, Clement of Alexandria who understands the entry of Moses into the darkness where God was to show 'that God is invisible and beyond expression by words' (Stromata, Book V, Ch. XII). Clement thinks this was Plato's view, and that Plato learned this wisdom from Moses, not an unusual belief amongst Christian thinkers of this time.

Augustine's Talk and Monica's Tears

The *Confessions* is the work of a former professor of rhetoric and one who knows that there are many who may doubt the genuineness of his recent conversion. In it Augustine is preoccupied with questions of words and true speaking, not only questions as to how we may speak truly of God, but how we can speak at all. It is an autobiography based around words. Even his account of infancy revolves around questions of speech. As a baby, he says, I knew only to suck and to weep. He underlines the account of his infancy with the fact that the Latin *infans* means literally 'without speech'. Notoriously, for Augustine, even the infant is not free from savage wilfulness and selfishness, but the acquisition of language allows the child to hone these to a new sharpness.

At school he was flogged for harmless play and praised for verbal fluency 'so that I might get on in the world' to 'excel in the skills of the tongue, skills which lead to high repute and deceitful riches' (*Conf.* I.9.14). Would any sound judge of the matter 'think it right for me,' he asks, 'to be beaten because I played ball as a boy, and was hindered by my game from more rapid progress in studies which would only equip me to play an uglier game later?' (*Conf.* I.9.15). He presents his schooling as in large part training in deceit and in self-deception. Learning the alphabet, learning to read and write, those were good skills to learn which still stand by him, but at school he was forced also to memorise

the wanderings of some fellow called Aeneas, while forgetting my own waywardness, and to weep over Dido, who killed herself for love ... I could weep over the death Dido brought upon herself out of love for Aeneas, yet I shed no tears over the death I brought upon myself by not loving you. O God ... (*Conf.* I.13.20)

As a youth he is taught to 'be more wary of committing some barbarism in speech than of being jealous of others who did not commit it when I did' (I.19.30). A student schooled in this way will be more greatly offended by someone who mispronounces the word for 'human being' than by one who 'flouts your commands by hating a fellow-human' (I.18.29). It is all training in mendacity. Indeed, the higher he ascends the academic ladder, the more accomplished he becomes in deceit of self and others.

All this is not without irony, for it is by means of words that he convinces us of their treachery, and we know from the contemporary sections of his *De doctrina Christiana* that Augustine certainly did not think rhetoric should be shunned by Christians, nor did he ever lose his love of Virgil.[4] Speaking is demonised in the text to a literary end, for nothing Augustine says in the *Confessions* is unconsidered. It is far from being a 'tell all', yet not for this less truthful. We have no reason to doubt that as a young man he was dismissive of his mother's Christian faith or that once he stole pears 'for the hell of it', but these incidents in the texts are signs which point beyond themselves. The theft of pears represents a moral nadir not because it was the worst thing

[4] On Augustine's Christian remastering of rhetoric, see Paul R. Kolbet, *Augustine and the Cure of Souls* (Notre Dame, Ind.: Notre Dame University Press, 2010) and Michael Cameron, *Christ Meets Me Everywhere: Augustine's Early Figurative Exegesis*, Oxford Studies in Historical Theology (New York; Oxford: Oxford University Press, 2012).

the young Augustine did. He admits to sexual excess but does not provide the details that might titillate more than elevate. The theft of pears by its motiveless triviality shows the degradation of one who, in bad company, delights in acting badly for its one sake, just as later, in the faithful company of the Church, he will delight in the good.

We do well then, to keep an eye throughout on the figure of Monica. She is Augustine's model Christian, emblematic of the simple faithful the bishop grew so much to admire, and sometimes of 'mother' Church. The autobiographical section of his book ends with her death at Ostia.

Monica provides a foil for of her son's worldly success and spiritual dereliction. While the young Augustine acquires the rhetorical skills that will gain him preferment, Monica is represented as a person of modest intellectual achievements. She is not a reader of Cicero, Homer or the Neoplatonists, yet it is she who, as Augustine comes to see, has been in possession of the truth which eluded him for all his intellectual athleticism ('You wanted to show me first and foremost how you thwart the proud and give grace to the humble' (VII.9.13)). His mother enables Augustine to make a point salient to any work of theology – that professors of theology are no more likely to be saved than those of simple faith and learning.

Monica has a part to play in the sub-plot concerning words and speech. As Augustine gains in rhetorical agility, she is described, at almost every mention, as incoherent with tears. In the end it is her tears that are heard.

You stretched out your hand from on high and pulled my soul out of these murky depths because my mother, who was faithful to you, was weeping for me more bitterly than ever mothers wept for the bodily death of their children ... and you heard her, O Lord, you heard her and did not scorn those tears of hers which gushed forth and watered the ground beneath her eyes wherever she prayed. (III.11.19)

What then happens in the Milan garden, the famous but under-described moment of his conversion? Desperate to become a Christian and with all the argumentation failing to do the trick, the great professor of rhetoric, throws himself down under a fig tree and sobs – the tears 'burst from my eyes like rivers, as an acceptable sacrifice to you' (VIII.12.28). In the midst of incoherence, he hears the voice of a child chanting, 'Tolle, lege, tolle, lege' – 'Pick it up and read', which he interprets as a command to read the Bible. This text, once dark and obscure, now speaks directly to him. He, like Moses, finds himself addressed.

In the garden – and it is partly Eden – the great word-smith is once again deprived of words – once again *in fans*. It seems that God's gift to this 'salesman of words', as he describes his early profession, is to deprive him of speech. When the new convert is considering how he may tactfully resign from his teaching post, 'so that young boys who were devoting their thoughts not to your law, not to your peace, but to lying follies and legal battles, should no longer buy from my mouth the weapons for their frenzy ... and resolved ... no more to offer myself for sale, now that you had redeemed me' (IX.2.2), he suffers a providential chest infection which makes it difficult to speak and so has an excuse to escape from his teaching obligations.

The symbolic overtones of a professor of rhetoric who loses his voice are not far to seek. But the question is, how may he ever speak again? Why, we might ask, if Augustine has become so critical of human speaking in the *Confessions*, does he not choose a life of silence after his conversion? This would seem an appropriate act of contrition for a former 'salesman of words', perhaps life in the desert as some kind of linguistic Simon Stylites – and indeed Augustine is worried as to how he can speak. He cannot abandon words – they are not bad in themselves:

I am blaming not the words, which are finely-wrought, precious vessels, but the wine of error mixed for us in them by teachers who are drunk themselves. (I.16.26)

How can he find his way to truthful speech? It is the crux of the *Confessions* that if words are the means of corruption so also are they the source of healing. More properly it is the Word who is this source, and the Word speaking through the words of other people and, pre-eminently, those of Scripture.

Augustine retreats to Cassiciacum with a few friends and students and immerses himself in the words of Scripture. In particular he reads the Psalms which he reads as songs of fire – 'how I was inflamed by them with love for you and fired to recite them to the whole world' and especially to the Manichees who had misled him and deluded themselves (IX.4.8).

Yet the process is gradual. Returning to Milan after the vacation, Augustine is encouraged by Ambrose to read the prophet Isaiah, but he can make nothing of it: 'So I put it on one side to be resumed when I had more practice in the Lord's style of language' (IX.5.13).

'The Lord's Style of Language'

The *Confessions* are as much to do with losing as with finding. Were he to write the lyrics to *Amazing Grace*, the refrain might be *I once was found but now am lost*, for the young Augustine knew well enough who he was and what he wanted – pleasure, success, the admiration of others. It is only with the address of the divine Other that Augustine's self-opacity becomes so entirely apparent to him. Yet this has not stopped some from detecting in Augustine's writings a confident grasp of his own subjectivity, whether in Cartesian or post-Kantian mode, which is paralleled by a confident grasp of God. In this argument (Augustine as the pre-cursor of Descartes) the subject, finding no certainties in the world, becomes by introspection directly certain of itself. Certainty of God becomes the correlate of this direct certainty of the self.[5]

This sounds too tinny and smooth to be Augustine. It is true that in the *Confessions* he discovers God to be 'more inward than my most inward part and higher than the highest element within me' (*Conf.* III.6.11), but this, in the light of continued insistence on God's incomprehensibility, is scarcely to resolve a mystery. Who, or what is God? Descartes, after coming to the certainty of his

---

[5] For an argument of this nature, see Jürgen Moltmann, *The Trinity and the Kingdom: The Doctrine of God*, 1st US ed. (San Francisco: Harper & Row, 1981), 14.

thinking self and judging that he could 'accept it without scruple as the first principle of the philosophy I was seeking', moves quite quickly on to other things which can be conceived 'very clearly and very distinctly', and from the fact he has doubted and must thus be imperfect, to the idea of a Perfect Being which has '*all the remainder of perfection that I knew myself to lack*' and so to be 'infinite, eternal, immutable, omniscient, all-powerful'. Easy then, for Descartes: first me, then God. But it is not so easy for Augustine: 'Who then are you, my God? What, I ask, but God who is Lord' (*Conf.* I.4). Not only does Augustine not know who he himself is, but he cannot say what God is:

For with what understanding does a human being grasp God, who does not yet grasp his or her own understanding itself, through which one desires to grasp him?[6]

After the chanting voice that leads him to read scripture, Augustine understands that *he has been addressed by God*. Indeed, he believes that God has already spoken to him before in many ways – through his mother, through Bishop Ambrose, through the things of Creation – but he could not hear it. He does not claim to know what God 'is' for Augustine will never tire of saying that what God is in Godself we shall never know, at least not in this life. In *De Trinitate* he cites Paul's first letter to the Corinthians to this effect:

'If anybody thinks he knows anything, he does not yet know as he ought to know. But anyone who loves God, this man is

---

[6] Augustine, *On the Holy Trinity, Doctrinal Treatises, Moral Treatises*, trans. Arthur W. Haddan, Vol. III (Grand Rapids, Mich.: William B. Eerdmans, 1980), Book V, Prologue 2. See also Book X.13.

known by him' (I Cor 8:2). Even in this case, you notice, he (Paul) did not say 'knows him', which would be a dangerous piece of presumption, but 'is known by him'. It is like another place (Galatians) where as soon as he has said 'But now knowing God', he corrected himself and said, 'or rather being known by God' (Gal 4:9).[7]

Augustine does not know 'what' God is as in a list of attributes, but after his conversion he knows 'who' God is in the word of address. He now knows he has been spoken to and understands that he can speak back, that is, pray. This new situation is underscored at the beginning of Book IX, the book that relates the time spent at Cassiciacum with his friends just after his conversion. There we find him making a confession we have not heard before – 'I was now talking with you …' (*Conf.* IX.1.1).[8]

Augustine and God as Being Itself:
in idipsum

Augustine tells us that his reading of the fourth psalm while on retreat at Cassiciacum pierces him to the core – 'How long will you be heavy-hearted human creatures?' The final verse of the psalm 'wrung a cry from the very depths of my heart'.

---

[7] Augustine, *On the Holy Trinity, Doctrinal Treatises, Moral Treatises*, Vol. III, Book IX, Prologue 1.

[8] I use Henry Chadwick's translation of the *Confessions* (Oxford; New York: Oxford University Press, 1991), unless otherwise specified, but think Boulding's translation of *in idipsum* as 'Being Itself' better captures Augustine's use of this term across his texts than does Chadwick's suggestion of 'the Selfsame' (Augustine, *Confessions*, trans. O. S. B. Maria Boulding (London: Hodder and Stoughton, 1997)).

In peace! Oh! In Being itself! What did it say? *I will rest and fall asleep.* Yes, who shall make war against us when that promise of scripture is fulfilled, *Death is swallowed up in victory?* In truth you are Being itself, unchangeable, and in you is found the rest that is mindful no more of its labours, for there is no one else beside you, nor need our rest concern itself with striving for a host of other things that are not what you are; rather it is you, *you Lord, who through hope establish me in unity.* (*Conf.* IX.11)[9]

Here then is one answer to the question 'Who are you, my God?': God is Being Itself. '*In peace!*', writes Augustine, '*Oh! In Being itself ... I will rest and fall asleep.*' It must be said that no modern translation of the Psalms will have such a sentiment. The NRSV has simply 'I will both lie down and sleep in peace: for you alone, O Lord, make me lie down in safety.' Augustine's identification of God with 'Being Itself' is here fortuitous, some would even say gratuitous, because he was using a Latin translation of the Psalms which we now believe does not reflect the best text. Augustine reads in his Latin Bible '*in pace in idipsum dormiam et requiescam*' ... in 'Being Itself' (Boulding), in *the Selfsame* (Chadwick) will I rest.[10] In an illuminating essay on Augustine's negative theology,

---

[9] Trans. Maria Boulding. Chadwick translates the first line 'in peace ... the selfsame ... I will go to sleep and have my dreams.'

[10] Perhaps the point at which to mention that 'self' often appears in English translations of Augustine where the Latin uses a variety of reflexive forms. This, and the fact that English uses reflexive pronouns such as *myself, yourself, oneself* which, as John Cavadini has pointed out, 'sound like possessive pronouns plus the noun "self"'. This, he says, 'can sound like there is a thing called "self", which is "mine"' (John C. Cavadini, 'The Darkest Enigma: Reconsidering the Self in Augustine's Thought', *Augustinian Studies* 38, no. 1 (2007): 119–32 at 121).

Tarsicius von Bavel says that 'according to Augustine, "Being", or better "To Be", is God's proper and highest name; it applies only to God'.[11]

For many modern philosophers, to call God 'Being Itself' shouts of ontotheology – the Christian theologian trading divine disclosure for a dubious piece of metaphysics. But this is to misread Augustine for, as Maria Boulding points out, *idipsum*, 'Being-Itself', is linked by Augustine, not only here but throughout his works, with the mysterious name for God as given to Moses from the burning bush – the 'I Am Who I Am'.

Augustine turns repeatedly to Moses and Exodus 3 in his writings, dozens of times in his Expositions of the Psalms alone. Various topics prompt him to reflect on the gift of the name – God's everlastingness and our transience, the Psalmist's injunction to 'call upon the name of the Lord' and what it might mean to know the name of the Lord.

At the beginning of Psalm 104 (in our numbering, Psalm 105) Augustine finds we are enjoined to 'Confess to the Lord and call upon his name' – a confession of praise.[12] We are to seek God always. In sentiments reminiscent of Gregory of Nyssa, he suggests that the finding of the beloved (God) does not 'put an end to the love-inspired search; but as love grows, so let the search for one already found become more intense'.[13] While the

---

[11] Tarsicius Jan van Bavel, 'God in between Affirmation and negation according to Augustine', in *Augustine: Presbyter Factus Sum*, ed. Joseph T. Lienhard, Earl C. Muller and Roland J. Teske (New York: P. Lang, 1993), 73–98 at 75, referring to Augustine, *Ennaratio in Psalmum* CXXXIV.4.

[12] Augustine, *Expositions of the Psalms*, trans. Maria Boulding, 6 vols. (New York: New City, 2000), Vol. III, 184.

[13] Augustine, *Expositions of the Psalms*, Vol. III, 187.

psalm itself makes no mention of either the burning bush or the 'I Am Who I Am', it does recount at length the story of God's great saving works, including the Exodus. It is reflection on the wonders done for the children of Israel that prompts Augustine to remind his listeners of

the occasion when God replied to Moses, who had asked him who he was, *I AM WHO I AM. Thus shall you say to the children of Israel, HE WHO IS has sent me to you* (Ex. 3:14) It is a rare mind that can understand this even in the smallest degree; and so it was that God mercifully accommodated his grace to human beings by going on to reveal his name in these terms, I am the God of Abraham, the God of Isaac and the God of Jacob. This is my name forever.[14]

In a move reminiscent of one we have seen in Philo, Augustine suggests that this name, 'the God of Abraham, the God of Isaac and the God of Jacob', is given in charity so that those who seek God, even if it is too difficult to see 'what God is', may reflect on the 'wonders he has wrought'.[15]

A short psalm of ascent (Ps 121, our 122) extracts nonetheless lengthy comment from Augustine, for there he reads that Jerusalem 'shares in Being-Itself'.[16] This brings him back to Exodus 3:

What is *idipsum*? It is simply *idipsum* Being-Itself. How can I say anything about it, except that it is Being-Itself? Grasp it if you can, brothers and sisters, for whatever else I may say, I

[14] Augustine, *Expositions of the Psalms*, Vol. III, 187–8. Augustine, *Expositions of the Psalms*, Vol. VI, 186–7.

[15] Augustine, *Expositions of the Psalms*, Vol. III, 188.

[16] Verse 3 in his Latin text: *Jerusalem quae aedificatur ut civitas, cujus participatio ejus in idipsum*. Augustine, *Expositions of the Psalms*, Vol. VI, 18.

shall not have defined Being-Itself. All the same, let us attempt to direct the gaze of our minds, to steer our feeble intelligence, to thinking about Being-Itself, making use of certain words and meanings that have some affinity with it.

What is Being-Itself? That which always exists unchangingly, which is not now one thing, now another. What is Being-itself, Absolute Being, the Self-same? That which is. What is That Which Is? The eternal, for anything that is constantly changing does not truly exist, because it does not abide – not that it is entirely nonexistent, but it does not exist in the highest sense.

Augustine turns to Exodus 3.16 to expand:

And what is That which Is if not he, who, when he wished to give Moses his mission, said to him, *I Am Who I Am* ... This is Being-Itself, the Self-same: *I Am Who Am, He Who Is has sent me to you.*

There follows an important clarification of who the 'I AM' is, which bring us to a further level of understanding the divine names tradition:

You cannot take it in, for this is too much to understand, too much to grasp. Hold on instead to what he who you cannot understand became for you. Hold onto the flesh of Christ ... Hold on to what Christ became for you, because Christ himself, even Christ, is rightly understood by this name, *I Am Who I Am*, inasmuch as he is the form of God. In that nature wherein he *deemed it no robbery to be God's equal*, there he is Being-Itself. But that you might participate in Being-Itself, he first of all became a participant in what you are *the Word was made flesh* (Jn. 1.14) so that flesh might participate in the Word.[17]

---

[17] Psalm 121 in Augustine, *Expositions of the Psalms*, Vol. VI, 18.

Even Moses, Augustine surmises, was terrified by the name 'He Who Is', but God had more to say to him: '*I am the God of Abraham, the God of Isaac and the God of Jacob; this is my name forever* (Ex. 3:15).' We are not to despair in our own mutability and failings because God tells us:

I am coming down to you because you cannot come up to me. *I am the God of Abraham, the God of Isaac and the God of Jacob.* Put your hope in Abraham's seed, that you may be strengthened to see the one who is coming to you from Abraham's seed.[18]

Often the trigger for Augustine's return to Moses and Exodus 3.14 is God's eternity – not the steely everlastingness of the god of Aristotle but rather in the sense of God's providential care. This is the God in whom there is no change. God alone is Being and the One through whom we have our being, the One who made us and who will save us – a frequent theme of the Psalms. The *I Am* is not frightening or distant, but the one who comes to us, who speaks to us, who Augustine believes spoke to him in the garden at Milan.

That the *I Am* of Moses is Christ is equally made evident in his sermons which touch upon the 'I Am' sayings in John's Gospels. We are created, but the *I Am* is the one through whom all things are made. In his second exposition Psalm 101 (our 102), reflecting on the eternity of God and the ephemeral nature of creatures (verses 23–24), Augustine encourages his listeners:

But do not despair, frail humanity. *I am the god of Abraham, the God of Isaac and the God of Jacob*, he says. 'You have heard what

---

[18] Psalm 121 in Augustine, *Expositions of the Psalms*, Vol. VI, 19.

I am in myself; listen now to what I am for your sake.' That eternity has called us, for the Word has burst forth from eternity... Ah, the wonder of it! The Word exists before time, and through him all time was made; he was born in time, though he is eternal life; he calls temporal creatures, and makes them eternal. This is what the psalm means by the generation of generations [throughout all generations, J. S.].[19]

What we see here is a theology of creation and participation and a distinctly Christian metaphysics in which God is fullness of Being and creatures have their being from God. To be clear – it was not the books of the philosophers but the Book of Exodus read in conjunction with the creation theology of Genesis, Isaiah and the Psalms, which laid the ground for a distinctive Christian metaphysics which Augustine has inherited and deploys. In the developed theology of *creatio ex nihilo*, creatures are not part of God, but receive their being from God who is the source of being. Otherwise, they 'participate' in being. The background for this is the doctrine of creation – for if a given 'thing' is not held in being by God then how, on this reasoning, could it 'be' at all?

Jean-Luc Marion has written an article 'Idipsum: The Name of God According to Augustine' in which he shows himself averse to any talk of 'Christian metaphysics.' Marion contends that 'the metaphysical and ontological interpretation of *idipsum* in Augustine may owe everything to the posterior and, in fact, modern Thomist tradition, and, as such, contradicts what Augustine meant to say'.[20]

[19] Augustine, Exposition 2 of Psalm 101, Vol. III/19; Augustine, *Expositions of the Psalms*, Vol. VI, 71.
[20] Jean-Luc Marion, '*Idipsum*: The Name of God according to Augustine', in *Orthodox Readings of Augustine*, ed. George E.

The assumption here seems to be that any metaphysical concept of God would be an attempt to grasp the divine but, as we have seen, the foundational teaching of *creatio ex nihilo* means that this grasping is never a possibility. The suggestion that an understanding of God as 'Being Itself' is a later Thomistic imposition on Augustine's texts is not convincing and it is unclear why Marion wants to make so tortured a claim – possibly based on phenomenology's overall resistance to metaphysics, unless he assumes that all who talk of God as 'Being Itself' are engaged in onto-theology, which is not the case.[21]

Marion is quite right to say that 'idipsum' is, for Augustine, an apophatic title, but this does not mean that no 'Christian metaphysics' is at work here. Rather, it is the marker of a distinctively Christian (and in Philo's case, Jewish) metaphysics to say that, as Creator and according to Exodus, God is 'Being Itself', even if we cannot say what that means. Providing, of course, we keep in place the absolute distinction enforced by the doctrine of *creatio ex nihilo*, which means God is in no sense a being amongst beings (not even the supreme one), there is no ontic continuity between God and creatures, even though all creatures exist only and solely through God's creative

Demacopoulos and Aristotle Papanikolaou (Crestwood, NY: St Vladimir's Seminary Press, 2008), 167–90 at 178. See also Thomas A. Carlson's introduction to Marion's *The Idol and the Distance: Five Studies*, trans. Carlson (New York: Fordham University Press, 2001) which suggests that any metaphysical concept of God would be an attempt to grasp or define God (xvii).

[21] If Marion's more modest claim were that Augustine was not aiming to devise a 'philosophy of being' and that he did not take from philosophical texts a 'philosophy of being' into which he shoe-horned Christianity, then I agree.

will. In Augustine (as in Philo) we see a radicalisation of antique understanding of the relation between the being of the world and the being of God, which is based on the biblical teaching about creation.

Whether we then speak about God declaring himself as 'the Existent' (which Marion favours) and the source of existing things, or as 'Being Itself' and the source of beings, is a matter of indifference as long as we keep in mind that this by no means suggests that we 'know' what God is in Godself, or that God is in ontic continuity with creatures, other than as their Creator (that is, we are entirely dependent on God for our being, but God is in no way dependent on us). Although neither Philo nor Augustine was intent on devising a philosophy of being, their writings and those of any number of early Christian writers transform the teaching on the origin of and nature of things and is thus reasonably called 'metaphysical' even if based and grounded in scripture.[22]

Tarsicius van Bavel writes that Augustine 'never ceases to stress the inaccessibility of God to human comprehension and the inadequacy of human language to speak truly about Him'.[23] We can say anything at all in naming God, but nothing worthily, 'God is everything for us: bread water, fountain, light, clothing, a house. Everything can be said about God, but nothing worthily. Nothing is more comprehensive than his deficiency (*inopia*).

---

[22] See David B. Hart, 'The Hidden and the Manifest: Metaphysics after Nicea', in *Orthodox Readings of Augustine*, ed. Demacopoulos and Papanikolaou, 191–226.

[23] Bavel, 'God in between Affirmation and Negation According to Augustine', 76.

God can be called Father as well as Mother.'[24] For all this Augustine is not simply in the position of Plotinus whose One, being beyond all distinction and even that of knower and known, cannot speak or be spoken of but only known in rapture.[25] We speak truly, if partially, of God, and pre-eminently by the words of Scripture in which the divine reality is accommodated to our understanding. We should not hesitate to use the metaphors of the Bible, for only rarely does scripture use non-metaphorical ascriptions. Rarely, but not never, for all the figurative ascriptions are dependent upon the name given to Moses, I Am Who I Am. Although our speaking will always be deficient, we have, according to Augustine, the obligation to speak, to correct error, in ourselves and in others, to praise God and to point ourselves to 'the mystery of the radical Other.'[26]

Augustine points us also in another direction. Human words, when they participate in love, are tokens of the Word through whom all things have their being. A warmth about human words and human teachers suffuses the *Confessions*, which is almost entirely absent from his earlier tract on words and teaching, the *De magistro*. That text reads like a Socratic dialogue, after the manner of Plato's *Meno* whose arguments it, on occasion, follows. Augustine engages his sixteen-year-old son, Adeodatus, on the subject of teaching, but for all his brilliance

---

[24] Bavel, 'God in between Affirmation and Negation According to Augustine', 74.

[25] See Bavel, 'God in between Affirmation and Negation According to Augustine', 73.

[26] Bavel, 'God in between Affirmation and Negation According to Augustine', 82–3.

Adeodatus is still the student led by his erudite father. The Divine teacher in Augustine's *Confessions* is, by contrast, much more courteous to his child, letting Augustine speak while the Deity, in what is no less truly a dialogue, remains the silent interlocutor. In the later writings the give and take between the one speaking and the one addressed, preacher and hearer, author and reader already participate in some way in the generosity of the Divine Word.

Seek the Face of God, Always

Augustine understands that in this life we are always seekers. One of his favourite biblical verses is, as for Nyssen, Philippians 3.13:

Above all there is this text: *Brothers*, he (Paul) says, *I do not consider that I myself have got there: one thing, though, forgetting what lies behind, stretching out to what lies ahead I press on intently to the palm of our upward calling from God in Christ Jesus. As many of us therefore as are perfect let us set our minds on this* (Phil 3:13). Perfection in this life, he is saying, is nothing but forgetting what lies behind and stretching out to what lies ahead intently. The safest intent, after all, until we finally get where we are intent on getting and where we are stretching out to, is that of the seeker. The certitude of faith at least initiates knowledge; but the certitude of knowledge will not be completed until after this life when we see *face to face* (I Cor 13:12). (*de Trin.*, Book IX, Prologue 1)

The same biblical verse inaugurates one of the most memorable passages of the *Confessions*, the conversation between Augustine and his mother, Monica, at Ostia, the port of Rome. Monica is about to sail home to North

Africa and, though neither she nor her son knew it, she will shortly die before making the trip. Mother and son stand at a window overlooking a garden, reminiscent of the garden of Eden and the garden in Milan where Augustine has heard God speak:

Forgetting what lay in the past, and stretching out to what was ahead (Phil 3.13), we inquired between ourselves ... what the eternal life of the saints would be like. (IX.10.23)

They speak of the things of God and in their speaking together are lifted up in ardent longing towards *the Selfsame* (*idipsum*). Moving beyond all bodily creatures, they arrived at 'the summit of our own minds' and, passing beyond these, briefly touch 'the land of never-failing plenty where you pasture Israel forever with the food of truth' before falling back to 'the noise of articulate speech' (*Conf.* IX.10.24).

The indebtedness to Plotinus in this account of their ascent is unconcealed and we see its stages – inquiry after the truth, movement beyond natural things, brief union with the One before a falling back. Sometimes to the embarrassment of his Christian readers, Augustine is quite prepared to retain what he thinks valid in the Platonists but here, at the summit of Monica's Christian life, the resemblance to Plotinus is marked. Has the bishop failed to notice that he is still wearing the garb of the philosophers, writing some ten years on? It is far more likely that these overt Neoplatonic references serve to make the oddities of this ascent, from a philosophical point of view, all the more apparent.

It is precisely Monica's presence which reveals the difference. In the first place the experience is shared, an impossibility in Plotinian union where the soul is no longer conscious that she is in the body, no longer conscious of herself as distinct from the One, and so could not be conscious of another person. The Christian unitive vision involves no such collapse of seeker into Sought. On the contrary, the promise of resurrection holds out that individuality will always be our condition. Ostia is no flight of the alone to the Alone but a foretaste of the life of the saints – which is indeed the topic of Augustine and Monica's conversation. It is through their speaking and shared longing that they are lifted up and touch 'the Selfsame', leaving the 'first fruits of our spirit' and returning again to 'the noise of articulate speech, where a word has a beginning and end' (IX.10.25).

And then there is the person of Monica herself. Ancient philosophy is better conceived as a way of life than a branch of study. This was its attraction and limitation.[27] Philosophical study involved practices, changes in diet and occasionally in dress. The Neoplatonism widely regarded in Augustine's day (and probably by himself) as the true philosophy involved such disciplines. Philosophy had stages of spiritual progress and beginners were restricted to certain texts. In the *Enneads* the philosopher progresses from ethics, to considerations of the sensible world and finally consideration of the divine things. Unitive experiences were rare, and the achievement of the adept. Porphyry, the student of Plotinus, made it clear that philosophy is not for ordinary people – not for those 'who practice manual trades

[27] See Pierre Hadot, *What Is Ancient Philosophy?* (Cambridge, Mass.: Harvard University Press, 2002), 154.

or who are athletes, soldiers, orators, or politicians, ... but people who have reflected on the questions, "Who am I? Where do I come from?" And who, in their diet and other areas, have established for themselves principles different from those which rule other ways of life.'[28] Monica, although praised by Augustine for intuitive philosophical grasp has not undergone the rigorous moral and intellectual training required for philosophical ascent. This was, for Augustine, a failing of Platonism – or rather the triumph of Christianity that it could win the unlearned to truths which the Platonist had never dared preach to them. The Plotinian soul of the adept elevates itself to a Deity who is attractive but by no means bends down to be known. Through the Incarnation, so Augustine had come to believe, God reaches out to the many and leads them home.

The ascent at Ostia is often contrasted with Augustine's earlier, and previously described, ascent in Milan – sometimes called the 'failed' Platonic ascent (VII.10.6). That the Ostia ascent is better we take for granted, but it's not immediately obvious why this should be so. Pierre Courcelle has made clear that the similarities between the two are striking – the same words, phrases and stages of progress.[29] At the time of the earlier ascent, Augustine is not yet baptised but already reading Christian scriptures. He makes a deliberate attempt to return to himself by means of a philosophical strategy (VII.10.16).

[28] Porphyry, *On Abstinence* (I, 27.I, cited in Hadot, *What Is Ancient Philosophy?*, 157).

[29] Pierre Courcelle, *Recherches sur les Confessions de Saint Augustin* (Paris: E. De Boccard, 1950).

The similarities alert us to the differences. The Milan account uses metaphors of vision throughout – Augustine enters a vision and sees a light. The verb, *videre*, is used six times. Ostia is more of an *audition*. Although it begins with a glimpse of the garden, terms of vision are avoided as Augustine and Monica move through words to the Word. Thus, one ascent is visual, the other auditory; one is philosophical and solitary, the other incarnational and participatory; one (it is said) unsuccessful whereas the other succeeds.

But perhaps instead of contrasting later success at Ostia with the early failure, we may note that in its own terms the philosophical ascent in Milan did not fail. Augustine tells us that by this means he saw an incommunicable light, the very light of creation:

The light I saw was not this common light at all … it was exalted because this very light made me, and I was below it because I was made. Anyone who knows truth knows it, and whoever knows it knows eternity. Love knows it. (VII.10.16)

Augustine did not doubt the veracity of this *seeing*. That was real enough: it is open to all who seek to understand through the things that are made (Romans 1.20). The disappointment of Milan is that what he saw left Augustine unsatisfied. Even the vision of the philosophical adept is not enough.

By a strategy of philosophical contemplation, Augustine has gone as far as one can by reason and has a vision of the light of creation, but even that elevated seeing is blind. At Milan, he is shown that although 'that which I might see exists indeed, I was not yet capable of seeing it'. His gaze is feeble. Here his sensory metaphors shift from the visual to the auditory, and then to those of taste. Trembling with love and dread, he *'seems to hear'* a voice, and that voice promises he will be fed

I *seemed to hear* your voice from on high: 'I am the food of the mature; grow then, and you will eat me. You will not change me into yourself like bodily food: you will be changed into me.' (VII.10.16)

The vision of light is exceeded by an elusive audition, a *seeming to hear* which holds beyond it the promise of eucharistic eating. Augustine is baffled:

'Is truth then nothing, simply because it is not spread out through space either finite or infinite?' ... Then from afar you cried to me, 'By no means, for *I am who am.*' (VII.19.16)

Ego Sum Qui Sum (Ex. 3:14). These words make clear to the attentive and Christian reader not just what Augustine has seen, but Who it is that addresses him: the very God who spoke to Moses. It is after hearing these words 'in the heart' that

no possibility of doubt remained to me; I could more easily have doubted that I was alive than that truth exists, truth that is seen and understood through the things that are made. (VII.19.16)

At Ostia, and by then baptised, Augustine no longer *seems to hear* but hears. He hears the words of Monica and his own words as they reflect on the words of Scripture. The two are lifted up into the Word. As they talked, he tells us, they touched the very edge of the Eternal:

then, sighing, we left the first-fruits of our spirit captive there, and returned to the noise of articulate speech a word that has a beginning and an end. (IX.10.26)

They ponder how different these human words are 'from your Word, our Lord, who abides in himself, and grows not old, but renews all things'.

Augustine and Monica fall back from this epiphany, as did Augustine in his Milan ecstasy, though not this time to disappointment but a sense of peace. As Christians they have the Word and each other in the communion of faith. By the gift of the Word in Scripture and their shared faith, they guide each other in love for they, too, are informed by the Word and participate already in the Word who feeds them from his altar as he will 'pasture Israel for ever with the food of truth'. The vision at Ostia is social, not solitary, for that is how we hear the Word – through Scriptures, preaching, the witness of others. These are the ligatures of love which bind us to one another and to God. Yet this Word is at the same time the *I AM Who I AM* who 'spoke' to him, when he could hear, in Milan.

At Ostia Monica's tears finally give way to her words as these are sublimed to the Word itself. In their holy colloquy mother and son are caught up into that Word, teaching and leading one another. All this is absent from his early solitary ascent. The ascent at Ostia is shared because the life of the saints is social. It is from other people that we learn to speak.

How fitting that Augustine should share this moment with his mother, who likely taught him to speak in the first place. At her death it is his turn to cry. He holds back his tears for many hours, in case he appeared weak and lacking in faith, but after a bath, in the privacy of his own room and before God, he weeps for his mother and for himself, strewing his tears 'as a bed beneath my heart'.

8

Aquinas

Philosophical Theology as Spiritual Practice

~

Introduction

There was a time, not long past, when what most students of philosophy of religion knew about Aquinas was that he had come up with 'Five Ways', or proofs for the existence of God (*Summa theologiae*, Ia.2). If their acquaintance was closer, they might have known that these led to a string of divine attributes (*S.T.* Ia.2–11). Independently they might have been taught a smattering on 'the doctrine of analogy' (*S.T.* Ia.13). Truncated in this way, the Aquinas of the *Summa theologiae* amounted to a medieval predecessor for modern philosophy of religion and those like John Locke who defined 'God' and sketched out the divine attributes.

The link looks fair enough: both Aquinas and Locke held out great promise for human reason and, while both denied the possibility that the idea of God could be innate, it seemed that both believed you could prove the existence of God and derive a certain number of the divine properties in doing so.

While this is probably unfair to Locke, it is certainly unfair to Aquinas who is writing centuries before Locke and at a time when what we call 'divine attributes' would largely have been discussed as 'divine names'. My suggestion is that the early questions of the *Summa theologiae*,

165

which we read as primarily concerned with demonstrating the existence of God and delineating the divine attributes, read quite differently if we see Aquinas as standing within a venerable divine names tradition, as surely he does. This means not only that he is referring back to theological predecessors who have written on the divine names, but that he knows these names of God through invocation and prayer, in liturgy, psalmody and the panoply of devotions that made up his Christian life as a Dominican friar. But first to revisit Locke.

On Locke and Aquinas

I have already mentioned Locke's pragmatic treatment of the word 'God':

The name God being once mentioned in any part of the world, to express a superior, powerful, wise, invisible being, the suitableness of such a notion to the principles of common reason, and the interest men will always have to mention it often, must necessarily spread far and wide, and continue it down to all generations. (*Essay Concerning Human Understanding*, Book I, Ch. 3, §10)

Warming to his theme, he later continues,

If we examine the *Idea* we have of the incomprehensible **supreme Being**, we shall find, that we come by it the same way; and that the complex *Ideas* we have both of God, and separate Spirits, are made up of the simple *Ideas* we receive from *Reflection*; *v.g.* having from what we experiment in ourselves, got the *Ideas* of Existence and Duration; of Knowledge and Power; of Pleasure and Happiness; and of **several other Qualities and Powers, which it is better to have, than to be without;**

when we would frame an *Idea* the most suitable we can to the supreme Being, we enlarge every one of these with our *Idea* of Infinity; and so putting them together, make our complex *Idea of God*. (*Essay Concerning Human Understanding*, Book II, Ch. 23, §33, my emphasis)

For Locke, it seems, that once we establish that there is a God, these divine 'qualities and powers' (others will call them 'attributes') just follow as belonging to a maximally perfect being or, in Locke's Enlightenment parlance, 'the Supreme Being'. It seems we can take qualities we admire in a powerful man or superman, 'enlarge every one' and arrive at God, or at least 'the Supreme Being' – a deity free from allegiance to any one particular religion, a product only of rational reflection.[1]

This austere and seemingly reasonable 'natural theology' – designed to be beyond religious sectarianism and held to be reasonable because it does not rely on revelation – must appear to us now as worryingly anthropomorphic. Locke's composite God, inflated from characteristics he admired in a powerful or superman, is the monstrous potentate criticised by Moltmann and many others.

Despite superficial resemblances, squeezing the Aquinas of the *Summa theologiae* into the categories of early eighteenth-century natural theology is like trying to fit a swimming cap over a full head of hair: certain bits will spring out.

---

[1] Locke was himself a serious Christian and reader of the Bible. It is his semantic strategy and not his faith that is in question here. On Locke's religion see Nathan Guy, *Finding Locke's God: The Theological Basis of John Locke's Political Thought* (London; New York: Bloomsbury Academic, 2019).

Locke, like many other post-Cartesian speculators, roughly takes the attributes as qualities God 'has' and sees in them a grammar of maximal perfection. His interests are predominantly epistemological. Aquinas, I shall argue, sees reflection on our naming and even our knowing God as more nearly a task of spiritual formation. His exploration of the names of God, and of how it is possible for us to name God at all, is akin to spiritual exercises in that their object, as with all Holy Teaching, is nothing less than our *salus*: our total well-being, or salvation. Aquinas, no less than Philo, Gregory and Augustine, is 'seeking God's face'.

Thomas spoke of the names and the naming of God throughout his life and writings, but for our purposes we turn initially to Questions 2–13 of the first part of his last work, the *Summa theologiae*. These questions are frequently discussed in philosophy of religion classes when the topics are faith and reason, proofs for the existence of God, analogy and religious language, and the classical attributes of God. They have been the subject of much study and many excellent books. My hope is that a focus on 'naming' may shed new light on the ensuing debates.

Aquinas writes as a scholastic theologian. We see little of the language of longing and desire found in Philo, Nyssen and Augustine, but he is nonetheless a God-besotted theologian, seeking always the face of God.[2] We should see that his treatment of knowing and naming God is more patristic, more biblical, more problematic and at

---

[2] On Aquinas as a spiritual writer, see Jean-Pierre Torrell, *Saint Thomas Aquinas*, Vol. I: *The Person and His Work* (Washington, DC: Catholic University of America Press, 1996).

the same time more generative than many accounts of Aquinas on religious language give credit.

Aquinas on the Un-nameable Creator

The first of all names to be used of God is HE WHO IS.
(John Damascene, *De fide orthodoxa*, I, 9)[3]

The preceding chapters have shown that the identification of God with 'Being Itself' and 'the source of all being' is not a medieval scholastic imposition but can be traced back to scriptural interpretation as early as the first century in Philo and becoming standard in Christian theology, both eastern and western. The prompt was reflection on the names given to Moses and the link between these and the doctrine of creation. From reflecting on what it might mean for God to be the Creator and not a creature, it follows for all these authorities that, strictly speaking, *God cannot be named by us*. Aquinas quotes John Damascene:

In this life our minds cannot grasp what God is in himself; whatever way we have of thinking of him is a way of failing to understand him as he really is. So the less determinate our names are and the more general and simple they are, the more appropriately they may be applied to God. That is why John Damascene says, *'The first of all names to be used of God is* HE WHO IS *for he comprehends all in himself, he has his existence as an ocean of being, infinite and unlimited.'*[4]

Here Aquinas, writing in the thirteenth century, cites John, a Damascus theologian of the eighth century,

---

[3] Cited by Aquinas, *S.T.* Ia.13,11 reply.
[4] Cited by Aquinas, *S.T.* Ia.13,11 reply.

whose words, in turn, echo those of Gregory Nazianzen, Archbishop of Constantinople in the fourth century. It is indeed a long lineage.[5]

Gregory Nazianzen made the exegetical link with Moses evident, even while writing in a metaphysical and mystical vein:

> God always was, and always is, and always will be. Or rather, God always Is. For Was and Will be are fragments of our time, and of changeable nature, but He is Eternal being. And this is the Name that He gives to Himself when giving the Oracle to Moses in the Mount. For in Himself He sums up and contains all Being, having neither beginning in the past nor end in the future; like some great Sea of Being, limitless and unbounded, transcending all conception of time and nature, only adumbrated by the mind, and that very dimly and scantily ... not by his Essentials.[6]

Aquinas is heir through many channels to these long-standing reflections which link knowing and naming God to the giving of the Name to Moses. Threads, themes and *above all* biblical citations standard to these earlier writings on naming God are present in Thomas's

---

[5] John Rist thinks it was probably Philo, as I also have suggested, who first 'made the move of distinguishing God's existence (we know *that* He exists) from questions about his nature (we do not know *what* He [*sic*] is, that is his *ousia*'. And that Philo does so because he wants to distinguish the Creator from the creature. John Rist, 'Augustine, Aristotelianism, and Aquinas: Three Varieties of Philosophical Adaptation', in *Aquinas the Augustinian*, ed. Michael Dauphinais, Barry David and Matthew Levering (Washington, DC: Catholic University of American Press, 2007), 79–99 at 84.

[6] Gregory of Nazianzus, '"The Second Oration on Easter', in *A Select Library of Nicene and Post-Nicene Fathers of the Christian Church: Second Series*, ed. Philip Schaff and Henry Wace (Grand Rapids, Mich.: William B. Eerdmans, n.d.), Vol. VII, 422–34 at 423.

texts. While we moderns tend to skip over these scriptural phrases as mere nods to biblical piety, for theologians of his time, steeped in the divine names tradition, they were important way marks and shorthands for a rich tradition of reflection.

Creation and Naming in Aquinas

By the time Aquinas wrote the *Summa theologiae*, treatises *de nominibus Dei* were an established genre. Indeed, Aquinas himself had written, as had his master Albertus Magnus, a commentary on *the Divine Names* of Pseudo-Dionysius, a markedly Neoplatonic work which grew in influence in western theology in the twelfth and thirteenth centuries.[7]

Yet for all his deference – and Aquinas cites Dionysius some 1,700 times – there is little in the *Summa* which marks him strictly as a disciple, and at times Aquinas introduces Dionysius' views only to qualify, if not apparently to contradict them.[8] We must add to this the philosophy of Aristotle who is, for Aquinas, 'the philosopher'. As a young student in Sicily he was amongst the first to study texts of Aristotle which had been lost for centuries to the Christian West and recovered from Muslim and Jewish sources. In the writings of Moses Maimonides, Aquinas found a stress

---

[7] Torrell reckons that Aquinas would have known this for a long time before he wrote his own commentary on it, having 'once recopied by hand the course that Saint Albert gave on Dionysius's text' (*Saint Thomas Aquinas*, Vol. I, 127).

[8] It would not be appropriate for Aquinas to openly contradict so hallowed a source, especially since the writer was thought at this time to have almost apostolic status, but Aquinas will persistently qualify in an argumentatively tighter direction.

on a teaching not taken from Aristotle but invoked by Islamic and Jewish theologians to counter Aristotle's views where they were seen to contradict scriptural understanding: the doctrine of *creatio ex nihilo*. This teaching would be fundamental to Aquinas' own mature theology.[9]

The great medieval theologians who worked on *creatio ex nihilo* – Al-Ghazali, Moses Maimonides and, following both, Thomas Aquinas – all contrast the God of Abraham with the prime mover of Aristotle. Maimonides is a case in point. From the tenth century Aristotle's works had marked influence on Jewish philosophy, mostly in virtue of his prestige in science and cosmology.[10] Yet Maimonides saw clearly the gulf between the views of the philosophers (including Aristotle, whom he admired greatly) and *creatio ex nihilo*, the teaching, as he believes, of Moses. Maimonides writes:

The theory of all philosophers whose opinions and works are known to us is this: It is impossible to assume that God produced anything from nothing, or that He reduces anything to nothing ... They therefore assume that a certain substance has co-existed with God from eternity in such a manner that neither God existed without that substance nor the latter without God.[11]

---

[9] The texts of Aristotle which Aquinas would have read would have already been altered by their Islamic editors to be more compatible with Abrahamic monotheism than Aristotle's originals. On this see Rist, 'Augustine, Aristotelianism, and Aquinas'.

[10] On the reception of Aristotle by Jewish theologians of the time, see Norbert Max Samuelson, *Judaism and the Doctrine of Creation* (Cambridge; New York: Cambridge University Press, 1994), 82 ff.

[11] 'For whilst we hold that the heavens have been created from absolutely nothing, Plato believes that they have been formed out of something ...'. Moses Maimonides, *The Guide of the Perplexed*, trans. M. Friedlander ([Chicago]: University of Chicago Press, 1963), Part II, Ch. 13, 172.

By contrast,

Those who follow the Law of Moses, our Teacher, hold that the whole Universe, i.e., everything except God, has been brought by Him into existence out of non-existence. In the beginning God alone existed and nothing else … He produced from nothing all existing things such as they are, by His will and desire. Even time itself is among the things created; for time depends on motion, i.e., on an accident in things which move, and the things upon whose motion time depends are themselves created beings, which have passed from non-existence into existence. We say that God *existed* before the creation of the Universe, although the verb *existed* appears to imply the notion of time; we also believe that He existed in infinite space of time before the Universe was created; but in these cases we do not mean time in its true sense. We only use the term to signify something analogous or similar to time. For time is undoubtedly an accident, and, according to our opinion, one of the created accidents.[12]

This passage is not only a full-blooded expression of *creatio ex nihilo* but demonstrates how adherence to that teaching must, of necessity, have an effect on religious language. 'Eternal' must mean something other when applied to the God of Moses than when applied to the Aristotelian god. The god of Aristotle is merely without beginning or end – everlasting in time. But the God of Moses, according to Maimonides, creates time itself. Many other things we say of God will need qualification. Maimonides in this passage draws attention to 'time' and 'exists' – there is no time 'before' creation and nor is God's 'existence' a simple existence in time.

[12] Maimonides, *The Guide of the Perplexed*, Part II, Ch. 13, 171.

This drive to transcendence presses Maimonides to an almost atheistic account of religious language.[13] Our names can carry no creaturely ascriptions. They must shed all bodilyness or anthropomorphism. He treats all the positive names and even biblical names of God with extreme austerity – to say that God is 'wise' is to deny he his foolish, to say that he is 'living' is to deny he is dead, since God is, for Maimonides, truly simple, and any declension into qualities is strictly speaking inappropriate. Even the four attributes judged to be essential – life, power, wisdom and will – are all to be considered, not with reference to the Divine essence, but with reference to things that are created: so 'He has power in creating things, will in giving to things existence as He desires, and wisdom in knowing what He created.'[14]

Whenever we speak of God *according to the language of the sons of man*, a certain looseness of expression is involved, even when we say that God is 'One':

Thus when we wish to indicate that the deity is not many, the one who makes the statement cannot say anything but that He is one, even though 'one' and 'many' are some of the subdivisions of quantity. For this reason, we give the gist of the notion and give the mind the correct direction toward the true reality

---

[13] God is 'One' and cannot possess essential attributes, according to Maimonides. He cannot be classed according to genus, nor can anything be predicated of him that suggests composition, multiplicity or change. See Maimonides, *The Guide of the Perplexed*, Part I, Chs. 50–64, especially 54, which treats of 'Moses our Master' and the revelations at Sinai. The parallels with Philo are remarkable although there's no reason to suspect direct indebtedness. For a treatment of Maimonides and Hermann Cohen, see Daniel Heller-Roazen, *No One's Ways: An Essay on Infinite Name* (New York: Zone Books, 2017), especially Ch. XIII.

[14] Maimonides, *The Guide of the Perplexed*, Part I, Ch. 55. See also Ch. 56.

of the matter when we say, one but not through oneness, just as we say eternal in order to indicate that He has not come into being in time. For when we say eternal, we speak loosely, as is clear and manifest, since eternal can only be predicated of a thing to which time attaches.[15]

The driver for this verbal parsimony, it needs to be stressed, is not Aristotle. Indeed, to defend his belief in a God who freely creates all that is, Maimonides feels obliged to *deny* one of that philosopher's central tenets – the eternity of the world. Despite his deference to Aristotle and despite this philosopher's prestige at that time in matters of science, Maimonides could not, for religious reasons, accept Aristotle's views on the eternity of the world.[16]

---

[15] Maimonides, *The Guide of the Perplexed*, Part I, Ch. 57. Maimonides says that attributes, such as 'the First' and 'the Last' are as metaphorical as speaking of God's 'ear' or 'eye'.

[16] Maimonides, like al Ghazali, seems to presume that *creatio ex nihilo* entails a beginning in time, that is, they seem to disallow the possibility that the Creator may have freely created an everlasting Universe. Aquinas, as already mentioned, allows this last possibility, although he believes that, as a matter of fact, the Universe is not everlasting. David Burrell puts it nicely: 'Maimonides simply presumes (as did Ghazali) that an everlasting universe leaves no room for free creation; in this he conflates *creatio ex nihilo* with *creatio de novo* – that is, not simply that nothing is presupposed to creation but that it takes place such that there is an initial moment of time. ... Aquinas declares his indebtedness to both by concurring with Maimonides that neither position – everlasting or temporal creation – admits of proof, and yet he refuses to foreclose the conceptual possibility of a free creator (in the biblical or Qur'anic sense) creating everlastingly ... He does concede that postulating an initial moment would make the case more evident ... but, strictly speaking, the case for creation *de novo* rests solely with revelation. ... (There is no conceptual difficulty with an eternal God creating an everlasting universe, precisely because one can distinguish the *eternity* which characterizes God alone from a temporality without beginning).' David Burrell, 'Freedom and Creation in the Abrahamic Traditions', *International Philosophical Quarterly* 40, no. 158 (2000): 162–71 at 168–9.

In Jewish understanding, but not in Aristotle's, God can exist without any universe. Furthermore, for Aristotle no questions can be asked about the purpose of the universe or the final cause of the heavens – there is no 'purpose' at that level in Aristotle's system. But these were questions which Maimonides felt the followers of Moses must ask. Aristotle's Prime Mover is as much a part of the cosmic order as that which is moved. There is no room for divine freedom or divine knowledge of particulars and, since the system is fixed, seamlessly ordered and without beginning or end, no room for miracles. Maimonides considered that Aristotle's particular 'eternal universe' must be rejected and *creatio ex nihilo* defended as a fundamental principle of the Jewish religion. It is, as he puts it, 'a high rampart erected around the Law'.[17] 'According to our theory, taught in Scripture, the existence and non-existence of things depends solely on the will of God and not on fixed laws.'[18]

Pseudo-Dionysius, Aquinas's other great source on divine names, sensuous though his prose may be, is as committed to the doctrine of *creatio ex nihilo* as is Maimonides. The teaching is key to both his 'Divine

---

[17] Maimonides, *The Guide of the Perplexed*, Part II, Ch. 17, 181. José Faur sets out Maimonides' views in the following way: 'The only possible relation between absolute monotheism and a world brimming with diversity is Creation *ex nihilo*, repudiating an ontological relation between God and the Universe .... Belief in the creation of the world', wrote Maimonides, 'necessarily requires that all the miracles are possible'. Consequently, 'Whoever believes in the eternity (of the world) does not belong at all to the congregation of Moses and Abraham'. Faur, *Homo Mysticus: A Guide to Maimonides's Guide for the Perplexed* (Syracuse, NY: Syracuse University Press, 1998), 89, citing Maimonides' Treatise on Resurrection, 30.

[18] Maimonides, *The Guide of the Perplexed*, Part II, Ch. 27.

Names' and the 'Celestial Hierarchy'. Indeed, keeping the doctrine of creation in mind may help make palatable, to those with otherwise little taste for it, what Dionysius means by participation.

For Dionysius God is 'the cause of everything, that is its origin, being and life.' God is 'the Life of the living, the being of beings, it is the Source and Cause of all life and of all being, for out of its goodness it commands all things to be and it keeps them going.'[19] In the 'Celestial Hierarchy' we read:

One truth must be affirmed above all else. It is that the transcendent Deity has out of goodness established the existence of everything and brought it into being. It is characteristic of the universal Cause, of this goodness beyond all, to summon everything to communion with him to the extent that this is possible. Hence everything in some way partakes of the providence flowing out of this transcendent Deity which is the originator of all that is. Indeed nothing could exist without some share in the being and source of everything. Even the things which have no life participate in this, for it is the transcendent Deity which is the existence of every being.[20]

'The Ways in Which God Does Not Exist'

Aquinas, as he turns to naming God, stands thus as the beneficiary of two great traditions – the Christian

[19] Pseudo-Dionysius, 'Divine Names', in *Pseudo-Dionysius: The Complete Works*, trans. Colm Lubheid (Mahwah, NJ: Paulist Press, 1987), 47–131 at 51.
[20] Pseudo-Dionysius, 'Celestial Hierarchy', in *Pseudo-Dionysius*, trans. Lubheid, 143–91 at 156.

Platonism of Augustine, Nazianzen and Dionysius and the Aristotle-inflected Judaism of Moses Maimonides.[21] He reconciles them at a point of convergence – the teaching of *creatio ex nihilo* – and from this he draws the implications for naming and knowing God.

To this end we need to appreciate something of the delicate architecture of the *Summa theologiae*. Question 1 sets out the nature and need for holy teaching (*sacra doctrina*) and states that, while philosophy has its place, divine revelation takes us beyond these things to what is needful for our *salus* – 'our whole welfare, which is in God'.[22] The Prologue before Question 2 lays out the astonishing plan of his work:

Because the fundamental aim of holy teaching is to make God known, not only as he is in himself, but as the beginning and end of all things and of reasoning creatures especially, we now intend to set forth this divine teaching by treating,

First, of God,

Secondly, of the journey to God of reasoning creatures,

Thirdly, of Christ, who, as man, is our road to God.

Questions 2–13 all seem to fall in the first of these tasks – 'treating first, of God'. But as we shall see, our

---

[21] While there is no time to go into it, the sharp division sometimes proposed between Platonists and Aristotelians at this period will not stand. The 'Aristotle' which Aquinas and, for that matter, Maimonides inherited from the Arabs was already modified in Neoplatonic, and monotheistic directions, and the Christian Platonists also used Aristotle.

[22] *S.T.* Ia.1, 1 reply. Thomas Gilby elaborates in a footnote – 'Well-being: *salus*, health, welfare, salvation – the last should not be confined to its negative connotation, of being saved from something' (Aquinas, *Summa theologiae*, trans. Thomas Gilby, OP (London: Eyre & Spottiswoode, 1967).

journey to God as well as Christ, who is our way to God, are already present in these early questions.[23]

The vital preliminary topic (Question 2) on 'whether there is a God' is broken down into three others (1. Is it self-evident that there is a God? 2. Can it be made evident? 3. Is there a God?).

Moses soon makes an appearance in the third of these questions *Is there a God?* The initial suggestion, which Aquinas will oppose, that there is 'no need to suppose that a God exists', is followed by

On the other hand (*sed contra*), the book of Exodus represents God as saying, *I am who I am.* (*S.T.* Ia.2, 3)

Exodus 3, a scripture central to the divine names tradition, now serves to open up Aquinas' discussion of the 'Five Ways'.

It is often remarked that, for all the attention they have subsequently received, the 'Five Ways' take up little space in the *Summa theologiae*. Here, as in the earlier *Summa contra gentiles*, God's existence is taken as given, and indeed there is some debate as to whether Aquinas intended them as proofs. What is clear is that, in the architecture of the *Summa theologiae*, the *Five Ways are used to set the stage for the extended discussion over Questions 3 to 13 as to how we can know and name God.*[24]

---

[23] See A. N. Williams, 'Mystical Theology Redux: The Pattern of Aquinas' Summa Theologiae', in *Spirituality and Social Embodiment* (Oxford: Basil Blackwell, 1997), 53–74. See also Fáinche Ryan, *Formation in Holiness: Thomas Aquinas on Sacra Doctrina* (Leuven: Peeters, 2007) on the Christoform nature *of sacra doctrina* (p. 114).

[24] Aquinas does, it seems, believe that these arguments work to prove an unchanged cause of change, a first cause, a non-contingent cause

It being evident that God exists, Aquinas supplies a Prologue to Question 3 which outlines his next objectives:

Having recognized that a certain thing exists, we have still to investigate the way in which it exists. *Now we cannot know what God is, but only what he is not*; we must therefore consider the ways in which God does not exist, rather than the ways in which he does. We treat then,

First, of the ways in which God does not exist,

Secondly, of the ways in which we know him, [Quae. 12]

Thirdly, of the ways in which we describe (or 'name' ed.) him (*tertio quomodo nominetur*) [Quae. 13].[25]

Accordingly, Aquinas addresses, through Questions 3–11, God's simpleness, perfection, goodness, limitlessness, existence in all things, unchangeableness, eternity and oneness. In contrast to Locke, these are not qualities God 'has', as he might 'have' red hair or an aquiline nose, but come under the general heading of 'the ways in which God does not exist'.[26] They do not, however, tell us nothing of God since, as Rudi te Velde has pointed out, this unfolding

of beings, and so on, to which he adds, 'to which everyone gives the name "God".' (Ia. 2,3). My point is not to say that they fail as such demonstrations, but one concerning the purpose they serve here in his text.

[25] I'm passing over this quickly as by now familiar ground. Note only that, while Aquinas very rarely criticises Aristotle, in Question 10, Article 3, 'does eternity belong to God alone?' Aquinas' answer is 'yes', whereas Aristotle held the universe to be eternal. To my mind nothing in the overall reach of the *Summa* is lost if we say that the 'Five Ways' do not work as proofs. One would then just begin with a statement of belief that God is the creator of all that is.

[26] The Prologue before Question 3 continues:

The ways in which God does not exist will become apparent if we rule out from him everything inappropriate, such as compositeness, change and the like. Let us inquire then of negations is subtended by a profound affirmation – that God is the creator – the uncaused cause of 'all changeable things and things that can cease to be'.[27] And while Aquinas may hold that he has demonstrated on neutral grounds that there is a God, it is clearly the Christian creator God who is under discussion. All these questions about simplicity, perfection, eternity and so on are exercises in thinking about what it is for God to be creator.

Simplicity, important also to Maimonides, is treated first (Question 3) and is key to all the negative ascriptions that follow.[28] Here we read, amongst other things, that God does not belong to a genus and that his existence is his essence. Philosophically recondite as these claims sound and may be, they here serve to elaborate the doctrine of creation and particularly the claim of both Dionysius and Augustine that God is Being itself and the source of all existing things.

First, about God's simpleness …
secondly, about God's perfection,
thirdly, about his limitlessness,
fourthly, about his unchangeableness,
fifthly, about his oneness' (Prologue before Question 3, my emphasis)

[27] See *S.T.* Ia.2, 3. Nor does Aquinas claim, as later Thomists will suggest, that God is *causa sui* – a term that does not antedate Descartes. On this and for exoneration of Aquinas of the charge of ontotheology, see Jean-Luc Marion, 'Thomas Aquinas and Onto-theo-logy', in *Mystics: Presence and Aporia*, ed. Michael Kessler and Christian Sheppard, Religion and Postmodernism (Chicago: University of Chicago Press, 2003), 38–74. The exoneration is all the more welcome given Marion had taken a different line in the first edition of *God without Being*.

[28] Torrell points out that in the earlier *Summa contra gentiles* priority had been given to the divine unchangeability, but now in the *Summa theologiae*, the starting point is divine simplicity (*Saint Thomas Aquinas*, Vol. I, 35.)

It is often said that Aquinas inherits the negative way (*via remotionis*) pursued in Questions 2–11 from Pseudo-Dionysius.[29] This is not entirely true. Aquinas knows many precedents in the Christian Platonist tradition, whom he cites. To this we should add that the 'negative way' came to him as readily, and perhaps with more clarity and urgency, from Maimonides. Aquinas indeed seems uncomfortable with some of Dionysius' more fulsome pronouncements. What he finds and embraces in Dionysius and the other Christian Platonists is the conviction that God is the creator from whom all flows, the one for whom all things long and in whose life all things share, even while the measured language of Maimonides and Aristotle, will often prove a more sympathetic vehicle for his thought.

'The Ways in Which We Know Him'

Thus far we have been speaking of 'the ways in which God does not exist (*quomodo non sit*)'. With Question 12, 'How God is known by creatures', we turn to how God is known by us (*quomodo a nobis cognoscatur*). We might expect something more positive and indeed we have it: God in himself 'is supremely knowable' and the blessed will see the essence of God. Aquinas cites I John, *We shall see him just as he is*. This is of utmost importance to Aquinas.[30] Yet while the blessed will see God – and almost the whole of this question is devoted to the beatific

[29] See, for instance, Torrell, *Saint Thomas Aquinas*, Vol. I, 31.
[30] Note the implicit Christology since the one we shall see *'just as he is'* is the risen Christ.

vision – the limitations to our knowledge of God in this life, limitations identified as far back as Philo, are still in place.[31] God as being itself is, Aquinas says, 'beyond all that can be known of him – this is what is meant by saying that he cannot be comprehended' (*S.T.* Ia.12, 1). The answers to most of the questions about our knowledge of God that follow are substantially negative. In Question 12, article 1, for instance, we read that the blessed will see the essence of God but, Aquinas adds, they will not comprehend it. He goes on to say that we cannot see God's essence with bodily eyes (article 3); that no creature will see God's essence by its own natural powers (article 4); that no created mind can comprehend the divine essence (article 7) and that no man in this life can see God's essence (article 11). Aquinas here seems to become impatient, repeating himself as if speaking to slow learners: 'The reason for this is that, as we have said, the way in which a thing knows depends on the way it has its being. Our souls, so long as we are in this life, have their being in corporeal matter' and 'the divine essence cannot be known through the natures of material things'.

It may seem surprising, then, after this crescendo of negations, that Aquinas' answer to Question 12, article 12 ('Can we know God by our natural reason in this life?') is an emphatic 'Yes'! We can know, and by implication all should know that God exists (see Romans 1:19) and

---

[31] For a fine reading of the importance of Question 12, see Ryan, *Formation in Holiness*, Chs. 3 and 4. Ryan cites Herbert McCabe: 'It is highly significant that almost the whole of Question 12, which is about the way we know God, is devoted to a discussion of the Beatific vision; such knowledge of God as we have in this life is so exiguous as to be hardly worth discussing' (84).

is the cause of all creatures, and that nothing created is in Him. Being the kind of creatures who know through experience, we cannot understand the divine essence in itself, but we can be led from effects to cause, and so know

that he exists and that he has whatever must belong to the first cause of all things which is beyond all that is caused.

We know about God's relation to creatures as their source. In the final article to this question Aquinas adds that this knowledge is deepened by the revelation of grace (*S.T.* Ia.12, 13). Were we reading him just as a philosopher, this might seem an irrelevance. Here it is important: 'By grace we have a more perfect knowledge of God than we have by natural reason.' Of course, even our natural knowledge of God, according to Aquinas, is graced, but in addition to this we have the prophetic visions, and God also *'has given us sensible signs and spoken words* to show us something of the divine'. We are at a distinct remove from Locke. Aquinas believes that, along with inspiring the prophets and biblical writers, God has actually spoken words – not many, but some. The instance Aquinas gives us is 'as at the baptism of Christ when the Holy Spirit appeared in the form of a dove and the voice of the Father was heard saying, *This is my beloved Son.*'

Although 'in this life revelation does not tell us *what* God is and thus joins us to him as to a known unknown', nevertheless revelation teaches us things we could not have known through natural reason, 'for instance that he is both three and one' (*S.T.* Ia.12, 13).[32] Revelation also

[32] In this article Aquinas once more cites Dionysius in setting up the question, only to qualify him in the reply. Ryan notes that, setting

gives us 'spoken words' such as 'this is my beloved Son'. But how can these words apply to (or name) the known unknown? That is the task for Question 13.

'The Ways in Which We Name God' (Question 13)

It is these two positive assertions – that we can by natural reason know God in this life and that this knowledge is deepened by revelation (*S.T.* Ia.12, 12 and 13) – which provide the problematic for Question 13, *de nominibus Dei.* We might put it thus: given we can know God, how can we name God? To the modern reader, if we can answer the first, epistemological, part of the question ('How can we know God?') it might seem that the second, 'How do we name God?' is a secondary consideration. Not so for Aquinas. He has received, from two sides, the strongest inducements to think God cannot be named – *at all*. And revelation, pre-eminently Scripture, is not for Aquinas (as arguably it was for Philo, Augustine and Dionysius) the entire solution, but a further part of the problem. We need to look at Question 13 with some care, not least because it is this question – and especially its treatment of analogy – which has led some to say Aquinas is here doing 'natural theology'.

up the question, Aquinas cites Dionysius to the effect that 'he who is best united to God in this life sees him as utterly unknown (*omnino ignoto*)', but in his reply this becomes the more modest 'revelation joins us to him as to an unknown (*quasi ignoto conjungamur*)', reflecting Thomas's Augustinian predilection to the view that we can only love what we know and so must, in some sense, know God (*Formation in Holiness*, 97).

While Questions 1–12 have all in their own way been concerned with what we can say of God, Question 13 bears the title, *de nominibus Dei*. Herbert McCabe translates this as 'theological language', and the introductory sentence as 'Having considered how we know God we now turn to consider how *we speak of him* (*procedendum est ad considerationem divinorum nominum*), for we speak of things as we know them' (my emphasis).

The translation, '*how we speak of* him', though not in itself wrong, nonetheless risks occluding the divine names tradition in which Thomas stands. That he was mindful of precedents would have been immediately evident to his contemporaries. Dionysius on the Divine Names is cited right away:

Article 1: can we use any words to refer to God?

First Point: It seems that we can use no words at all to refer to God. For Dionysius says, *Of him there is no naming nor any opinion.*[33]

Triangulating between the eloquent Platonism of the Fathers and Dionysius, and Maimonides' sober warnings on the dangers of anthropomorphism, Aquinas gives a succinct summary of the implications for religious language of confessing belief in God as 'Creator of all that

[33] *De div. nom.* I, cited in Aquinas, Prologue to Question Ia.13. More fully Dionysius says 'Indeed the inscrutable One is out of the reach of every rational process. Nor can any words come up to the inexpressible Good, this One, this Source of all unity, this supra-existent Being. Mind beyond mind, word beyond speech, it is gathered up by no discourse, by no intuition, by no name. It is and it is as no other being is. Cause of all existence, and therefore itself transcending existence, it alone could give an authoritative account of what it really is' (Pseudo-Dionysius, 'Divine Names', 49–50).

is': certain terms cannot be used of God because God is altogether simple. He thus has no accidental properties and is non-temporal. We cannot define God or point to God (ostensive reference) since 'he is not available to the senses.' However, the source of our problem is also the beginning of a solution. God cannot, as creator, be defined or delimited by us, but we can and do know God as creator, and 'How *we refer* to a thing depends on how *we* understand it' (*S.T.* Ia.13, 1 reply).

Just as we do not see the essence of God but know God from creatures (Aquinas's answer to *quomodo a nobis cognoscatur*), so *quomodo nominetur* (how we name God) is from our knowledge of creatures.[34] Aquinas is quite clear on this: 'It is the knowledge we have of creatures that enables us to use words to refer to God, and so these words do not express the divine essence as it is in itself' (*S.T.* Ia.13, 1).

Simply referring to God poses no great problem. Aquinas points out that we do not need a definition in terms of essential properties for successful reference – it is enough to point to 'something understood, for so long as we know something, in whatever way, we can point it out'. So we can 'point to' God as 'the God who spoke to Moses' or 'the God of Abraham, and of Isaac, and of Jacob' without invoking any essential properties.[35] We can point to God as the creator of all that is, for instance, however much we fail to understand fully what that means. This insight is at the root of Thomas's distinction

---

[34] See Preface to Ia.3.
[35] Aquinas appears to have anticipated Saul Kripke's 'rigid designation'. I have discussed in *Metaphor and Religious Language* (Oxford: Oxford University Press, 1985).

between our mode of signifying (*modus significandi*) and the 'that' which is signified (*res significata*). We understand our mode of signifying but cannot claim to comprehend the 'that' which is signified.

This is all helpful, but we are still not out of the realm of negation, so Article 2 moves to the awkward question that any beginner might well ask: '*do any of the words we use of God express something of what he is?*' (Ia.13, 2).

The negative names of God, the names Aquinas has already discussed in questions 2–11, pose little problem, speaking as they do of *what God is not*. But Aquinas believes we need not and cannot be restricted to a diet of negations. It is not just that we *want* to have positive names of God – we already possess them from revelation and even from God's own speaking, as at the baptism of Jesus when the voice from heaven said 'This is my beloved Son.' The question remains how even these names can apply to a transcendent and utterly simple God.

Dionysius had said 'of him there is no naming nor any opinion'. Taken seriously Dionysius presents a challenge to biblical revelation itself. Does our language of God, even that given in Scripture, *signify anything*? What are we saying when we say that God is 'wise' or 'good' or is 'the living God' – which are all, let it be stressed, *biblical* terms?

Aquinas tells us that 'When a man speaks of the "living God" he does not simply want to say that God is the cause of our life, or that he differs from a lifeless body.' Here he has Maimonides in mind: Maimonides, as we have seen, applies such strictures to divine transcendence, that to say, 'God is living' could mean no more than 'God is not like an inanimate thing.' Aquinas observes that to say,

'God is good' cannot mean just that 'God is the cause of goodness in things', for God is also the cause of bodies, and we don't say God is a body (*S.T.* Ia.13, 2). He argues that some of the words we use of God do express something of what God is. It follows that some (positive) things may be said literally of God (article 3), a point of departure from both Maimonides and Dionysius.[36] Of course all our names for God are, of necessity, taken from our human speech about creatures – we have no speech but human speech. Many scriptural ascriptions are metaphors, such as that God is 'a rock' or 'a lion'. These are all evidently qualified by materiality. But certain perfection terms – Aquinas mentions 'being,' 'good' and 'living' – are not tinged with materiality and so can literally apply to God, as long as we are mindful of the fact that *'what' they signify belongs to God* (in fact even more to God than to creatures 'for these perfections belong primarily to God and only secondarily to others'), but *our way of signifying* these perfections (*modus significandi*) is tailored to creatures and thus inadequate. Olivier-Thomas Venard puts it nicely: for Thomas our 'discourse about God can be literally true without our knowing how'.[37]

---

[36] Here he again makes evident his difference from Dionysius, whose views are set up in posing the question of article 3, can we say anything literally about God? 'Now according to Dionysius it would be truer to say that God is not good or wise or any such thing than to say that he is. Hence no such thing is said literally of God' (Ia.13, 3).

[37] Oliver-Thomas Venard, OP, 'Extending the Thomist Movement from the Twentieth to the Twenty-First Century: Under What Conditions Could There Be a "Literary Thomism"?', in *Faithful Reading: New Essays in Theology and Philosophy in Honour of Fergus Kerr, OP*, ed. Karen Kilby, Simon Oliver and Fergus Kerr (London: T&T Clark, 2012), 91–112 at 97.

It may seem that Aquinas has here given with one hand only to take away with the other, for he has told us there are some terms that can be predicated literally of God, only to say our understanding of them will always be inadequate. What kind of knowledge do we have then? But this is to misunderstand his purpose. Aquinas is *not*, in any of the questions tackled under Question 13, concerned with how we 'know' God – that has been dealt with in article 12. He is concerned with how we name, or 'speak of' God – with how our religious language has sense. Otherwise put, his concerns are not primarily epistemological but semantic, though the two are inevitably intertwined. We *know* that God is 'good', or 'living' or 'being' first and foremost because Scripture gives us these names, as it does 'rock' and 'lion'. These are *all scriptural names* for Aquinas, but some can be used literally and others metaphorically.

We are now well on the way to analogy. Aquinas has established to his satisfaction that certainly biblical names may be used of God literally, as opposed to metaphorically. This does not, however, mean that what is said of God and of creatures is said *univocally*. God differs far more from any creature than any one creature does from another: to say 'God is wise' (another perfection term for Aquinas, and predicated literally of God) is not the same as to say 'Homer is wise', for 'no word when used of God means the same as when it is used of a creature'. Yet our speaking is not mere equivocation. Instead, we speak 'analogically, for we cannot speak of God at all except in the language we use of creatures, and so whatever is said both of God and creatures is said in virtue of the order that creatures have to God as to their source and cause in which all the perfections of things pre-exist transcendentally' (*S.T.* Ia.13, 5).

The handling of analogy is brief. It seems Aquinas does not think analogical or 'proportional' uses of language are per se unusual or especially problematic, nor is analogical speech used only when we are speaking of God. He gives as examples of analogical speech 'health' in a complexion, 'health' in a man and 'health' in a diet (which contributes to health in a man). Analogy seems to be a semantic tool and not an epistemological strategy – in Wittgensteinian vein it describes a kind of language use. All of which makes even more astonishing the acreage of writing on the so-called 'doctrine of analogy', not even to mention the *analogia entis* which, as is frequently noted, is not part of the *Summa* but a later development.[38]

Natural Theology or Scriptural Language?

Now to what David Burrell has called the neuralgic point: is Aquinas, through this theory of analogy, making claims to a natural knowledge of God? Some such fear is behind Barth's famous dismissal of the *analogia entis* as the 'invention of the Antichrist' – what he calls 'the misery

---

[38] On this see various of the essays in Thomas Joseph White, ed., *The Analogy of Being: Invention of the Antichrist or the Wisdom of God?* (Grand Rapids, Mich.; Edinburgh: William B. Eerdmans, 2011). And, John R. Betz's excellent introduction to Erich Przywara, *Analogia Entis: Metaphysics: Original Structure and Universal Rhythm* (Grand Rapids, Mich.: William B. Eerdmans, 2014), especially 5.1. Heidegger and 'Onto-Theology'.

of the so-called natural knowledge of God in the sense of the Vaticanum'.[39] Others, of course, praise Aquinas for just what Barth condemns – seeing analogy as a means by which we can attain knowledge of God through natural reason alone. Aquinas does believe we can know certain things of God by natural reason, for instance that God exists, as did St Paul. But to see Aquinas on analogy as engaged in a natural theology that generates detailed information about the divine essence is to misread, or at the very least vastly over-read, the *Summa*. Analogy is not here a device by means of which we *know* things about God which *we could not otherwise know* but a semantic strategy. Indeed, Aquinas is not speaking about *what we know* of God, or even the *ways in which we know God* (which, as mentioned, has been the subject of Question 12), but *how we speak of God*, how we name God or, we might say, how our talk about God has meaning. And this is as much a problem for the names taken from revelation, the scriptural names, as for any others! Indeed, it will sharpen our reading of Question 13 if we think of the problem he is facing as one presented *most acutely* by the claims of scripture.

All the terms discussed in Question 13 are names given in Scripture: God is 'wise', God is 'good', God is the 'living God'. This is just as we would expect, for the divine names tradition is above all concerned with reflection on the *revealed* names of God. Dionysius is clear on this point – all our names must be taken from Scripture. (The same

---

[39] He later moved away from this position. Karl Barth, *Church Dogmatics*, ed. Geoffrey William Bromiley and Thomas F. Torrance (London: T&T Clark, 2009), I.1, xiii.

is true of Al-Ghazali's *Ninety-Nine Beautiful Names of God*, all of which are from the Qur'an or the hadith.) In the very first paragraph of his *Divine Names* Dionysius states that 'we must not dare to resort to words or conception concerning that hidden deity which transcends being, apart from what sacred scriptures have divinely revealed' (49).

It is improbable that Thomas should ignore Dionysius' directive when he came to writing his own treatise *de nominibus Dei*. This point may be obscure to modern readers, many of whom assume that names like 'One', 'Good' and 'Being' are taken solely from philosophical reasoning. But for Dionysius and Aquinas, and many others preceding them, these were first and foremost *biblical* and revealed names, even if found to have corroboration in the works of the philosophers: *One*, given in Deuteronomy 6.4. 'Hear, O Israel: the LORD is our God, the LORD is one'; *Good*, from Mark 10.18, and *Being*, from long established readings of Exodus 3. Indeed, the fifth chapter of Dionysius' *Divine Names* is given over to the name, *Being*.

We have seen that Dionysius and Maimonides, in their different ways, both press religious language towards an entire collapse in meaning. And here is Aquinas's problem: driven by *creatio ex nihilo* and the radical divine transcendence this compels, even biblical terms ('names') run the danger of becoming vapid. He invokes analogy, not as a means of *acquiring* knowledge about God, but to explain how certain positive terms, pre-eminently names given in revelation, can communicate something of the divine reality. Barth should be in entire agreement.

Naming and Participation: Analogy Qualified

But if Aquinas is not John Locke, then neither is he Ludwig Wittgenstein. A Christian metaphysic supports his view that certain words are predicated literally of God (*S.T.* Ia.13, 3). This is not on the basis of his theory of analogy, which explains semantically what is going on, but on the basis of his theology of creation and participation.[40]

Instead of saying that goodness in a created being discloses something of the goodness of God, Aquinas says that goodness is real in created beings because their created state participates in the supreme goodness of God.

A participational ontology is apparent in his citation of Augustine:

'God is good' does not mean 'God is not evil,' or 'God is the cause of goodness in things' but it means that what we call 'goodness' in creatures pre-exists in God in a higher way. Thus God is not good because he causes goodness, but rather goodness flows from him because he is good. As Augustine says, *Because he is good, we exist.* (*S.T.* Ia.13, 3)

What these perfection terms signify belongs to God and indeed even more to God than to creatures 'for these perfections belong primarily to God and only secondarily to others'. To say God is 'good' is not just to say what God does but to 'say what he is' (*sed etiam essentialiter*),

---

[40] For a splendid account of Aquinas on participation, which draws on Rudi te Velde, David Bentley Hart and others, see Andrew Davison, *Participation in God: A Study in Christian Doctrine and Metaphysics* (Cambridge: Cambridge University Press, 2019).

even while we cannot fully understand what this might be in God.[41]

To sum up, analogy is discussed in the *Summa theologiae* as a semantic tool and not an epistemological strategy. It does not to *determine* what we can say positively of God, still less what we can know of God – above all Scripture does that. An epistemology is present – of course we must know about God – but it is a Christian epistemology, grounded in the doctrine of creation.[42] Aquinas' account of analogical predication shows how our names, even scriptural names, which derive their meaning from what we know of creatures, may be ordered to the God who brings about creation. It is thus a way of explaining how our terms signify in this unique situation of metaphysical dependency. Here semantic and metaphysical points fuse.

A particular case in point is the disputed term 'being'. 'Being' for Philo, Augustine, Dionysius and Aquinas is a divine Name, and that 'God is Being Itself' a disclosure given to Moses at the burning bush. 'Being' indeed has for Aquinas a degree of primacy as a divine Name. But, as Armand Maurer notes, this is not because the name 'being' expresses the ineffable essence of God as it is in itself. No

---

[41] Not least because God is simple, so the perfection terms we use for God 'signify what is one'. They are not synonymous, however, for they signify in different ways, just as 'what pre-exists in God in a simple and unified way is divided amongst creatures as many and varied perfection' (Ia.13, 5 reply).

[42] Thomas's 'view of how our minds are related to the world is interwoven with his doctrine of God: no epistemology without theology.' Fergus Kerr, *After Aquinas: Versions of Thomism* (Malden, Mass.: Blackwell Publishers, 2002), 30. This is far from being an epistemological or 'propositional theory of revelation' such as perhaps we see in Francisco Suárez in the sixteenth century and criticized by Jean-Luc Marion in *Givenness and Revelation*.

name could do that! But 'because creatures participate in being as the primary gift of God, he is named and praised suitably and principally by the name of being before all other names'. The name Being 'praises God insofar as creatures are related to him by participating his gifts'.[43]

We should notice, when discussing Aquinas on religious language, that he introduces his clarification of those perfection terms used *'primarily of God and derivatively of creatures'* with a citation from Ephesians 3: *'I bow my knees to the Father of our Lord Jesus, from who all fatherhood in heaven and on earth is named'* (*S.T.* Ia.13, 6 *sed contra*). Here Aquinas, in a move astonishing to most modern theologians but not perhaps to Karl Barth, simply declares that the name 'father' (like 'One', 'good' and 'Being') applies primarily to God and derivatively to creatures – although 'from the point of view of our use of the word, we apply it first to creatures because we know them first'. We are now very far from John Locke and reminded once again that Aquinas was a *Magister in Sacra Pagina*. With this citation from Ephesians, he leads us, in the *Summa theologiae*, into Questions 33 through 43, which treat of the Trinitarian names of God: the Name 'Father', the Name 'Word', the Name 'Image', the Name 'Holy Spirit', the Name 'Love' and the name 'Gift', all names given to us in Scripture and the means by which we may be drawn into the life of God.

---

[43] Armand A. Maurer, 'St Thomas on the Sacred Name "Tetragrammaton"', in *Being and Knowing: Studies in Thomas Aquinas and Later Medieval Philosophers*, ed. Armand A. Maurer (Toronto, Ont.: Pontifical Institute of Mediaeval Studies, 1990), 59–69 at 61.

9

Conclusion

Calling and Being Called

~

In the marriage service of the Sarum Rite of medieval England, the heavenly choir was invoked to proclaim the names of the Most High God over the bridal couple: Messiah, Emmanuel, Firstborn, Alpha, Omega, Lamb, Serpent, Goat, Lion, Word, Worm, Splendour, Bridegroom.[1] This book began by noting that at some time in the early modern period philosophers and theologians spoke less and less about divine names and more and more of 'divine attributes', with these understood as features of the divine nature which could be determined by reason alone.

---

[1] The full sequence, chanted between the Epistle and the Gospel, reads:

'Let the heavenly choir now proclaim the names of the most high God:
Messias, Saviour, Emmanuel, Sabaoth, Adonai
Only-begotten, Way, Life, Hand, Homoousion,
Beginning, Firstborn, Wisdom, Strength
Alpha, Head, the End and the Omega
Fountain and Origin of goodness, Paraclete and Mediator,
Lamb, Sheep, Bull-calf, Serpent, Goat, Lion, Worm
Bone, Word, Splendor, Sun, Glory, Light and Image
Bread, Flower, Vine, Mountain, Gate, Stone of stumbling,
Angel and Bridegroom, Pastor, Prophet, Priest,
Deathless, Lord, God Ruler of All, and Jesus
Save us, to whom be glory through all ages.'
I'm grateful to Eamon Duffy for this translation.

Descartes' demonstrable deity – infinite, eternal, immutable, omniscient, omnipotent – has not proved religiously attractive. Resistance to the imposition of this God of the philosophers onto the texts of the Bible is a long-standing feature of Protestant criticism of natural theology. More recently, philosophical abstraction in naming God has come under fire by at least one cardinal and a pope.[2] On my account, however, we should not simply purge offensive language. We need not cease speaking of God as 'eternal', 'almighty', 'infinite', 'One' and even as 'Being Itself' – all appellations with biblical warrant. Better would be to return to seeing these not as free-standing philosophical determinations but as divine names profoundly anchored in Scripture. This is how they were seen by generations of theologians and spiritual writers before us. Neither do we need to dismiss metaphysics, or even metaphysics employed when thinking of God as 'Being Itself', but it should be a Christian metaphysics anchored in our confession of God as creator.

Divine perfections like 'eternal', 'almighty' and 'One' are triangulated in our practices of naming God with hundreds of other names by which Christians, Jews and Muslims praise and call upon the name of the LORD – that is, by which we pray. Even the seemingly abstract attributions take their place, not in a bare list of assertions but as fibres of a thickly braided rope of signification woven throughout and from the scriptural texts.

---

[2] See the discussion below of Walter Kasper's *Mercy: The Essence of the Gospel and the Key to Christian Life* (New York: Paulist Press, 2014).

Why 'Names'?

What in this book I have been calling 'names', philologists, textual and biblical scholars discuss for their purposes as epithets, titles, ascriptions and designations. I
prefer to speak of them as 'names' and this is because of
what *we do* with names. We *use* names to do things – all
names and not just the names of God. We use names tax-
onomically to designate and identify, certainly, but this
is only a subset of the uses we have for names and not
the most useful subset if our topic is naming God. We
use names to summon, to beseech, to cajole, to reproach,
to endear and to praise. Indeed, a term only becomes a
'name' by virtue of some speaker or group of speakers
using it as such. 'Refuge' and 'fortress' are not in themselves names of God but become names when we use them
as such following the Psalmist's invocation – 'My refuge
and my fortress' (Ps 91.2). With names we must say, after
Wittgenstein, 'don't ask for meaning, ask for use'. It
may sound as though this evacuates our speech of meaning, but this is not so. It is a question of where meaning
resides. Names are used for particular purposes. Meaning
does not reside in bare lists of words sitting on a piece of
paper. We can put it concisely this way – names do not
name God. People using names name God. Christians
(and we can add Jews and Muslims) stand as heirs to practices of naming, and to myriad names, unfolded across
times, places and speakers in their sacred texts.

It might seem, then, that the best way to conclude a
book on naming God would be to provide a long list of
God's names – perhaps a list of biblical names comple-
mented by those recently found helpful in worship. This

is a worthy, but perhaps impossible, task. I want to ask not 'which are the names of God?' or even 'which are the most appropriate names for God?' but 'what is involved in the *very activity of naming God?*' for 'naming God' is a practice.

How Do Christians Name God?

Paul Ricoeur is one of the few modern philosophers to have reflected deeply on naming God. A committed Protestant working within a French philosophical academy which was, for most of his career, deeply hostile to religious belief, Ricoeur was wary of being seen as a theologian disguised as a philosopher and distrustful of imposing the God of the philosophers onto the God of the Bible, and particularly of any claim to 'onto-theological knowledge'.[3] Only towards the end of a long career did he speak of where his philosophy and his faith met, and did so in a clutch of essays which dealt with naming God.[4] His conversation partners were biblical scholars rather than theologians or philosophers of religion

[3] See Paul Ricoeur, 'Biblical Readings and Meditations' (originally 1995), in his *Critique and Conviction: Conversations with François Azouvi and Marc de Launay*, trans. Kathleen Blamey (Cambridge: Polity Press, 1998) 139–70 at 150. He later claimed to believe he was too cautious, especially in thinking any talk of God as 'Being Itself' was ontotheology in the form critiqued by Heidegger and Jean-Luc Marion in the first edition of Marion, *God without Being: Hors-texte* (Chicago: University of Chicago Press, 1991). See Paul Ricoeur, 'From Interpretation to Tradition', in André LaCoque and Paul Ricoeur's *Thinking Biblically: Exegetical and Hermeneutical Studies*, trans. David Pellauer (Chicago: University of Chicago Press, 1998), 331–61, Marion similarly retracted the accusation that the great scholastics were engaged in 'onto-theology' in a new chapter to the second edition of his book.
[4] 'Naming God', in Ricoeur, *Figuring the Sacred: Religion, Narrative, and Imagination*, ed. David Pallauer, trans. Mark I. Wallace

for, as a hermeneutical philosopher, Ricoeur interested himself in texts and interpretation. Like Wittgenstein he was aware that naming, even naming God in the Bible, was not something to be read flat off the page, and, like Augustine, he knew that naming like language itself is a social possession.

Ricoeur begins his earliest foray, the essay simply entitled 'Naming God', with a characteristically modest confession of faith:

Few authors have the gift or talent to write, 'What I believe'. Yet more than one listener to Christian preaching may stand ready to describe the ways they understand what they have heard. I am one of those listeners.[5]

Faith, he writes by clarification, 'inasmuch as it is a lived experience, is *instructed* – in the sense of being formed, clarified and educated – within the network of texts that in each instance preaching brings back to living speech'.[6] This is what it is to inhabit a biblical religion.

To be inducted into a biblical religion is like learning a language. No one name of God is adequate. The very word *God* cannot 'be understood as a philosophical concept, not even "being" in the sense of medieval philosophy or in Heidegger's sense'.[7] The word *God* is a 'suspended word' in the Bible, whose meaning is unfolded across its texts – for instance the word *God* says 'more

(Minneapolis: Fortress Press, 1995), 217–35 at 233. The essay was originally published in *Union Seminary Quarterly Review* 34, no. 4 (1979): 215–27 and is the earliest of this sequence of Ricoeur's essays I will discuss.

[5] Ricoeur, 'Naming God', 217.   [6] Ricoeur, 'Naming God', 218.

[7] Ricoeur, 'Naming God', 227. The reference is to Heidegger's God of 'onto-theology'.

than the word "being" because it presupposes the entire context of narratives, prophecies, laws, wisdom writings, psalms, and so on. The referent "God" is thus intended by the convergence of all these partial discourses.'[8]

Turning to the title of his essay, he writes: 'I can name God in my faith because the texts preached to me have already named God.'[9] This naming of God occurs across the scriptural texts. Names arise in narrative, legal, prescriptive, hymnic and epistolary writings. They appear in the Psalms, in Wisdom literature, in the Prophets and in the Law. Names appear in acts of invocation, lamentation, praise and disputations and by means of metaphor, simile, metonymy and synecdoche.

Ricoeur is no simple biblicist. By lodging his confession of faith and 'naming God' within what he calls 'Christian preaching', he acknowledges that he has received, and continues to receive, his faith from others – from prophets, psalmists and the writers of gospels and epistles but also the writings of spiritual masters, living Christians and scholars of scripture. The naming of God is a corporate and not just a private matter. Our faith is mediated by language, and religious language is given to us by others as a living practice.[10]

---

[8] Ricoeur, 'Naming God', 228. See also Ricoeur, 'From One Testament to Another' (1991), trans. Barnabas Aspray in *Modern Theology* 33, no. 2 (2017): 235–42.

[9] Ricoeur, 'Naming God', 218.

[10] 'Biblical Readings and Meditations', 140. Ricoeur writes, 'religion is like a language in which one is either born or has been transferred by exile or hospitality; in any event, one feels at home there, which implies a recognition that there are other languages spoken by other people' (145). Ricoeur, deeply influenced by Buber and Rosenzweig and a friend of Emmanuel Levinas, was deeply resistant to supersessionism. See *Critique and Conviction*, 164.

Ricoeur places historical criticism amongst the types of reading of the Bible, alongside 'canonical' readings, which attract his attention as a hermeneutical philosopher. Christians (and Jews) receive their scriptures as a whole and pray their scriptures as a whole, so when the Christian recites the Psalms and invokes the LORD, it is indeed the God of Abraham, and of Isaac and of Jacob, and also the God of Jesus Christ.

Can We Name God Newly?

The historical figures discussed earlier in this book (Philo, Gregory of Nyssa, Augustine, Dionysius, Aquinas) restricted their discussion of names for the most part to names given in the Bible. We will naturally ask 'but can we name God newly?' The answer is 'yes', and that this has always been done. Indeed, if naming is a practice then we not only can but inevitably will name God newly each time we pray, just as no cup of water from the spring is the same cup of water on a successive day.[11] We can find new names as well. Poets do this at every turn. If I invoke 'the God Pascal met in fire', I have named God newly, yet new names will usually be braided in with the old if they are to speak to a community of believers. Fashions in naming change, which is a sign not of loss but of vitality and response to lived conditions. In the early church, a church which knew plagues and devastating

---

[11] See, for instance, Wilda C. Gafney, *A Women's Lectionary for the Whole Church* (New York: Church Publishing 2021), which includes an appendix of God's names and divine titles.

illnesses, Christ was often named 'physician' on the basis of the parable of the Good Samaritan. In the fourteenth century Christ was named as 'mother' by Julian of Norwich, binding together strands of what both Christ and mothers do – bearing us, bleeding and feeding us. We may call Christ 'my chevalier', as does Gerard Manley Hopkins in *The Windhover*, and his poem will make good the significance of the name. I may invoke God in prayer as 'my Carolina wren' and those who know me may understand something of its significance for me but will not mean much – without a good deal of back story – in a sermon preached in Zimbabwe. The canonical scriptures act not as a prison house of naming God but as the shared point of departure. Scripture is still *being performed* in this sense and is always renewing itself in the life of the faithful.[12] Is there, then, a 'best' name for God?

Is There a 'Best Name' for God?

Towards the end of his discussion of the *Divine Names*, Aquinas turns his attention to 'the most appropriate name for God'. This cannot but be alarming, given the continued insistence of all the writers in the divine names tradition, and of Aquinas himself, that no name for God is adequate. Even more troubling, it may seem, is Aquinas's answer to the question: 'Qui est' – 'the One Who Is' is, he considers,

---

[12] Paul Ricoeur cites Albert the Great, 'Scripture grows with those who read it.' 'Experience and Language in Religious Discourse' (1992), in *Phenomenology and the 'Theological Turn': The French Debate*, by Dominique Janicaud et al. (New York: Fordham University Press, 2000), 134

the most appropriate name for God (*S.T.* Ia.13, 11). What can we make of this? Does it even make sense to ask what is the most appropriate name of God?

As already mentioned, the authorities Aquinas has before him converged in believing that 'the One Who Is' and 'Good' are the two most appropriate names of God, yet this cannot fully exonerate Aquinas if he is to speak not just out of the past but into the present. In our own time no name has met with more hostile response than 'Being', or 'Being Itself', both of them variants of *Qui est*. We could fill a dossier with the criticisms: not biblical, not personal, a philosophical interloper, and – after Heidegger – the God of ontotheology before whom we can neither dance nor pray.

Let me cut quickly to a salient criticism, not least because it comes from a Catholic theologian of great distinction, Cardinal Walter Kasper. In *Mercy: The Essence of the Gospel and the Key to Christian Life* (a work endorsed and developed by Pope Francis in his own book, *The Name of God Is Mercy*), Cardinal Kasper argues that 'divine mercy' as a name for God has been criminally neglected. He points the finger at the 'handbook theology' which dominated Catholic seminary education of the nineteenth century. There he finds the divine attributes 'that are derived from God's metaphysical essence as Subsistent Being itself (*ipsum esse subsistens*) are the focus of the handbooks: simplicity, infinity, eternity, omnipresence, omnipotence and other attributes'.[13] How, he asks, does this correspond with the biblical understanding of God who suffers with his creatures, who is with the poor

---

[13] Kasper, *Mercy*, 10–11.

and for the poor? Here, says Kasper, 'we should merely point out that, within the parameters of the metaphysical attributes of God, there is scarcely room for a concept of mercy, which derives not from the metaphysical essence, but rather from the historical self-revelation of God'.[14] Does then Aquinas not stand condemned for privileging a designation which takes us far from scriptural witness and, as a historical legacy, leads western theology in modernity onto the spiritually barren ground of 'the God of the attributes'? Are we not at the cusp of the degradation wherein God becomes 'an entity' – the 'most perfect being', as Descartes would have it?[15] This is 'ontotheology', a fully immanentist logic where God becomes one entity amongst others.

By way of apology we must ask: *in what sense* did Aquinas believe 'the One Who Is' to be the most appropriate name for God? Aquinas knew and pondered and prayed hundreds of names of God which he understands to be at the same time names of Christ – Counsellor, Flower, Font of Wisdom, Beautiful, Light of the World, Physician, Bridegroom – he found dozens of names of Christ in his commentary on Isaiah alone.[16] A glance at

[14] Kasper, *Mercy*, 10–11. The criticism clearly relates to the discussion of 'the most appropriate name for God' in *S.T.* Ia.13, 11 and to the discussions in *S.T.* Ia. 2–11 which unfold from the so-called 'Five Ways' of God's simplicity, perfection, goodness, limitlessness, existence in all things, unchangeableness, eternity and oneness.

[15] On this see Jean-Luc Marion, 'The Essential Incoherence of Descartes' Definition of Divinity,' in *Essays on Descartes' Meditations*, ed. Amélie Oksenberg Rorty (Berkeley: University of California Press, 1986), 297–338 at 320.

[16] See Henk Schroot's excellent *Christ, the 'Name' of God: Thomas Aquinas on Naming Christ* (Leuven: Peeters, 1993).

his prayers shows that there can be no sense in which Aquinas regarded 'Qui est' as the *only or even best name* for God, displacing names like 'Redeemer', 'Saviour', 'Lord' and even the name 'God' itself. What do we mean then by 'the most appropriate name of God'? Given our modern predilection to think of names as definitions, we naturally think 'the most appropriate name' must mean something like 'the best description'. The context for Aquinas, however, and his contemporaries and predecessors in the divine names tradition, was different. It was praise – for as Dionysius had stressed, standing in a line that can be traced back as far as Philo, the names are not the means by which we *define* or describe the divine essence for that cannot be done, but the means by which we *praise* God for his gifts. It is in this context and by treating reflection, even philosophical reflection, on the divine names as a spiritual exercise or meditation, that 'the One Who Is' comes into its own. Our question should be 'what is the most appropriate name by which to praise God for God's gifts to us?'

It is helpful to compare Aquinas' discussion of the 'most appropriate name' with the writings of his contemporary and Parisian colleague, Bonaventure. Bonaventure's *Itineraria mentis in Deum, The Soul's Journey into God*, bears in the title its objectives of spiritual formation and presents the names of God as the subject for our meditation. Bonaventure devotes the fifth and sixth chapters of *The Soul's Journey into God* to the names 'Being' and 'Good'. In a work with only seven chapters, the emphasis on these two titles gives us a glimpse into the then-contemporary practice of meditating on the Divine Names.

Bonaventure tells us that John Damascene, 'following Moses', says that '*He Who Is*' is God's primary name (Ex. 3.14) and that Dionysius, 'following Christ', says God's primary name is 'the Good', with reference to Mark 10.18 and Luke 18:19 where Jesus asks 'why do you call me good? No one is good but God alone'. Bonaventure does not choose between these two divine names but devotes his fifth chapter to the Divine Unity through its primary name which is 'Being' and the sixth to the Blessed Trinity, whose name is 'Good'.

It is important to remember that both 'Being' and 'Good' were for Bonaventure and Aquinas, as for Dionysius and others before them, not only *scriptural* names for God but names of the highest order because, unlike names taken from human praise such as 'our rock' and 'my fortress', 'the One Who Is' and 'Good' were understood to be divine self-designations – names which, in scripture, God was credited with giving to Godself.[17]

Aquinas, while considering 'the Good' as a fundamental name of God, nonetheless privileges *Qui est*, 'the One Who Is' – the name revealed to Moses – as the most appropriate name. This reflects the increasing weight he gives to *creatio ex nihilo*. While always important to him, by the time of writing the *Summa theologiae* Aquinas had made further study of the *Guide to the Perplexed* and found in Maimonides a great ally on this teaching on creation. If Maimonides did not, as we have seen, give what Aquinas

---

[17] This does not preclude the fact that Dionysius, an influence on both Bonaventure and Aquinas, found these names for God in his Neoplatonic sources as well.

regarded as an entirely satisfactory account of naming God, he nonetheless understood the doctrine of *creatio ex nihilo* to protect many of his convictions – on the sovereignty of God, on human and divine freedom and on miracles – to name but a few.[18]

Aquinas provides three reasons for privileging *Qui est* and anchors them in his sources: first, because of its meaning, as not signifying any particular form but rather existence itself; second by virtue of its universality or indeterminacy for, citing Damascene, 'In this life our minds cannot grasp what God is in himself', and third, because of its tense, 'for it signifies being in the present and this is especially appropriate to God whose being knows neither past nor future, as Augustine says' (*S.T.* Ia.13, 12, citing *de Trin.* V.2).

Thomas cites Augustine here but is at the same time faithful to Maimonides who, expanding in the Guide for the Perplexed on the name given to Moses, explains that all the names of God in scripture derive from God's actions, with the exception of the Tetragrammaton (Book I, Ch. 61–63). The Tetragrammaton alone is God's nomen proprium (Shem-ha-meforash) and is

---

[18] Torrell suggests that Aquinas learned his apophaticism from Maimonides as derivative from the strong sense of the divine transcendence. *Saint Thomas Aquinas*: Vol. I: *The Person and His Work* (Washington, DC: Catholic University of America Press, 1996), p. 122). Yet the idea, with respect to God, that our denials are more apposite than our affirmations was frequently articulated by Augustine and any number of Latin and Greek fathers. Not only the *Summa theologiae* and the *Summa contra gentiles*, but his writing on Lombard's *Sentences* are prefaced, Torrell notes, by apophatic declarations. Aquinas simply pursues this in a more analytic fashion in the *Summa Theologiae*.

so because, being derived from hayah, it conveys the notion of absolute existence. God exists, not in the ordinary sense, says Maimonides, but as the one who 'has never been and never will be without existence.' (Book I, Ch. 63).[19]

This brings us again to *creatio ex nihilo*. God is, at every moment, the source and cause of all our being, of all that is. For this reason Aquinas believes 'the One Who Is' to be a more fundamental name than 'Good' – or rather, while 'Good' may be foundational insofar as it treats of God as cause, 'to be' is presupposed in being a cause. We could say the same of a name like 'Mercy' or 'Redeemer'. Both those names, however central, depend on there *being anything at all in the first place* for mercy and redemption to be even necessary.[20]

There is in Aquinas a developed philosophical reflection on what it means for God to be 'the One Who Is' as it relates to creatures. While *creatio ex nihilo*, the teaching so central for him, is not in itself a discussion of the finely

[19] There is an extensive theological and philosophical literature generated by Aquinas' understanding of God as 'the One Who Is' and 'Being Itself'. While deeply interesting to some, it can easily draw us into debates as to 'what God is' instead of 'who God is for us', which is my purpose. I would highly Rudi te Velde's chapter 'The Heart of the Matter: What God Is (Not)', in his *Aquinas on God: The 'Divine Science' of the Summa Theologiae* (London: Ashgate, 2006), for his discussion of *ipsum esse per se subsistens* (81) and the attributes in these early chapters. As te Velde says, this formulation should not be taken as 'positively expressing the essence of God, but is rather a substitute for a definition' (81). Let me also add that this philosophical debate, while not for everyone, is not remote from meditation and prayer.

[20] Friedrich Schleiermacher makes the same point in *The Christian Faith*. See Janet Soskice, 'Being and Love: Schleiermacher, Aquinas and Augustine', *Modern Theology* 34, no. 3 (July 2018): 480–91.

tuned creaturely order (something we might call 'the theology of creatures'), out of *creatio ex nihilo* comes this key understanding: all the world, 'all that is', is gift. Our own being and that of all creatures is gift.[21] God alone 'is' and we (and angels, earthworms, stars and planets) have at every moment our own being from God.

'All that is, is gift.' The startling Latin formulation – *ipsum esse per se subsistens* – preserves this fundamental truth. Yet the conviction that only God is 'being itself' does not mean that creatures and we ourselves have diminished being. The theology of participation is an outflowing of understanding how it is we creatures 'truly are', independent and free yet neither as fragments of God or separate from God. Indeed, as I have tried to stress, God's ultimacy and intimacy are one: God is closer to us and to all things than our own hands and feet. It is something of a paradox that a formulation which sounds

---

[21] Andrew Davison notes that *creatio ex nihilo* 'is the foundation for participatory theology, and it is the foundation because to call creation *out of nothing* is to say "all things come from Thee"'. He goes on to translate a key section of Aquinas's doctrine of creation in a way that captures the participatory insistence:

'Every being in any way existing is from God ... (so that while) God is Being itself, founded in himself by his own nature ('self-subsisting being itself' – *ipsum esse per se subsistens* – ... all beings apart from God are not their own being, but participate (or share) in being (received from God). (*S.T.* Ia.44.1).

Cited in Andrew Davison, *Participation in God: A Study in Christian Doctrine and Metaphysics* (Cambridge: Cambridge University Press, 2019), p. 23. This whole study can be recommended, along with Hans Boersma's *Heavenly Participation*. For an account which also touches on human freedom see also David Burrell, 'Creator/Creatures Relation: "the Distinction" vs. "Onto-theology"', *Faith and Philosophy: Journal of the Society of Christian Philosophers* 25, no. 2 (2008): 177–89.

so remote – *ipsum esse per se subsistens* – is concerned to preserve the intimate relation of God to all creatures and, for Aquinas, the theology of participation spills out from the biblical name, 'the One Who Is'.[22]

To conclude 'the One Who Is' or 'Being Itself' does not define the divine essence. It is rather a name of praise, a name which is *a name for us*, a name which denominates our foundational relation to God as the Giver of Gifts – not just our being but all created being.

Is reflecting on the names of God and specifically on the name 'Qui est' still spiritually resonant in our age? I would say 'yes', and more so than ever. We might try this thought experiment, or if you prefer meditation, on some different divine names. Take, for instance, the names 'Life' and 'Truth' – both of which are biblically given and even candidates for being names in the special category of 'divine self-designations', since we read in John's Gospel 'Jesus said to him, "I am the way, the truth, and the life"' (John 14.6). We might say that 'truth' is a profound gift, but can we say that 'truth' is a gift for living creatures apart from reasoning human beings? Is 'truth' a gift for cattle, or for roses or for stag beetles? Only in an extenuated sense. It might seem then that the divine name 'Life' is better in terms of its broader reach, for all those creatures have life and have this from God. But what if, for instance, you were the 'sun and the moon' or the 'dews and the sleet' or the 'light and dark'? These

---

[22] It is also the case that Aquinas believed we could prove there was an 'uncaused cause' and that his discussion of *ipsum esse per se subsistens* uses Aristotelian terminology, but his *Summa theologiae* unfolds from his belief in *creatio ex nihilo*, which is not an Aristotelian teaching at all. In fact, quite the opposite as I have said.

are not 'living things', but they are all creatures. All are invoked by the three young men in the fiery furnace of the Book of Daniel to praise and bless the Lord. Psalm 148 is an avalanche of requests that the sun and moon, dragons and deeps, fruit trees and cedars, bears and cattle, worms and feathered fowl join us in praising the LORD.

Sun and moon, like ourselves and cattle and sparrows, owe their entire being to the one who is 'Being Itself'. Without God they, like us, simply would not be. 'The One Who Is' thus does not supplant other divine names but grounds them – Way, Truth, Life, Beauty, Mercy, Bread of Heaven.

This is where *creatio ex nihilo* and God as the 'I AM' turns from scriptural metaphysics to reverential awe. Once aware of this move, we spot it across western spiritual writings, beautifully encapsulated by Julian of Norwich in the famous 'showing' of the hazelnut. In this she sees the world as a tiny thing, about the size of a hazelnut, in the palm of her own hand:

I looked at it thoughtfully and wondered, 'What is this?' And the answer came, 'It is all that is made.' I marvelled that it continued to exist and did not suddenly disintegrate; it was so small. And again my mind supplied the answer, 'It exists, both now and forever, because God loves it.'[23]

In short every thing and each particular thing owes its existence at every moment to the love of God. Nothing could be more secure. That we *are*, that anything is at all,

---

[23] Julian of Norwich, *Revelations of Divine Love*, trans. Clinton Wolters (London: Penguin, 1966), Ch. 5. It is important that it is *her* hand and not God's hand.

constitutes the foundational blessing and the primordial ground for praise.

The Gift of Naming

Given the plentitude of divine names across the Scriptures, why do those Jews and Christians interested in naming God return so often to Moses at the burning bush? *YHWH*, the proper name of Israel's God, is invoked elsewhere and earlier in the biblical writings even according to canonical chronology. In Genesis 4 Eve uses the name *YHWH*, and the name, 'God of Abraham and of Isaac and of Jacob' appears in Genesis 50.[24] If the names given to Moses, even the name 'the One Who Is', do not have their significance from this one encounter but cumulatively across the panoply of texts which disclose the divine identity, then why return with such frequency to discussing the burning bush?

By way of an answer, we must get away from the notion that Exodus 3 is only about the gift of the Name, or of several linked and dependent names, and consider instead what the narrative sequence does – that is, not just what the text *says* but what the text *shows us* about Israel's God. This is the strategy of the Rabbinics scholar, José Faur in his remarkable, *Golden Doves with Silver Dots*.

'Scripture teaches that God has a name', writes Faur of Exodus 3, and this 'means that God is semiologically accessible'. The phrase 'semiologically accessible'

---

[24] By canonical chronology I mean the sense of chronology given in the texts themselves, where creation would antedate Moses and the burning bush. Scholars of the Hebrew Bible have their own dating of these texts.

214

lacks poetry but Faur's point is apt – in the context of Moses' request for a name, the consequent back and forth between God and Moses *displays* the fact that his God can be addressed. This is the primordial disclosure to which the text attests – a Holy One who both calls and who can be called upon.

It is not a magical or esoteric relation. On the question as to whether Moses' request for God's name has over-tones of name magic, Faur points out that in the Hebrew Bible the 'act of naming does not imply power over the thing named. According to the Rabbis, Adam named the animals, but also God' (an observation, although Faur doesn't make it, that puts the naming of Eve in a new light). He continues:

Rather than magical theology, knowledge of God's name involves the possibility of addressing Him and receiving a response, that is to *pray* to God. Indeed, the biblical expression 'to call upon the name of the Lord' is synonymous with prayer.[25]

At a pivotal point in the Exodus narrative, the encounter at the burning bush underscores the belief that God is a 'speaking' God and a 'hearing' God and does so by means of the gift of names. Perhaps we might better speak of the *gift of naming*. God has heard the cry of Israelites enslaved in Egypt, even without their vocal prayer. Moses hammers the point home. 'For whatever great nation has

---

[25] José Faur, *Golden Doves with Silver Dots: Semiotics and Textuality in Rabbinic Tradition*, Jewish Literature and Culture (Bloomington: Indiana University Press, 1986), 39, citing *Bereshit Rabba* XVII, 4. Adam's naming of Eve does not, on this argument, suggest power over her.

a god so near to it as YHWH our God is whenever we call
to him', says the Deuteronomic Moses to the Israelites as
a prelude to setting out the statutes (Deut 4. 7). This God
can hear the needy, can hear slaves and even non-Jews
(Deut 24.14–22) with a 'hearing' that entails 'seeing'.[26]
The Tetragrammaton, with its cryptic gloss, the 'I Am
the One who is with you' remains, not as authorising a
positive ontology, but as the unnameable name which
sends us back to the narratives and unites the narratives
with Laws, Prophecy and Psalm.[27]

'And Now I Was Talking with You'
(Augustine, *Confessions*, Book IX)

Does starting with Moses mean forgetting Christ? Does
Aquinas in privileging *Qui est* as the 'most appropriate
name for God' remain faithful to Maimonides at the
expense of his Christian faith? Is the Christology of
the *Summa*, as has sometimes been suggested, an after-
thought appended to a super-structure of philosophical
monotheism? These questions are not just for Aquinas
but for the whole legacy of Christian reflection on naming God which takes as its stepping-off point Moses and
the burning bush. So then, does starting with Moses
mean forgetting Christ?

By no means. Let us return, for instance, to Augustine
preaching on Psalm 121 (122), He reminds his listeners

---

[26] The plight of Hagar, the slave girl driven out by Sarai, is heard. She
gives her son with Abraham the name, Ishmael, meaning 'God has
heard', and she praises God with a new name, *El Roi*, which might be
translated 'God of seeing' (Gen 16).

[27] Ricoeur, 'Naming God', 228

that Moses, when he asked for a name, was told *I AM WHO I AM:* "'This is Being-Itself,'" says Augustine, "the Self-same: *I AM WHO AM, HE WHO IS has sent me to you*'". Augustine then cautions his flock: 'You cannot take it in, for this is too much to understand, too much to grasp. Hold on instead to what he who you cannot understand became for you. Hold onto the flesh of Christ.'[28]

The 'I AM WHO I AM' we cannot understand. But 'who God is for us', that we can understand. Augustine continues with a clarification of how he understands the Exodus passage: 'Hold on to what Christ became for you, because Christ himself, even Christ, is rightly understood by this name, I AM WHO I AM, inasmuch as he is the form of God. In that nature wherein he *deemed it no robbery to be God's equal* (Phil 2.6), there he is Being-Itself.' Augustine's reference is to the 'Christ hymn' in Philippians 2.6. The passage is commonly drawn upon to illustrate the humility of Christ, taking the form of a servant, but the same hymn astonishingly unfolds the mystery of Christ by identifying Jesus with the Name of the Lord. This is not to say that the name 'Jesus' is the name *YHWH* but that *Jesus himself is the Name of the Lord*, dwelling with the people (Isa 45.23–4).[29] Jesus is thus named 'the Name', the very divine presence.

Augustine makes the conflation, common in Patristic and Medieval thought but occluded in modern western theology until relatively recently, between Jesus and the

---

[28] Augustine, *Expositions of the Psalms*, trans. Maria Boulding, Vol. VI (New York: New City, 2000), 18.

[29] Aquinas, too, believed that Christ is 'the Name' of the LORD, following St Paul and various New Testament passages on glorifying the 'Name'. See Schroot, *Christ, the 'Name' of God*, Ch. 3.

One who summoned Moses from the burning bush.[30] Christ is the 'I AM', the creator and the redeemer. This identification of Christ and the 'I AM' is entirely biblical. The Prologue of John's Gospel, with its strong echoes of the creation narratives of Genesis, identifies the Word Incarnate with the Word through whom all things came into being.[31] This identification is made by Jesus himself in the various 'I AM' sayings of John's Gospel. 'Before Abraham was, I AM', says Jesus in John 8.58, a self-identification with the one God, creator and redeemer.[32]

On the lips of the Johannine Jesus the 'I Am' takes us back to Exodus 3 but also to the 'I AM' sayings of Deutero-Isaiah where, in a sequence of divine self-designations, YHWH declares that he *alone* is God and creator.

> For thus says YHWH,
> who created the heavens
> (he is God!),

---

[30] See Orthodox, and especially, Sinaitic icons of Mary as the burning bush, where the Theotokos is sometimes pictured inside the bush, sometimes as containing it.

[31] Martin Hengel writes that 'as narrated Christology the Fourth Gospel is grounded throughout in the Old Testament ... no New Testament writing has such a wealth of titles and designations provided from there and Judaism: the Anointed, Messiah, King, Rabbi, Rabbouni, Son of God and Son of Man, the Lord, the Holy One of God, the Elect, Only-Begotten, the Prophet, the Lamb of God, the Light of the World, the True Vine, the Good Shepherd, and – not least – the absolute *ego emi* or even theos himself. Beyond question "salvation comes from the Jews" (John 4.22).' *The Prologue to the Gospel of John as the Gateway to Christological Truth*, in *The Gospel of John and Christian Theology*, ed. Richard Bauckham and Carl Moss (Grand Rapids, Mich.: William B. Eerdmans, 2008), 271.

[32] Richard B. Hays, writing of Luke's Gospel, speaks of 'a narrative world, thick with scriptural memory'. *Reading Backwards* (London: SPCK, 2015), 59.

who formed the earth and made it
(he established it;
he did not create a chaos,
he formed it to be inhabited!):
'I AM YHWH, and there is no other.' (Isa 45.18)

In developed Jewish and Christian monotheism, the creator is the redeemer. God alone creates and God alone redeems – the two belong together.[33] The Pauline literature frequently alludes to Christ's role in creation, identifying him with Word or Wisdom. This is famously so in I Corinthians:

for us there is one God, the Father, from whom are all things and for whom we exist, and one Lord, Jesus Christ, through whom are all things and through whom we exist. (I Cor 8.6)

And in Colossians:

He is the image of the invisible God, the firstborn of all creation; for in him all things in heaven and on earth were created, things visible and invisible, whether thrones or dominions or rulers or powers – all things have been created through him and for him. (Col 1.15)

Outside of the Pauline writings, the author of the Epistle to the Hebrews begins by saying

in these last days he (God) has spoken to us by a Son, whom he appointed heir of all things, through whom he also created the worlds. He is the reflection of God's glory and the exact imprint of God's very being, and he sustains all things by his powerful word. (Heb 1.1–3)

---

[33] See Richard Bauckham, *Jesus and the God of Israel* (Milton Keynes: Paternoster, 2008).

As in John's Prologue, this is all the language of creation.[34]

Attentive to names and to naming, we can turn to that most Jewish and thus least read and understood of the New Testament writings – the Book of Revelation.[35] The book opens with a theophany which is itself a divine self-designation:

'I am the Alpha and the Omega', says the Lord God,
who is and who was and who is to come, the Almighty.
(Rev 1.8)

This one verse contains four or five divine names, all of which would be already familiar to early followers of Jesus who knew their Hebrew scriptures. In the resounding sequence of divine self-designations that follow, *God and Christ* are both called 'Alpha and Omega' and 'First and the Last'. These names are themselves glosses of *YHWH*, whose only full interpretation in the Old Testament is in Exodus 3 where, as we have seen, a sequence of word-play expands on the Tetragrammaton and its similarity to the Hebrew verb 'to be'.

The distinctive name, 'First and Last', is not of New Testament coinage but appears as a divine self-designation a number of times in Deutero-Isaiah:

[34] This is not to say the developed Christology and doctrine of creation can be simply read off these biblical writings, but these are seed corn. For a contesting view on early Christology monotheism and a summary of the vigorous debate amongst biblical scholars, see Brittany E. Wilson, *The Embodied God* (Oxford: Oxford University Press, 2021), especially Ch. 3.

[35] Here I am drawing on Richard Bauckham's *The Theology of the Book of Revelation*, New Testament Theology (Cambridge: Cambridge University Press, 1993). See also Richard B. Hays, 'Jesus in the Apocalypse of John', in his *Reading with the Grain of Scripture* (Grand Rapids, Mich.: William B. Eerdmans, 2020), 285–302.

Thus says the LORD (YHWH), the King of Israel,
and his Redeemer, the LORD of hosts:
'I am the first, and I am the last;
besides me there is no god.' (Isa 44.6, see also 41.4)

And in Isaiah 48.12 where this name (and the Name) are
associated with creation:

I am He; I am the first, and I am the last.
My hand laid the foundation of the earth,
and my right hand spread out the heavens;
when I summon them, they stand at attention.
    (Isa 48.12b–13)

According to Richard Bauckham this divine self-
designation in Deutero-Isaiah – the first and the last –
'encapsulates the understanding of the God of Israel as the
sole Creator of all things and sovereign Lord of history,
which Deutero-Isaiah so magnificently expounds and asserts
polemically against the idols of Babylon'.[36] In the Book of
Revelation this same name underscores the identification of
Jesus Christ with the Creator, the Holy One of Israel:

Do not be afraid: I am the first and the last, and the living one.
I was dead, and see, I am alive forever and ever; and I have the
Keys of Death and of Hades. (Rev 1.17b–18)

The 'first and last' is the one who will redeem all things
having created all things. Compare here the song of the
living creatures in Revelation 4.8:

Holy, holy, holy,
the Lord God the Almighty,
who was and is and is to come.

[36] Bauckham, *The Theology of the Book of Revelation*, 27.

with the Praise the twenty-four elders accord God as Creator:

> You are worthy, our Lord and God,
> to receive glory and honour and power,
> for you created all things,
> and by your will they existed and were created. (Rev 4.11)

The creative and redeeming God is the 'eternal' God of scripture, the One who always was, and is, and always will be. Jesus is identified with the names of this One, eternal God within the texts of the New Testament, not by borrowing from Greek metaphysics, but through a cascade of names and titles from the Hebrew Bible.[37]

Much more could be added about naming Jesus as 'Lord', for 'Lord' similarly is a gloss on the Tetragrammaton, or rather it is a circumlocution since devout Jews did not articulate the name *YHWH* but instead said – and often wrote in their texts – 'Adonai'. Naming Jesus 'Lord' then takes us back to *YHWH* and the many invocations, supplications and praises of the LORD in the

---

[37] Richard Bauckham writes that 'we should think of the Jewish monotheistic understanding of God in the Second Temple period in terms of the identity of God rather than of the divine nature'. 'Monotheism and Christology in Hebrews I', in *Early Jewish and Christian Monotheism*, ed. Loren T. Stuckenbruck and Wendy E. S. North, Journal for the Study of the New Testament Supplement series (London; New York: T&T Clark International, 2004), 167–85. Extensive work has been done on this 'early high Christology' and I pass the reader on to the many excellent works by biblical scholars, including Larry Hurtado and N. T. Wright. The background, as it were, is the nineteenth-century prejudice towards thinking the earliest understanding of Jesus was as a simply Galilean teacher and that only after the incursion of later (and gentile) thought did Jesus become God. For a summary and some counter-argument see Wilson, *The Embodied God*, Ch. 3.

Hebrew Bible, invisible to readers of the Bible whose translations give simply LORD.[38]

In *Confessions*, Book VII, Augustine tells us of a spiritual ascent attempted prior to his conversion experience. He was guided by 'the Platonic books', but his account of the experience is shot through with Christ. Augustine describes being taken to the light that is not the light of day ('It was superior because it made me'). He saw Being and trembled because he himself was not yet Being. He nonetheless despairs, crying 'Surely truth cannot be nothing, when it is not diffused through space, either finite or infinite?' And you cried from far away "Now I AM WHO I AM" (Ex. 3.14).'[39]

At this stage in his journey Augustine does not, in his terms, 'know Christ'. The name of Christ, at least as a name by which he can call upon his God, will appear only later in the *Confessions*. But that *it is Christ* who speaks to him at this juncture is made clear by the voice he seems to hear from on high: 'I am the food of the fully grown; grow and you will feed on me. And you will not change me into you like the food your flesh eats, but you will be changed into me' (*Conf.* VII.10.16)

This is eucharistic feeding. The voice that says 'you will feed on me' is the same, self-announced 'I am who

---

[38] On this see C. Kavin Rowe, 'Romans 10:13: What Is the Name of the Lord?', *Horizons in Biblical Theology*, Vol. 22 (2000) and Rowe's *Early Narrative Christology: the LORD in the Gospel of Luke*. See also Richard B. Hays who draws on Rowe and others in his immensely helpful discussion of the New Testament's deployment of the Old, *Reading Backwards*.

[39] Augustine, *Confessions*, trans. Chadwick, Book VII.10.16. This is by contrast with the divine ascent which he and his mother, Monica, share later in Ostia.

I am' who speaks to him in his despair. It is this same guide who, he can later see, even at the beginning of his seeking, was guiding him all the way.[40] In what seems a deliberate literary strategy, Augustine conceals the 'mystery' of Christ in the early books of the *Confessions*. He will only *know that it is* Christ who has addressed him and carried him throughout his life when he can call Christ by name – or pray, which amounts to the same thing. 'And now I was talking with you', Augustine will later announce (*Conf.* Book IX). Christ is not 'almost absent' from the *Confessions* or Augustine's early life, but everywhere present, if only one knows how to hear his voice.[41]

Something similar occurs in the *Summa theologiae*, though not with the literary elegance we find in the *Confessions*. It is not as though Aquinas labours through a number of matters in 'natural theology' (an anachronism in any case) and then gets around to questions of Trinity and revelation. For Thomas and all his contemporaries, the 'I AM WHO AM' is already Christ as witnessed in John's Gospel, in Paul and in the Book of Revelation: the one who was, and is, and is to come. Christ is the God whose presence to us as the source of being is unfolded in those first questions of the *Summa*. This is made textually evident at numerous junctures, for instance in *Summa theologiae* (Ia.3, 3) when, in a *sed contra* to a question on

---

[40] 'With you as my guide I entered into my innermost citadel and was given power to do so because you had become my helper (Ps 29.11)' (*Conf.* VII.10.16).

[41] 'Thereby I submitted my neck to your easy yoke and my shoulders to your light burden (Matt 11:30), O Christ Jesus "my helper and redeemer" (Ps 18:15) ... And now I was talking with you, Lord, my God, my radiance, my wealth, and my salvation' (*Conf.* IX.1.1).

divine simplicity, Aquinas tells us 'God is not only called living but life: *I am the way, the truth and the life.*' These three Christic self-designations Aquinas takes, without pausing, to be names of God.

The Summoned Self

Hear, O Israel: the LORD is our God, the LORD alone. You shall love the LORD your God with all your heart, and with all your soul, and with all your might. (Deut 6.4–6)

To be a Christian, or a Jew, is to stand as one who has been addressed. Rarely is this in the dramatic manner described in scripture of Moses and the prophets, or even of the disciples in the New Testament who hear Jesus say 'Follow me.' More often it is through reading scripture, hearing the preacher, the voice of friends, the beauty of the created order. The Christian life is one of call and response.

Having confessed himself to be a 'listener to Christian preaching', Paul Ricoeur makes clear in the rest of 'Naming God' and his other essays which touch on the same theme that understanding oneself as having been addressed, or summoned, is central not only to his Christian faith but also to his diagnosis of the philosophical hubris he finds in western modernity. Ricoeur writes that to 'confess that one is a listener is from the very beginning to break with the project dear to many, and even perhaps all, philosophers: to begin without any presuppositions'.[42] For the philosopher to listen to Christian preaching, two kinds of hubris must be knocked down, writes, Ricoeur. The first is that of metaphysical knowledge – 'one must let

---

[42] Ricoeur, 'Naming God,' 217.

go (*se depouiler*) of every form of onto-theological knowl-edge'.[43] However, there is a 'second hubris' even more invisible 'no longer metaphysical but transcendental'. It is the presumption of self-founding, 'the beginning of self by and from the self'. Listening, says Ricoeur, excludes founding oneself. And listening to Christian preaching requires 'abandoning a more subtle and more tenacious pretention than that of onto-theological knowledge. It requires giving up (*dessaissement*) the human self in its will to mastery sufficiency and autonomy. The Gospels' statement that "Whoever would save his life will lose it" applies to this giving up.'[44] His point is both spiritual and philosophical.

In 'The Summoned Subject', Ricoeur writes of a subject which understands itself as always constituted by being in relation and always in response. As such it 'diametrically opposes itself to the philosophical hubris of a self that absolutely names itself'.[45] Ricoeur takes as his biblical template the prophet, as one who is called by God, usu-ally in solitude and by name. The religious relation of call and response has a strong sense of 'I hear', writes Ricoeur in another essay, where the superiority of the call of the Most High 'is recognized, avowed, confessed'.[46]

---

[43] As mentioned, at the time of writing this essay he feared the medieval had amalgamated God and being, a fear he later saw was groundless.

[44] Ricoeur, 'Naming God', 224.

[45] 'The Summoned Subject in the School of the Narratives of the Prophetic Vocation' (1988), in Ricoeur, *Figuring the Sacred*, 269–75 at 262.

[46] Paul Ricoeur, 'Experience and Language in Religious Discourse', in Janicaud et al., *Phenomenology and the Theological Turn*, 129. Ricoeur is expanding on the difficulties a phenomenology of experience of religion must confront.

Ricoeur speaks of religion as 'like a language into which one has either been born or has been transferred by exile or hospitality; in any event, one feels at home there'.[47] One learns a language by hearing and being spoken to, and one is inducted into Christian faith by reading the Bible, hearing it preached or participating in liturgy, and in doing so one learns names of God and the practices of naming God. When Christians name Jesus as 'the Lamb of God', they do not do so simply because John the Baptist named Jesus this way, or because the Book of Revelation does the same, but reach back to the sacrificial lamb of the first Passover itself. When Christians pray to God as Creator and Redeemer, they can do so, at least in part, because Isaiah already did. When they call out to Jesus in prayer, they do so, at least in part, because the Psalmist has said that the LORD 'is near to all who call on him, to all who call on him in truth' (Ps 145.18). Jesus' self-designation, 'I am the bread of life', immediately follows his discussion of Moses and the manna in the desert (John 6).

That God can speak and be spoken to should strike us as astonishing, and indeed sophisticated pagans found it so. Yet Hebrew Scripture consistently has God calling, summoning and addressing – not only the prophets and the leaders, but common people as well. And with equal frequency we find people calling back – calling upon their God by name or with many names. And although the human beings may be the only creatures who 'call upon

---

[47] Ricoeur, 'Biblical Readings and Meditations', 145. He adds, 'which implies a recognition that there are other languages spoken by other people'.

the Name of the Lord', in biblical terms the whole of creation is semiologically connected. God 'calls' all creatures into being in the first chapters of Genesis. The disclosure to Moses at the burning bush of the *Qui est*, reaches back into the creation narratives and forward to the promise of salvation. 'The One Who Is' called all things into being and called Moses by name. There is no need to choose between those who invoke a personal God and those who, over the centuries, have reflected on God as 'Being Itself'. That God is the same God.

It is by the Jewish scriptures that Christians know that God can be the Holy One who is wholly present. There we read that God addresses individuals like Moses or Abraham and directs them on their way and that *YHWH*, the Name, can 'dwell' with his people in the Tabernacle and the Temple.[48] Without this legacy of Hebrew Scriptures, the Christian doctrine of the Incarnation, that the Word was made flesh and dwelt amongst us, is inexplicable.[49]

This calling and creating God can be with the people – indeed with all creatures and all creation – at every moment and in every place without ceasing to be the transcendent God. This, as I have argued, is not *despite* but *because* God is the Creator. God is not distant from creatures but wholly present to them in every moment,

---

[48] See Michael Wyschogrod, *The Body of Faith: God and the People of Israel* (Northvale, NJ: Jason Aronson, 1996). The Tabernacle was the dwelling place of *YHWH*, or the Name, when the Israelites wandered in the desert and later in the Temple. The origins of the Christian doctrine of the Incarnation, that is to say, are to be sought in Jewish practice.

[49] On this from a Jewish perspective, see Wyschogrod, *The Body of Faith*, Preface and Ch. 1.

creating and sustaining them, which amounts to the same.[50] God's ultimacy and God's intimacy are one. Christian belief is not a 'flight to another world', for the deity does not inhabit an elusive elsewhere. There is only 'all that is' and God wholly present to 'all that is'.[51]

We are still called to name God newly. 'Who do you say I am?' asks Jesus. To be a Christian or a Jew, is to stand before the one through whom we have our being and know that we did not make ourselves. It is to break with any claim to self-founding. It is, in this sense, always to be brought back to the 'I AM' who spoke to Moses and to whom Moses spoke. It is to feel the call of the very ground of our being.[52] As we listen for the summons of God, we may also hear the summons of God's creatures demanding our attention and love.

Naming, calling, praising and praying belong together, and while we, for the moment, believe human beings

---

[50] There is no 'God-world binary' because God is not a 'thing' alongside the world but the One who holds all that is in being.

[51] Dominique Janicaud, sceptical of French phenomenology's 'theological turn', invokes this misplaced binary. A strong dose of *creatio ex nihilo* might cure him (Janicaud et al., *Phenomenology and the 'Theological Turn'*, 35). It is this teaching of creation that makes the biblical understanding of 'call and response' substantially different, or at least of a greater plenitude, than that of phenomenological accounts of 'call and response' like that of Jean-Louis Chrétien whose aims are not primarily theological but to transform phenomenology. These accounts may work to dispossess us of our egocentrism but runs the danger of remaining epistemic, or at least anthropocentric, whereas the 'call and response' of the Creator God unites us with all creatures, who are similarly called.

[52] For a superb philosophical and spiritual exercise on this theme, see Peter Ochs, 'Morning Prayer as Redemptive Thinking', in *Liturgy, Time and the Politics of Redemption*, ed. Randi Rashkover and C. C. Pecknold (Grand Rapids, Mich.: William B. Eerdmans, 2006), 50–87.

are the only creatures who can call upon the Name, we are by no means the only creatures who God summons and to whom God speaks. The disciples, finding their boat swamped by a storm, cry 'Lord, save us! We are perishing!' Jesus then waking rebukes the winds and the sea and there is dead calm. Who is this, the disciples ask themselves, 'that even the winds and sea obey him?' (Matt 8.23–7). (Mark 4.41, Matt 8.10). The answer can be found in Psalm 65. It is the LORD, the very One who summoned wind and water into being in the first instance who summons them now.

BIBLIOGRAPHY

Anderson, John M. *The Grammar of Names*. Oxford Linguistics. Oxford: Oxford University Press, 2007.

Aquinas. *Summa Theologiae*. Trans. Thomas Gilby, OP. London: Eyre & Spottiswoode, 1967.

Augustine. *Confessions*. Trans. O. S. B. Maria Boulding. London: Hodder and Stoughton, 1997.

    De doctrina christiana. Trans. R. P. H. Green. Oxford Early Christian Texts. Oxford: Clarendon Press, 1995.

    Expositions of the Psalms. Trans. Maria Boulding. 6 vols. New York: New City, 2000.

    On the Holy Trinity, Doctrinal Treatises, Moral Treatises. Trans. Arthur W. Haddan. Vol. III. Grand Rapids, Mich.: Eerdmans, 1980.

    Tractates on the Gospel of John. The Fathers of the Church. 5 vols. Washington, DC: Catholic University of America Press, 1988.

Augustine, and Henry Chadwick. *Confessions*. Oxford; New York: Oxford University Press, 1991.

Barth, Karl. *Church Dogmatics*. Ed. Geoffrey William Bromiley and Thomas F. Torrance. Study ed. London: T&T Clark, 2009.

Bauckham, Richard. *Jesus and the God of Israel*. Milton Keynes: Paternoster, 2008.

    'Monotheism and Christology in Hebrews 1'. In *Early Jewish and Christian Monotheism*, ed. Loren T. Stuckenbruck and Wendy E. S. North. Journal for the Study of the New Testament Supplement Series, 167–85. London; New York: T&T Clark International, 2004.

    The Theology of the Book of Revelation. New Testament Theology. Cambridge: Cambridge University Press, 1993.

Bavel, Tarsicius Jan van. 'God in between Affirmation and Negation According to Augustine'. In *Augustine: Presbyter Factus Sum*, ed. Joseph T. Lienhard, Earl C. Muller and Roland J. Teske, 73–98. New York: P. Lang, 1993.

Benjamin, Mara H. *Rozensweig's Bible: Reinventing Scripture for Jewish Modernity*. Cambridge: Cambridge University Press, 2009.

Blowers, Paul M. *Drama of the Divine Economy: Creator and Creation in Early Christian Theology and Piety*. Oxford Early Christian Studies. Oxford: Oxford University Press, 2012.

Boulnois, Olivier. *Être et représentation*. Paris: Presses universitaires de France, 1999.

'Les noms divins: Négation ou transcendence?' *Revue de Théologie et de la Philosophie* 150, no. 4 (2018): 315–33.

Bouteneff, Peter. *Beginnings: Ancient Christian Readings of the Biblical Creation Narratives*. Grand Rapids, Mich.: Baker Academic, 2008.

Brichto, Herbert Chanan. *The Names of God: Poetic Readings in Biblical Beginnings*. New York; Oxford: Oxford University Press, 1998.

Brueggemann, Walter. 'Exodus 3: Summons to Holy Transformation'. In *The Theological Interpretation of Scripture: Classic and Contemporary Readings*, ed. Stephen E. Fowl, 155–72. Cambridge, Mass.: Blackwell 1997.

Buber, Martin. 'On Word Choice in Translating the Bible: In Memoriam Franz Rosenzweig'. In *Scripture and Translation*, ed. Martin Buber and Franz Rosenzweig, 73–89. Bloomington: Indiana University Press, 1994.

Burnyeat, Miles. 'Platonism in the Bible: Numenius of Apamea on Exodus and Eternity'. In *The Revelation of the Name Yhwh to Moses: Perspectives from Judaism, the Pagan Graeco-Roman World, and Early Christianity*, ed. George H. Van Kooten. Themes in Biblical Narrative, XIV, 139–68. Leiden: Brill, 2006.

Burrell, David. *Aquinas: God and Action*. London: Routledge and Kegan Paul, 1979.

'Creator/Creatures Relation: "the Distinction" vs. "Onto-theology"'. *Faith and Philosophy: Journal of the Society of Christian Philosophers* 25, no. 2 (2008): 177–89.

'Freedom and Creation in the Abrahamic Traditions'. *International Philosophical Quarterly* 40, no. 158 (2000): 162–71.

Butler, Judith. *Excitable Speech: A Politics of the Performative*. New York; London: Routledge, 1997.

Cameron, Michael. *Christ Meets Me Everywhere: Augustine's Early Figurative Exegesis*. Oxford Studies in Historical Theology. New York; Oxford: Oxford University Press, 2012.

Cavadini, John C. 'The Darkest Enigma: Reconsidering the Self in Augustine's Thought'. *Augustinian Studies* 38, no. 1 (2007): 119–32.

Chadwick, Henry. *Confessions*. Oxford: Oxford University Press, 1998.

'Philo.' In *The Cambridge History of Later Greek and Early Medieval Philosophy*, ed. A. H. Armstrong, 137–57. Cambridge: University Press, 1967.

Childs, Brevard S. *Exodus: A Commentary*. Old Testament Library. London: Scm, 1974.

Chrétien, Jean-Louis. *The Call and the Response*. Perspectives in Continental Philosophy. 1st English language ed. New York: Fordham University Press, 2004.

Colson, F. H. *Philo*. The Loeb Classical Library. London: Heinemann; Harvard University Press, 1966.

'Translator's Introduction'. In *Philo*. The Loeb Classical Library. London: Heinemann, 1929.

Courcelle, Pierre. *Recherches sur les Confessions de Saint Augustin*. Paris: E. De Boccard, 1950.

Cumming, Sam. 'Names'. In *The Stanford Encyclopedia of Philosophy*, ed. Edward N. Zalta, 2019. https://plato.stanford.edu/archives/fall2019/entries/names/.

Dahl, N. A. 'Philo and the Rabbis on the Names of God'. *Journal for the Study of Judaism in the Persian, Hellenistic, and Roman Period* 9 (1978): 1–28.

Daniélou, Jean. *Gospel Message and Hellenistic Culture*. Trans. John Austin Baker. A History of Early Christian Doctrine before the Council of Nicaea, Vol. 2. London: Darton, Longman and Todd, 1973.

Davies, Graham. 'The Exegesis of the Divine Name in Exodus'. In *The God of Israel: Studies of an Inimitable Deity*, ed. R. P. Gordon. University of Cambridge Oriental Publications, 139–56. Cambridge: Cambridge University Press, 2007.

Davison, Andrew. *Participation in God: A Study in Christian Doctrine and Metaphysics*. Cambridge: Cambridge University Press, 2019.

de Certeau, Michel. *The Mystic Fable*, Vol. I: *The Sixteenth and Seventeenth Centuries*. Chicago: University of Chicago Press, 1992.

Derrida, Jacques. 'How to Avoid Speaking: Denials'. In *Derrida and Negative Theology*, ed. Harold G. Coward and Toby A. Foshay, 73–142. Albany: State University of New York Press, 1992.

Dillon, John. *The Middle Platonists: A Study of Platonism 80 B.C. To A.D. 220*. London: Duckworth, 1977.

Edwards, M. J. *Origen against Plato*. Ashgate Studies in Philosophy and Theology in Late Antiquity. Aldershot: Ashgate, 2002.

Faur, José. *Golden Doves with Silver Dots: Semiotics and Textuality in Rabbinic Tradition*. Jewish Literature and Culture. Bloomington: Indiana University Press, 1986.

Homo Mysticus: A Guide to Maimonides's Guide for the Perplexed. Syracuse, NY: Syracuse University Press, 1998.

Gafney, Wilda C. *A Women's Lectionary for the Whole Church*. New York: Church Publishing, 2021.

Gerson, Lloyd P. *God and Greek Philosophy: Studies in the Early History of Natural Theology*. London: Routledge, 1994.

Goodman, Lenn Evan. *God of Abraham*. New York; Oxford: Oxford University Press, 1996.

Guyette, Fred. 'The Genre of the Call Narrative'. *Jewish Studies Quarterly* 43, no. 1 (2015): 51–9.

Guy, Nathan. *Finding Locke's God: The Theological Basis of John Locke's Political Thought.* London; New York: Bloomsbury Academic, 2019.

Hadot, Pierre. *Philosophy as a Way of Life: Spiritual Exercises from Socrates to Foucault.* Trans. Michael Close. Oxford: Basil Blackwell, 1995.

What Is Ancient Philosophy? Cambridge, Mass.: Harvard University Press, 2002.

Harrison, Verna E. F. 'The Care-Banishing Breast of the Father: Feminine Images of the Divine in Clement of Alexandria's *Paedagogus* I'. *Studia patristica* 31 (1997): 400–12.

'The Fatherhood of God in Orthodox Theology'. *St Vladimir's Theological Quarterly* 37, nos. 2–3 (1993): 185–212.

Grace and Human Freedom According to St Gregory of Nyssa. Lewiston, NY: Edwin Mellen Press, 1992.

Hart, David B. 'The Hidden and the Manifest: Metaphysics after Nicea'. In *Orthodox Readings of Augustine*, ed. George E. Demacopoulos and Aristotle Papanikolaou, 191–226. Crestwood, NY: St Vladimirs Seminary Press, 2008.

Heller-Roazen, Daniel. *No One's Ways: An Essay on Infinite Name.* New York: Zone Books, 2017.

Hume, David. The Natural History of Religion (1757, 1777), 1.1, Hume Texts Online, davidhume.org.

Janicaud, Dominique, Jean-Francois Courtine, Jean-Louis Chretien, Michel Henry, Jean-Luc Marion and Paul Ricoeur. *Phenomenology and the 'Theological Turn': The French Debate.* Perspectives in Continental Philosophy. New York: Fordham University Press, 2000.

Kaplan, David. 'Dthat'. In *Syntax and Semantics*, Vol. 9, ed. Peter Cole, 221–43. New York: Academic Press, 1978.

Kasper, Walter. *Mercy: The Essence of the Gospel and the Key to Christian Life.* New York: Paulist Press, 2014.

Kaufman, Gordon D. 'Evidentialism: A Theologian's Response'. *Faith and Philosophy: Journal of the Society of Christian Philosophers* 6, no. 1 (1989): 35–46. https://doi.org/10.5840/faithphil1989613.

'Reconstructing the Concept of God: De-Reifying the Anthropomorphisms'. In *The Making and Remaking of Christian Doctrine*, ed. Sarah Coakley and David A. Pailin, 95–115. Oxford: Clarendon Press, 1993.

Kenny, Anthony. *The God of the Philosophers*. Oxford: Clarendon Press, 1979.

Kerr, Fergus. *After Aquinas: Versions of Thomism*. Malden, Mass.: Blackwell Publishers, 2002.

Kister, Menahem. 'Tohu Wa-Bohu: Primordial Elements and Creatio Ex Nihilo'. *Jewish Studies Quarterly* 14 (2007): 229–56.

Kolbet, Paul R. *Augustine and the Cure of Souls*. Notre Dame, Ind.: Notre Dame University Press, 2010.

Lacan, Jacques, and Anthony Wilden. *Speech and Language in Psychoanalysis*. Baltimore, Md.: Johns Hopkins University Press, 1981.

Le Grys, James. 'Names for the Ineffable God: St. Gregory of Nyssa's Explanation'. *The Thomist* 62, no. 3 (1998): 333–54.

Lehrman, Rabbi Dr S. M., ed. *Midrash Rabbah, Exodus*. London: The Soncino Press, 1939.

Levenson, Jon D. *Sinai and Zion: An Entry into the Jewish Bible*. New Voices in Biblical Studies. Minneapolis: Winston Press, 1985.

Locke, John. *An Essay Concerning Human Understanding*. Chicago: Gateway Editions, 1956.

Lossky, Vladimir. *The Mystical Theology of the Eastern Church*. Cambridge: Clarke, 1991.

Louth, Andrew. *The Origins of the Christian Mystical Tradition: From Plato to Denys*. Oxford: Oxford University Press, 1981.

Ludlow, Morwenna. *Gregory of Nyssa, Ancient and (Post)modern*. Oxford: Oxford University Press, 2007.

MacDonald, Scott. 'The Divine Nature: Being and Goodness'. In *The Cambridge Companion to Augustine*, ed. Eleonore Stump and Norman Kretzmann, 71–94. Cambridge University Press, 2001.

Maimonides, Moses. *The Guide of the Perplexed*. Trans. M. Friedlander. Chicago: University of Chicago Press, 1963.

Marion, Jean-Luc. 'The Essential Incoherence of Descartes' Definition of Divinity'. In *Essays on Descartes' Meditations*, ed. Amélie Oksenberg Rorty, 297–338. Berkeley: University of California Press, 1986.

'*Idipsum*: The Name of God According to Augustine'. In *Orthodox Readings of Augustine*, ed. George E. Demacopoulos and Aristotle Papanikolaou, 167–90. Crestwood, NY: St Vladimir's Seminary Press, 2008.

The Idol and the Distance: Five Studies. Trans. and intro. Thomas A. Carlson. New York: Fordham University Press, 2001.

On Descartes' Metaphysical Prism: The Constitution and the Limits of Onto-theo-logy in Cartesian Thought. Trans. Jeffrey L. Kosky. Chicago: University of Chicago Press, 1999.

'Thomas Aquinas and Onto-theo-logy'. In *Mystics: Presence and Aporia*, ed. Michael Kessler and Christian Sheppard. Religion and Postmodernism, 38–74. Chicago: University of Chicago Press, 2003.

Maurer, Armand A. 'St Thomas on the Sacred Name "Tetragrammaton"'. In *Being and Knowing: Studies in Thomas Aquinas and Later Medieval Philosophers*, ed. Armand A. Maurer, 59–69. Toronto, Ont.: Pontifical Institute of Mediaeval Studies, 1990.

May, Gerhard. *Creatio Ex Nihilo: The Doctrine of 'Creation out of Nothing' in Early Christian Thought*. Edinburgh: T&T Clark, 1994.

McFarland, Ian A. *From Nothing: A Theology of Creation*. Louisville, KY: Westminster John Knox Press, 2014.

Moberly, R. W. L. *The Old Testament of the Old Testament: Patriarchal Narratives and Mosaic Yahwism*. Overtures to Biblical Theology. Minneapolis: Fortress Press, 1992.

Moltmann, Jürgen. *The Trinity and the Kingdom: The Doctrine of God*. 1st US ed. San Francisco: Harper & Row, 1981.

Mortley, Raoul. *From Word to Silence*. 2 vols. Bonn: Hanstein, 1986.

From Word to Silence, Vol. I: *The Rise and Fall of Logos*. Bonn: Hanstein, 1986.

Nazianzus, Gregory of. 'On the Theophany, or Birthday of Christ'. In *A Select Library of Nicene and Post-Nicene Fathers of the Christian Church: Second Series*, Vol. VII, ed. Philip Schaff and Henry Wace, 345–51. Grand Rapids, Mich.: William B. Eerdmans, n.d.

'The Second Oration on Easter'. In *A Select Library of Nicene and Post-Nicene Fathers of the Christian Church: Second Series*, Vol. VII, ed. Philip Schaff and Henry Wace, 422–34. Grand Rapids, Mich.: William B. Eerdmans.

Nyssa, Gregory of. *Commentary on the Song of Songs*. Archbishop Iakovos Library of Ecclesiastical and historical sources, No. 12. Brookline, Mass.: Hellenic College Press, 1987.

Contra Eunomium I: An English Translation with Supporting Studies. Vigiliae Christianae, Supplements, Vol. 148. Ed. Miguel Brugarolas, trans. Stuart George Hall. Leiden: Brill, 2018 (e-book).

Contra Eunomium II: An English Version with Supporting Studies. Proceedings of the 10th International Colloquium on Gregory of Nyssa (Olomouc, 15–18 September 2004). Ed. Lenka Karfíková, Scot Douglass and Johannes Zachuber; trans. Stuart George Hall. Leiden: Brill, 2007 (e-book).

From Glory to Glory: Texts from Gregory of Nyssa's Mystical Writings. Ed. Jean Daniélou and Herbert A. Musurillo. Crestwood, NY: St Vladimir's Seminary Press, 1979.

Gregory of Nyssa: Life of Moses. Ed. and trans. Abraham J. Malherbe and Everett Ferguson, Preface by J. Meyendorff. Classics of Western Spirituality. New York: Paulist Press, 1978.

Ochs, Peter. 'Morning Prayer as Redemptive Thinking'. In *Liturgy, Time and the Politics of Redemption*, ed. Randi Rashkover and C. C. Pecknold. Grand Rapids, Mich.: William B. Eerdmans, 2006, 50–87.

Osborn, Eric. *The Beginning of Christian Philosophy*. Cambridge: Cambridge University Press, 1981.

'Negative Theology and Apologetic'. In *The Via Negativa*, ed. Raoul Mortley and David Dockrill, Supplement to Prudentia, 49–63. Auckland: Prudentia, 1981).

The Oxford Dictionary of the Jewish Religion. Ed. R. J. Zwi Werblowsky and Geoffrey Wigoder. Oxford: Oxford University Press, 1997.

Philo. *On the Creation of the Cosmos According to Moses*. Ed. and trans. David T. Runia. Philo of Alexandria Commentary Series Vol. 1. Leiden; Boston: Brill, 2001.

Przywara, Erich. *Analogia Entis: Metaphysics: Original Structure and Universal Rhythm*. Grand Rapids, Mich.: William B. Eerdmans, 2014.

Pseudo-Dionysius. *Pseudo-Dionysius: The Complete Works*. Trans. Colm Luibheid. Mahwah, NJ: Paulist Press, 1987.

Radice, Roberto. 'Philo's Theology and Theory of Creation'. In *The Cambridge Companion to Philo*, ed. Adam Kamesar, 124–45. Cambridge: Cambridge University Press, 2009.

Rajak, Tessa. *Translation and Survival: The Greek Bible and the Jewish Diaspora*. Oxford: Oxford University Press, 2009.

Recanati, François. *Direct Reference: From Language to Thought*. Oxford: Blackwell, 1993.

Ricoeur, Paul. 'Biblical Readings and Meditations' (originally 1995), in *Critique and Conviction: Conversations with François Azouvi and Marc de Launay*, trans. Kathleen Blamey, 139–70. Cambridge: Polity Press, 1998.

Paul Ricoeur, 'Experience and Language in Religious Discourse', in *Phenomenology and the 'Theological Turn': The French Debate*, by D. Janicaud, J. F. Courtine, J. L. Chrétien, M. Henry, J. L. Marion, and P. Ricoeur. New York: Fordham University Press, 2000.

'From Interpretation to Tradition', in *Thinking Biblically: Exegetical and Hermeneutical Studies*, by André LaCoque and Paul Ricoeur, trans. David Pellauer, 331–61. Chicago: University of Chicago Press, 1998.

'Naming God', in *Figuring the Sacred: Religion, Narrative, and Imagination*, ed. David Pallauer, trans. Mark I. Wallace, 217–35. Minneapolis: Fortress Press, 1995. Originally published in *Union Seminary Quarterly Review* 34, no. 4 (1979): 215–27.

'The Summoned Subject in the School of the Narratives of the Prophetic Vocation' (1988), in *Figuring the Sacred: Religion, Narrative, and Imagination*, ed. David Pallauer, trans. Mark I. Wallace, 269–75. Minneapolis: Fortress Press, 1995.

Rist, John. 'Augustine, Aristotelianism, and Aquinas: Three Varieties of Philosophical Adaptation'. In *Aquinas the Augustinian*, ed. Michael Dauphinais, Barry David and Matthew Levering, 79–99. Washington, DC: Catholic University of American Press, 2007.

Rosenzweig, Franz. '"The Eternal": Mendelssohn and the Name of God'. In *Scripture and Translation*, ed. Martin Buber and Franz Rosenzweig, 99–113. Bloomington: Indiana University Press, 1994.

'Scripture and Luther'. In *Scripture and Translation*, ed. Martin Buber and Franz Rosenzweig, 57–69. Bloomington: Indiana University Press, 1994.

Rosenzweig, Franz, and Martin Buber. 'A Letter to Martin Goldner'. In *Scripture and Translation*, trans. Lawrence Rosenwald with Everett Fox, 189–92. Bloomington: Indiana University Press, 1994.

Runia, David T. 'Naming and Knowing: Themes in Philonic Theology'. In *Exegesis and Philosophy: Studies on Philo of Alexandria*. Collected Studies, 69–91. Aldershot: Variorum, 1990.

Philo of Alexandria and the Timaeus of Plato. Leiden: E. J. Brill, 1986.

Philo of Alexandria and the Timaeus of Plato: Academisch Proefschrift ... Vrije Universiteit Te Amsterdam. Amsterdam: VU Boekhandel, 1983.

'Philo, Alexandrian and Jew'. In *Exegesis and Philosophy: Studies on Philo of Alexandria*, 1–18. Aldershot: Variorum, 1990.

Ryan, Fáinche. *Formation in Holiness: Thomas Aquinas on Sacra Doctrina*. Leuven: Peeters, 2007.

Sammon, Brendan Thomas. *The God Who Is Beauty: Beauty as a Divine Name in Thomas Aquinas and Dionysius the Areopagite*. Eugene, OR: Pickwick Publications, 2013.

Samuelson, Norbert Max. *Judaism and the Doctrine of Creation*. Cambridge; New York: Cambridge University Press, 1994.

Schroot, Henk. *Christ, the 'Name' of God: Thomas Aquinas on Naming Christ*. Leuven: Peeters, 1993.

Searle, John R. *Speech Acts: An Essay in the Philosophy of Language*. London: Cambridge University Press, 1969.

Sedley, D. N. *Creationism and Its Critics in Antiquity*. Sather Classical Lectures. Berkeley: University of California Press, 2007.

Seeskin, Kenneth. *Searching for a Distant God: The Legacy of Maimonides*. New York; Oxford: Oxford University Press, 2000.

A Select Library of Nicene and Post-Nicene Fathers of the Christian Church: Second Series. Ed. Philip Schaff and Henry Wace. Edinburgh; Grand Rapids, Mich.: T&T Clark; William B. Eerdmans, 1988.

Sonderegger, Katherine. *Systematic Theology*, Vol. I: *The Doctrine of God*. Minneapolis: Fortress Press, 2015.

Soskice, Janet. 'Being and Love: Schleiermacher, Aquinas and Augustine'. *Modern Theology* 34, no. 3 (July 2018): 480–91.

Metaphor and Religious Language. Oxford: Oxford University Press, 1985.

'Why *Creatio Ex Nihilo* for Theology Today?' In *Creation Ex Nihilo: Origins, Development, Contemporary Challenges*, ed. Gary A. Anderson and Markus N. A. Bockmuehl, 37–54. Notre Dame, Ind.: University of Notre Dame Press, 2018.

Sterling, Gregory E. '"The Most Perfect Work": The Role of Matter in Philo of Alexandria'. In *Creation Ex Nihilo: Origins, Development, Contemporary Challenges*, ed. Gary A. Anderson and Markus N. A. Bockmuehl, 99–118. Notre Dame, Ind.: University of Notre Dame Press, 2018.

Stump, Eleonore. *The God of the Bible and the God of the Philosophers.* Milwaukee, Wisc.: Marquette University Press, 2016.

Stump, Eleonore, and Norman Kretzmann. 'Eternity'. In *Concept of God*, ed. Thomas V. Morris, 219–52. Oxford: Oxford University Press, 1987.

'Theologically Unfashionable Philosophy.' *Faith and Philosophy* 7, no. 3 (1990): 329–39.

Swinburne, Richard. *The Coherence of Theism.* 2nd ed. Oxford: Oxford University Press, 2016.

Tanner, Kathryn. *God and Creation in Christian Theology: Tyranny or Empowerment?* Oxford: Basil Blackwell, 1988.

te Velde, Rudi. *Aquinas on God: The 'Divine Science' of the Summa Theologiae.* London: Ashgate, 2006.

Torrell, Jean-Pierre. *Saint Thomas Aquinas*, Vol. I: *The Person and His Work.* Washington, DC: Catholic University of America Press, 1996.

Turner, Denys. *The Darkness of God: Negativity in Christian Mysticism.* Cambridge: Cambridge University Press, 1995.

van den Berg, Robert. 'Does It Matter to Call God Zeus?', in *The Revelation of the Name YHWH to Moses: Perspectives from Judaism, the Pagan Graeco-Roman World, and Early Christianity*, Themes in Biblical Narrative, 169–83. Leiden: Brill, 2006.

Venard OP, Oliver-Thomas. 'Extending the Thomist Movement from the Twentieth to the Twenty-First Century: Under What Conditions Could There Be a "Literary Thomism"?' In *Faithful Reading: New Essays in Theology and Philosophy in Honour of Fergus Kerr, Op*, ed. Karen Kilby, Simon Oliver and Fergus Kerr, 91–112. London: T&T Clark, 2012.

White, Thomas Joseph, ed. *The Analogy of Being: Invention of the Antichrist or the Wisdom of God?* Grand Rapids, Mich.; Edinburgh: William B. Eerdmans, 2011.

Wilken, Robert Louis. *The Christians as the Romans Saw Them.* New Haven: Yale University Press, 1984.

Williams, A. N. 'Mystical Theology Redux: The Pattern of Aquinas' Summa Theologiae'. In *Spirituality and Social Embodiment*, 53–74. Oxford: Basil Blackwell, 1997.

Williams, Rowan. *The Edge of Words: God and the Habits of Language*. New York: Bloomsbury Continuum, 2021.

Williams, Rowan. *Looking East in Winter: Contemporary Thought and the Eastern Christian Tradition*. New York: Bloomsbury Continuum, 2021.

Wilson, Brittany E. *The Embodied God*. Oxford: Oxford University Press, 2021.

Winston, David. 'Philo of Alexandria'. In *The Cambridge History of Philosophy in Late Antiquity*, ed. Lloyd P. Gerson, 235–57. Cambridge: Cambridge University Press, 2010.

Wyschogrod, Michael. *The Body of Faith: God and the People of Israel*. Northvale, NJ: Jason Aronson, 1996.

Yourgrau, Palle. *Demonstratives*. Oxford Readings in Philosophy. Oxford: Oxford University Press, 1990.

INDEX